MW01491031

# ALTERNATIVE ECONOMICS 101

# TAX Your Imagination!

### The road to a debt-free & inflation-free economy.

Steve Consilvio

Copyright © 2014 Steve Consilvio
ISBN-13: 978-1505478594
ISBN-10: 1505478596
Printed by CreateSpace

# Table of Contents

## Introduction — 1

## 1. Money — 9
*The Past and Future* : 10
*Money Between Generations* : 12
*Thoughts, Feelings and Actions* : 14
*Money as an Object of Trade* : 18

## 2. Who Owns the Money? — 20
*Empires and Commonwealths* : 21
*Who Owns The Money?* : 24
*Origins of Organizations* : 27
*The Illusion of Choice* : 28
*Checks and Balances* : 29
*The Wheels of Confusion* : 32
*Debt* : 36
*Societies* : 39
*How do we share the bounty?* : 43

## 3. What is a Budget? — 46
*The Basic Math of a Budget* : 51

## 4. What is Inflation? — 57
*Supply and Demand Theory* : 58
*What is inflation?* : 62
*The Inflation Sequence* : 63

## 5. What are Boom and Bust? — 70
*Percentages & Compounding* : 70
*Monopoly* : 72
*Capitalism & Socialism* : 74
*Regulated Economies* : 74
*Revolutions* : 75

## 6. What is the Cost of Living? — 77
*Wealth Profiles* : 85

## 7. The Politics of Money — 89
*Religion* : 91
*Rights and Revolutions* : 92
*The Role of Government* : 93
*Transactional Economics* : 95
*What is Fair?* : 101
*The Rat Race* : 104

## 8. What is the GDP/GNP? 106
## 9. The National Debt is the Inverse of Inflation 112
## 10. What is a Ponzi Scheme? 121
## 11. Big History: The Anatomy of Ideas 130
*What is the priority? : 135*
*Comparing religion within revolutionary movements : 135*
*Cognitive Dissonance : 138*
*Comparative Analysis : 139*
*False Choices : 141*
*Wisdom versus Truth : 143*
*Dissonance of Means and Ends: Equality or Inequality? : 145*
*Ideas Rule : 147*
*Virtue is Consistent : 149*
*History is a Mess : 150*

## 12. The Anatomy of Contradictory Ideas 155
*Heroes and Villains : 161*
*Mapping Anger : 163*
*Silence is Not Harmony : 164*
*Enlightenment : 165*
*Know Thyself : 169*
*The virtue model : 171*
*The model in flux : 173*
*Hierarchy: Slavery versus Liberty : 175*
*Prejudice and Virtue : 177*
*What are Virtues? : 178*
*Virtue in Religion, and its Opposite : 179*
*Virtue in Politics, and its Opposite : 180*
*Virtue in Economics, and its opposite : 181*
*Consistency : 182*
*Finding Balance : 184*
*Money and the zero-sum game : 185*
*Hypocrisy and Internal Division : 187*
*Feeding the wolves inside of us : 187*

## 13. The Anatomy of Hierarchy 191
*Indoctrination as Prejudice : 193*
*Chasing Revenue is desperate, not democratic : 194*
*Common Patterns : 195*
*False Language Distinctions : 196*
*The light and dark, young and old : 199*
*Organized Failure : 203*
*Organized Success : 205*
*Groupthink : 206*
*Build or destroy? : 210*

## 14. What is Modern Finance? 212
*The social setting of Modern Finance : 212*
*The Rise of Commerce : 214*
*The Origin of Modern Finance : 216*
*France : 218*
*The Problem with Gold : 220*
*Cognitive Dissonance in America : 224*
*Robert Morris: America's version of John Law and Solon : 225*
*Power and personal opportunity : 227*
*Developing a Currency : 228*
*The Temptation of Speculation : 229*
*The Civil War and Banking : 231*
*The Income Tax : 237*
*Dissonance of Ownership : 238*
*Wall Street and the Role of Gold : 239*

## 15. The FIRE Economy and C=M+L 241
*Interest: the control of land and money : 243*
*The Land Bondage System : 244*
*The Social Consequence : 246*
*Government's equal: the Bank : 248*
*Bubbles and Real Estate : 250*
*Understanding Wall Street : 250*
*Wall Street as Community : 253*
*Housing Reform : 255*
*Stewardship : 256*
*What is Value? : 257*
*The Power and Place of Percentages : 258*
*C=M+L: Capital equals Money Plus Labor : 259*
*The FIRE Economy : 264*
*The problem with insurance and government : 265*
*Moving Forward : 266*

## 16. What is to be Done? 267
*The Choice: Fascism or Commonwealth : 267*
*The Problem: Inflation and Debt and Inequality : 269*
*Reforms for the Individual : 270*
*Reforms for Local Government : 274*
*Reforms for State Government : 277*
*Reforms for Federal Government : 278*
*Reforms for Businesses and Banking : 280*
*Liberty : 284*
*Personal Responsibility : 284*
*One Caveat : 286*

# Introduction

"The War Is Over!" Four simple words that bring a rush of relief to humanity. They are the community version of *"I Love You"* in importance. Both phrases represent a significant change to the status quo, and the satisfaction of a deep longing. Peace and love are a gift that we give to one another. Unlike a zero-sum game, the more you give, the more you will have. Less loneliness is more happiness. Less conflict yields more harmony. Peace, love and abundance represent a wise society living up to its potential in both a public and a personal way.

Life is a miracle. Everything that grows is a wonder, whether a grain of wheat, or stars being born in a distant galaxy. Life is full of rhythm, which we hear in our love of music, the waves crashing on the beach, and the wind rustling through the trees. The world is alive in the short space between our ears, too. How we think is more important than what we think. Negativity breeds negativity, optimism breeds optimism.

A rich and full life is ours for the taking and the sharing, **IF** we think broadly about our place in the universe and are willing to both give and receive. Courage, compassion and reason (aka the Lion, the Tin Man and the Scarecrow) are what it takes to be a complete person. There is no place like our home, the Earth. We are in Oz, or the Garden of Eden. Pick your metaphor. The choices we make are real, and have real consequences. We reap what we sow.

Thoreau wrote: *"There are a thousand hacking at the branches of evil to one who is striking at the root, and it may be that he who bestows the largest amount of time and money on the needy is doing the most by his mode of life to produce that misery which he strives in vain to relieve."* His statement takes no prisoners. Not only are the wealthy philanthropists criticized, but also the ministers of justice (i.e. Government), and the common man who cannot discern the brush from the root. No wonder he spent so much time alone. This book takes a similarly wide view, but is a bit more charitable in recognizing that *'their'* errors are a lot like *'my'* errors. We are all alike in our strengths and weaknesses. We are both victim and the crime.

Mark Twain wrote: *"It is easier to fool a man than to convince him that he has been fooled."* My goal is to explore how we have fooled ourselves, and document a new way of discerning the economy. It is based on my previous confusion. Always remember that this is a work of redemption. *"How could I have been so stupid?!"* No matter what you believe, this book will probably challenge some of your basic beliefs. Give it time, and keep an open mind. It is easier to let go of lies than to attempt to hold onto them through denial.

We need to understand success, so we can teach it to others, and we also need to understand failures, to fix them and avoid them. Sometimes these two things are hard to separate. The most ruthless win every war. The victory of killing machines masks the failure of winning the peace through diplomacy. Wars generally end only when the means to conduct them are exhausted. Victory is not necessarily progress, but does offer another chance to get it right.

Democracy was supposed to put an end to the nonsense of endless killing, but instead has become another excuse for war. Clearly the King was not wholly to blame for the fiscal and emotional failures of society. Monarchy, democracy, communism, federalism and con-federalism, Christian, Islamic and Jewish states all share similar human shortcomings regarding economics and war. Individuals organized to defeat empires soon act like empires themselves. Fear, jealousy and greed combine in infinite combinations to divide us and lead us astray from peace and prosperity. Our reasoning gets clouded by negative emotions that are passed between generations as stereotypes, prejudices and faux commonsense.

History might seem to indicate that we cannot agree on anything, yet in our hearts we all want the gifts of peace and love. What prevents us from giving the gifts that we knew instinctually as a child? How did we grow from innocence to an unrecognizable beast?

The answer lies in what we teach our children and what we were taught as children. The status quo that Thoreau criticized was a cultural conditioning that the ends can justify the means, and that habits need not be analyzed or corrected. The mores of society are stronger than the laws and can constitute a systemic corruption of right and wrong. While the good is not the enemy of the perfect, it is important to define principles clearly. There is no worse example of the ends justifying the means than the banality of profit.

The basis of every society is the give and take between generations. At the beginning and end of our lives we must rely upon others. This will never change. Monarchy and nobility, like other caste systems, kept some families ensconced in privilege and another families ensconced in misery. Democracy challenged this structure and gave everyone the freedom to compete on merit, or so it is claimed.

A quick review reveals that families with power and wealth still benefit from privilege, and hereditary advantage or favors remains the primary determinator of success. Rich or poor, time remains the great equalizer. We only have one life to live, and we can live it hiding from the truth or embracing it.

Monarchy and agrarianism waned as mercantilism and competition grew. The new profit-driven financial system that has resulted demands a stressful bloodless war of everyday life. It perpetually victimizes the next generation. Stewardship has been redefined as hoarding for yourself and giving the leftovers to your kids. There is no natural symbiotic relationship with time or one another, but an accounting-driven rush to accumulate a financial advantage that will last longer than the next bust. The future is something to be feared and 'prepared for' because financial problems are allegedly unpredictable. Institutions and individuals both follow the same philosophy.

Give and take are natural, but profit is an accounting trick: 2+2=5 (25% mark-up or 20% Gross Profit). The exchange is captured on the ledgers of modern business. Profit may seem like a small issue, and impossible to alter, but it is terribly important and man-made. Volatility is bust: 5=2+2. Prediction is not needed. It is cause and effect. The laws of mathematics will not yield to human desire or denial. We must respect mathematical truth or suffer the consequences.

There is a good reason why all prophets have warned about profit. It disrupts the natural equilibrium of life. Apologists will point to democracy and capitalism as a great success in channeling our genius and aggression in a socially beneficial way. After all, the population has grown immensely. That must indicate success, right? The Earth has grown smaller with instant communication, rapid transit, and productive output. Nevertheless, the yearning for peace and love continues. Inequality continues unabated. War is common.

Competition is not freedom. What people want most of all is the ability to live, love and trade with confidence and ease. Ambition and competition are a type of madness that makes everyone, including the next generation of rising winners, miserable. The ease of the modern lifestyle has not extended into our financial life. Rather, there is a widening disparity between the two. Public national debts are common worldwide. Our success is a house of cards.

In 1793, a Native American from Delaware complained that *"[Your] money to us is of no value, and to most of us unknown."* For modern man, money has become everything. It is the means to the ends, the measure of success, and the obstacle.

How many people today would like to live without the worry of money? Probably everyone! People want work that is rewarding, and an exchange of time for goods that maintains a pleasant and stress-free existence. Simple middle-class values are all anyone has ever wanted, whether in the form of a Marxist brotherhood, Sharia law, Native American spiritualism, a hippie commune or the religious independence of a new colony. Peace, love, comfort and predictable security have been in demand since the dawn of time. Why do we rob each other of the only gift we can give? And how?

There must be a systemic explanation of a systemic problem. As populations and material output has grown, imbalances have endured. New bosses and new philosophies have all yielded the same shortcomings. Economics is not the study of scarcity, as it is sometimes claimed. The wastefulness of the modern world indicates that there is a distribution problem, not a production shortage. Economics should study how we created depravity in a world of plenty.

As in the Garden of Eden, we have managed to screw up a free lunch. From sailing ships to spaceships, trade and technology have been transforming the status quo regularly for thousands of years. The Native Americans liked the inventions that the Europeans brought. New products changed their lives, just as new products change our lives today. Technology and growth cannot be the cause or the solution to inequality. To change the economy, we must focus on understanding how the economy actually functions. Facts and emotions must balance with reality.

Clashes of culture are never one-sided. Thousands of nations of Native Americans were living side-by-side on the North American continent in relative peace and economic equality. They were highly advanced politically. The Europeans, in contrast, could not maintain peace among a dozen nations and never knew equality. They brought their bad habits to the new continent. With profit-driven trade came trade alliances, and the Native Americans were soon poor, politicized and divided.

The vision of independence in the American colonies was for all men to live independent and free as yeoman farmers. Unfortunately, changing mores is more difficult than changing laws or replacing lawmakers. Merchants competing creates a competing political environment. Few are self-employed anymore, much less living independently in a rural landscape. The American plan was obsolete at the outset. The King was not wholly to blame for the economic landscape. The last three centuries provide a great deal of empirical evidence regarding paper money and deficit financing that we need to integrate into a comprehensive economic philosophy.

This book focuses on economics, the role of money, the pressure of competitive capitalism, and the mathematical underpinnings of contradictions in how we think and act. It challenges the status quo, various schools economic thought, and covers a wide breadth of seemingly obvious facts. Read between the lines. All items discussed are related to each other. Every link in both the capitalist and socialist chains are weak. Islamists wanting to overthrow both systems have fared no better. Blaming the modern West is as empty as blaming the tradition of monarchy.

What follows is an alternative economic understanding, based on math, money and time flow. A good name for it would be Transactional Economics or perhaps neo-transcendentalism. It unifies micro and macro theory, and challenges the basic assumptions of neo-conservativism, neo-liberalism, progressives and Islamists. It is heretical by many standards, yet still manages to build bridges to everyone. Half truths have some good in them, but the other half needs to be mated with mathematical accuracy.

The problems we face are ubiquitous. We cannot escape the consequences of our own choices. I have had the experience of living the 'American Dream' of bootstrapping a small business and operating successfully for many years. I have combined that experience, the events of 9/11, and my knowledge of history to arrive at a theory of how our troubles as a species developed.

Trade within and between generations is sharing our respective genius. We all contribute to the happiness of one another, or to our misery. It is important to know the root of which one is which, so we can nurture our genius and halt our folly.

The first assumption challenged is our understanding of money. The Native Americans were right that they did not need it. In an industrialized world, however, money can be a useful tool. If we are going to use money, then we must understand the full cycle of trade. What goes around must come around. War is everyone reaping what they sowed.

Math must balance (2+2=4, 4=2+2). Justice demands equality and consistency.

All the chapters lead up to the final one, which is a vision of how to transition our economy. It is brief and specific and strikes the root as quickly as possible. People have a tendency to regard change as radical, but all improvement requires change and letting go of the past. What I suggest are timid reforms in comparison to all the regulation, auditing and panic that currently exists.

To have an enduring peace and prosperity, all that is required is our writing down different numbers. The problem is in our accounting methodology, and it is there where we must make changes. It is practically effortless, but critically important for everyone to understand the why and the how. Good intentions and blind obedience are no substitute for a conscious understanding of right and wrong. Children must be taught to understand, not obey. Only doing the right thing for the right reason can endure.

The modern world can have zero debt, zero inflation, full employment, a high standard of living, with stable, satisfying and sustainable relationships with each other, across borders, between generations and with the Earth. A little courage, some empathy, and better math more cleverly applied, are all that is required to improve our world.

New mores need to replace the old mores. War, waste and stress are caused by how we trade. There is a better way to trade, and a better world is possible. If these changes are adopted, sometime in the future, people will be able to say "The Economic War is Over!"

# 1. Money

Inflation and debt are wreaking havoc on mankind. Because of these imbalances, jobs related to finance and *'selling stuff'* are widespread. We are inundated with advertising, false promises and fear. Earning money, by any means possible, is the baseline for survival. Farmers are worried about the Futures value of their crop as much as they are about the weather. They can feed hundreds and thousands of people, but they are not sure if they will be able to feed themselves. The difference between production and consumption can be described as *The Fiscal Gap*. The value of labor evaporates into a maze of numbers and drives an unending desperation.

Large organizations survive primarily because of access to credit. Size is not the problem. Big organizations are necessary to service large populations and build complex products. Attacking the existence of corporations is like destroying the forest to liberate the trees. Small and large businesses need to co-exist, and individuals with them. Borrowing is a method for surviving The Fiscal Gap.

Self-sufficiency is obsolete. Large populations cannot be supported without trade. The modern world is co-dependent, and finance is a constant problem. A debate rages concerning who or what caused the money problem and the best way to solve it. The fear surrounding money is as visceral as hunger. We must conquer both our fears and all the other problems that we have created,

Money separates man from animals. Animals may fight over territory, mates and food, but never over money or religion. Man, in contrast, is driven and controlled by the importance of abstract ideas. Money is an abstract idea, just like religion. Abstract thought gives us the ability to think, cooperate and build, but money also shares characteristics with mental illnesses.

Money gives man both great joy and great trouble. Man will steal, cheat, lie and kill for money; he will lose sleep with worry or excitement. Man will sell his pride, his dignity and his body for money. Money is a tool that can be used to bully individuals, businesses or nations. Almost everyone has been on both the giving and receiving end of monetary punishment and reward. The belief that money is real makes man strong and weak, happy and sad, intelligent and crazy.

The rich have lots of money, but they cannot escape the worries of the poor who have little. The rich find themselves with a burden to protect their money from others. Money does not buy freedom, as every hobo knows, but often demands more vigilance. The poor majority constantly complains about the wealthy minority. The wealthy have advice and sympathy for the poor. Nobody wants to be or to stay poor, or for the poor to even exist.

### The Past and Future

The discussion about money has lasted centuries over similar issues: taxes, prices, privileges, debts, needs and budgets. None of this angst would be possible without first accepting intellectually that money is real and a necessary part of society. The obsolescence of money is usually a key element of the imaginative future. A science fiction story like Star Trek depicts the end of money and substitutes a vaguely defined credit system. Today, however, money continues to be accepted as the supreme arbitrator of fairness and value.

We are all enslaved by a belief of what constitutes a fair exchange in the trade contract. We seldom agree, but we tolerate one another enough that we can trade regularly. When values change, it is either good or bad for a particular party. We have recently seen the price of gold increase, and people are trading their colored dirt (gold) for colored paper (dollars). This is the trading of one object of abstract value for another object of abstract value.

While gold has practical usage applications, money does not. Money's only purpose is as a chit in trade. Money can be whatever the parties agree to value. Money is an intellectual agreement. In the past, books, pepper, beads and tulip bulbs have all been used as currency. Star Trek credits are just an electronic version of traditional money. With computerized banking and finance, it is fair to say that the future has arrived. Most money today exists as an electronic entry in a numeric ledger.

Money is a benign tool that allegedly facilitates cooperation. It is quid pro quo: this object for that object. Whether moral, amoral or immoral, it is usually for sale. Money, in theory, makes trade easier by providing an impartial choice to every transaction. People can sell whatever they have to anyone, rather than barter with a specific person who has what they need and wants what they have. Money dramatically increases the opportunity to buy and sell every product. It is an efficient idea on the surface, but we have thousands of years of empirical evidence that money is a complex problem, too.

Money is an idea just like any other idea; it can be true or false, good or bad, right or wrong. The young, like Adam and Eve, have no understanding of money. Money is a concept that must be learned, the same as nakedness. A child grows believing that everything is free and shared, and he must learn of the cost, method and effort required to earn money from strangers. He is taught to count, to share, to charge, to save, to spend, to invest, to plan and to complain. Innocence is lost. Money is a source of embarrassment. We hide our finances the same way we cover our nudity. Money is the shame of mankind.

**Money Between Generations**

Every child is born into a world where elders control the wealth and rules. In addition to the fiscal gap, there exists a perpetual generation gap, income gap, and power gap. A child learns about money, and then discovers that he has none. These divides are why revolutionaries tend to be young. They have nothing, and nothing to lose. Whereas conservative elders have everything, and everything to lose. The elders only recently have wrestled control from the previous generation, and suddenly the young spring upon them trying to wrestle their control away. Democracy makes all adults politically equal, in theory. It does nothing to make the next generation financially equal. People fight to retain their inheritance, even though they did nothing to earn it. Monarchy was an inheritance of political power, but the conflict was always financial.

The young will steal what the elders refuse to share. As we have seen with the music industry, the law makes sharing illegal: the children must pay. Definitions of adulthood pivot on the concept of financial independence: to be able to sell ones own labor so as to buy the labor of others. The criminal impulse circumvents trade and substitutes force or stealth.

Every revolution is based on the criminal activity of the young against the old. The first lawmakers of every nation were originally lawbreakers. Once in power, their perspective changes. The disobedient expect to be obeyed.

Most elders are not thinking long-term about the next generation. They are too busy battling the Fiscal Gap, and focus on one another for control and ownership. Greed is a personality trait, a legally protected behavior, and often mandated as a fiduciary responsibility. Even people who are not greedy behave greedily. Moral reasoning is considered to be disruptive of the marketplace. The needs of others are never to be considered of greater importance than the immediate desires of ones own group. These attitudes are the seed of revolution between the powerful and powerless. Crimes are committed by both the high and low. Only the scale of the theft differs.

Competitive conflicts between groups and individuals are often accepted as the *'invisible hand'* of a free market. In fact, people are competing as equals in a corrupted marketplace. The Fiscal Gap is not caused by personal corruption; it is caused by the rules of the game. The math is corrupt.

If the economy were a computer program, then it should be described as buggy or malware.

Truth may be the first casualty of war, but dissonance arrives first. The belief that good things can come from bad choices is a characteristic of blind ambition. Radicals follow the example set by previous radicals, and conservatives follow the example set by previous conservatives. Honesty, contentment and compassion are for the losers. Revolutions are a battle between two groups that are dishonest, discontent and merciless.

The circumstances of boom and bust and inheritances ensure that our individual finances are as unique as a fingerprint. Volatility is the most common experience because the system is riddled with contradictions. The economy breeds the fear that makes solving issues more difficult.

This book seeks to explain the problems of inflation and debt, and offers possible solutions. An understanding of the system is necessary before attempting a repair. We need to do a better job for ourselves and for the next generation. The symptoms of the current money system are worse than the problems it was intended to solve.

**Thoughts, Feelings and Actions**

Money is ubiquitous. Like any habit, it is something we do without thinking. We lack self-awareness. Many economic philosophers have described economic behavior as a state of unconscious reasoning or animalistic instinct. This is contradictory since the use of money itself is based upon abstract reasoning. Theories of economics like *'survival of the fittest,'* champion self-interest and self-reliance. They are a result of the application of observations in nature to the behaviors of men. These claims suggest that money decisions lack personal objective capacity and moral reasoning. Problems in the economy are regarded as 'natural' mathematical events, like an autumn harvest, rather than as an addiction, which is the harming of oneself through unhealthy choices.

Far from being unconscious, money decisions are some of the most conscious actions we make. We are responding to many different stimuli, which make it seem confusing. The natural law and invisible hand claims of a self-regulating marketplace are dead wrong. Inflation is best explained with a mathematical model, since it is a mathematical event. A valid economic theory should encompass abstract reasoning, recognize the role of emotions, and be based on math, not invisible forces.

Economic history is a story of cause and effect, the same as any other phenomenon. Cause and effect are the basic components of all scientific inquiry. The hands at the end of our arms are visible. The actions we take determine the consequences. Ideas determine how we act, not instinct or habit. By following the math, we can understand the problems and the successes. We make choices with unintended mathematical consequences, and those consequences should not be dismissed easily. Our trouble stems from false economic theories. We do not understand the connection between our actions and the consequences.

Our feelings about money arise from our beliefs about money. Money is primarily an intellectual agreement. As a result, it has many facets: cultural, mathematical, personal, traditional and national. Economic philosophy has the same characteristics as people. It can be fraught with schizophrenic tendencies. Money is both commonsense and utter nonsense. Money can be its own form of mental illness.

The dictionary definition of schizophrenia is *"a long-term mental disorder of a type involving a breakdown in the relation between thought, emotion, and behavior, leading to faulty perception, inappropriate actions and feelings, withdrawal from reality and personal relationships into fantasy and delusion, and a sense of mental fragmentation. A mentality or approach characterized by inconsistent or contradictory elements."* This conflict between what we think, feel and do will be discussed in depth later.

Thoughts, feelings and actions are distinct groupings. There is a condition called cognitive dissonance, too, which is probably a precursor to schizophrenia. Cognitive dissonance is the uncomfortable feeling of holding two contradictory ideas simultaneously. Contradictory ideas will lead to contradictory emotions and contradictory behavior. In other words, there can be contradictions both between groups and within the groups.

People who are clinically schizophrenic are often in the headlines for a crime they have committed, but the dissonance that money represents is a broad cultural event. Men think, and think they need money. In trying to convince children of the importance of money, we create a self-fulfilling prophesy; we teach them to be both greedy and generous. Our dissonance becomes their dissonance. We should recognize dissonance as a form of mental illness. Money is a traumatic stress.

Economic policies that result in unintended consequences are caused by our contradictions. We have made counting money important. When counting and applying value cognitive dissonance begins to emerge. We teach 2+2=4 in math class, and teach 2+2=5 in business class. False mathematical equations are contradictions. The amount of profit depends upon the percentage applied. Percentages are used in many areas, not just business. Government taxes and banking interest are also percentages.

The tension over opposite ideas comes to a head in the political process, which is primarily a debate over multiple versions of false economic theory. We have to decide which math is true: 2+2=4 or 2+2=5? They cannot coexist.

| DISSONANCE | DISSONANCE | DISSONANCE |
|:---:|:---:|:---:|
| **ABSTRACT** | **EMOTIONAL** | **PHYSICAL** |
| 2+2=4 | LOVE | BUILD |
| 2+2=5 | HATE | DESTROY |

Schizophrenia is "a long-term mental disorder of a type involving a breakdown in the relation between THOUGHT, EMOTION, and BEHAVIOR."

When experiencing cognitive dissonance, one is unsure which ideas to change, to jettison or merge. Our power of abstraction gives us doubts about our certainty, especially after our plans have failed. The clinically schizophrenic succeed in denial of doubt while maintaining incompatible ideas. Attackers, like Timothy McVeigh in Oklahoma, or Jared Loughner in Arizona, are convinced of the superiority of their contradictions. Their extremism, however, is an incremental extension of common contradictions. Their anger stemmed from a belief about money and trade.

The angst, anger and delirious pleasure that money generates indicates that something is amiss. Paper money was intended to make life and trade easier, but history reveals that it made things more difficult, too. Volatility and emotional extremes indicate a lack of proper understanding and management.

Money is the most poorly engineered system on the planet, especially in modern times. Compare the abundant art of renaissance Florence, Italy that was created for pleasure, to the drab urgency of a tollbooth building that force motorists to wait in an unnecessary bottleneck. We have more kinds of money, more people, more productive capacity, more knowledge and seemingly less common sense. We have excess, yet lack art, peace, and economic security. This is not a random occurrence, but the inevitable result of cause and effect fueled by conscious choices. We lack the mathematical appreciation for how we arrive at unintended and unwanted consequences.

## Money as an Object of Trade

Animals are enslaved by their physical instincts, whereas man, in contrast, is enslaved by both physical needs and abstract beliefs. The most powerful idea is the validity of money as a mode of exchange. Money is an object that may change shape or size or color. It can be colored dirt or colored paper. It can have different numbers and pictures printed on it, but somewhere, somehow, there is a valuation that is applied to money that is widely accepted, at least temporarily. This is an important clue to diagnosing the problem.

The alleged ability to make a judgment regarding the value of different objects as fair or unfair when trading with one another is at the center of every exchange. You can buy a chicken with money, or you can buy an egg. The great question is not, *'Which came first, the chicken or the egg?'* The great question is *'How many eggs are worth one chicken?'*

Trade and cooperation are vital to human existence. Primitive tribes have a social structure made up of differing families contributing to the needs of the whole. Despite size and technology, we are still the tribe on mankind. Age, gender and skill within the social contract divide roles. Divisions of labor are a natural event, and part of a group effort of mutual responsibility towards the common goal of survival. Commonwealth is the natural state of man; slavery and fascism are unnatural.

Within the social contract, the younger and the elder consume without producing. Production falls to those in mid-life, roughly from 20 to 65 years old. We are all part of a dynamic life, both giving and taking.

The proper purpose of money is for the good of all the people. As a practical matter, the system needs to produce and distribute the wealth of society. One sign of a wise and successful society is that neither the young nor the old are expendable, and no subgroup is burdened disproportionately. Everyone should have the opportunity to participate and share the results. Many hands make light work.

Money is a bridge between the long and short term, the near and far, the slow and fast, the weak and strong, the young and old. The bridges between money and value and purpose are collapsing. We must repair them.

# 2. Who Owns the Money?

When the Pilgrims arrived at Plymouth harbor in 1620, the English Civil Wars and the establishment of the Commonwealth of England would occur twenty-nine years into the future. The rise of modern finance was ninety-five years in the future. The first steam engine was hundreds of years away, and electricity a century after that. The Mayflower Compact, which was written before the Pilgrims touched shore, lays out a framework that embodies the virtues of a commonwealth.

The word commonwealth means for the public good or general welfare. The idea of commonwealth is the basis of the society that we currently enjoy. The opposite of commonwealth is fascism, where the strong bully the weak and the many serve the few. Fascism and slavery are evil twins. One is generally regarded as a political term and the other as an economic term, but they hold in common the idea of the few taking advantage of the many, and a top-down society. Contrasting world-views of commonwealth and fascism are still common in society. This is a primary dissonance. Fascism can easily become part of any hierarchal relationship, regardless of the organizational type. A merciless autocrat, whose hand on the rod of law is swift and heavy can head a family, business, church or government. Fascism, in part, drove the Pilgrims to flee Europe. Fascism was part of the colonization of the world that followed. The world's most famous fascist was the Pharaoh of Egypt. Whether or not you accept Moses, the evidence of an Egyptian empire still stands. Empires always have fascist characteristics.

## Empires and Commonwealths

Empires are highly stratified, authoritarian and plunder-driven organizations. Commonwealths are based on a belief that all men are equal, but invariably set up some form of hierarchal authority. In a commonwealth, we have a shared responsibility toward one another and a moral duty to the next generation. The wealth of society is shared for the enjoyment of all. The concept of stewardship extends to the whole next generation, not to the royal inheritance for a narrow familial advantage. The words republic and commonwealth share the same meaning. The United States of America was formed as a republic, and overthrew the tradition of monarchy, but the idea was planted one-hundred fifty years earlier by the Pilgrims. The idea that *'All men are created equal'* was part of a continuing search for a just society, where the few did not take advantage of the many.

---

### The Primary Dissonance

| FASCISM | COMMONWEALTH |
|---|---|
| *Many Serve the Few* | *All Serve One Another* |
| **SLAVERY** | **TRADE** |

---

The problem of how shares get distributed, and who makes the decision, is the role of politics. The new commonwealth in America quickly fell prey to old European habits of authority. Those in power see the sacrifices of others as natural and necessary for order. There were complaints about taxation as early as 1632. The people of Watertown, Massachusetts did not want to pay for a fort in neighboring Cambridge. The fort sheltered the soldiers, not the people, and antagonized the natives. It did not offer them any protection, and made the colonists poorer. They demanded a vote, which is fondly recalled by the townspeople as the first demand for no taxation without representation in the new world.

One hundred and fifty years later, the same colony would contribute willingly to buy arms for their own fledgling government. The arms stored in Lexington were viewed as an act of disobedience by the colonial government. Reluctant subjects were transforming into adversaries. In the aftermath of *'the shot heard around the world,'* (1775) Paul Revere would flee Boston and would hide in Watertown, where one of his duties was to print money!

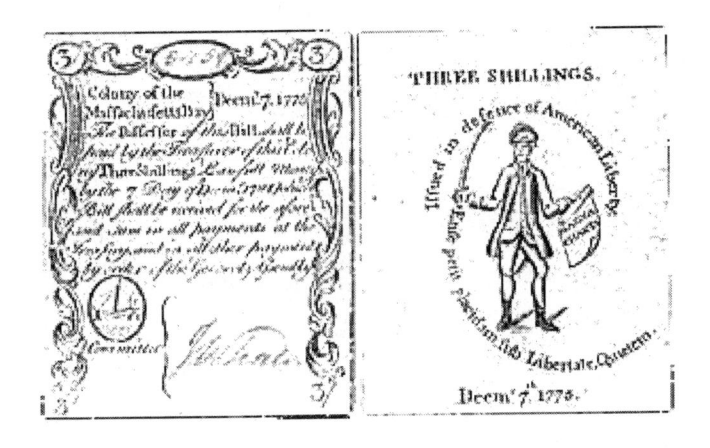

Politics are often about somebody being afraid of something, and of wanting a law to placate their fear. Violence, money and laws have a long sordid history. It is the nature of fascism to take too much, and then to demand more to protect what was taken. The more imbalanced the society becomes, the more the imbalance compounds, until the few have all, and the many have nothing.

Fear masquerades as commonsense. The rebel becomes as illogical as the authority he opposes. All violence is fascist. The rebel, in setting himself up as a champion, expects others to serve his needs, too. Trust and diplomacy are regarded as weak and dangerous on both sides. Both sides would rather kill their adversary and destroy their wealth, than share their wealth and live in peace. War is consumptive like a fire. Lives, labor and material wealth are exchanged for a heap of ashes.

The rebels, and those in authority, never recognize that they are fascists. They see themselves as champions over a self-defined evil: each other. In the course of their actions, they inflict harm trying to protect the thing they love. Hitler loved Germany, and in the process destroyed it. Hitler is an example of an extreme fascist, but a schoolyard bully is just as much a fascist. It is not the scale of success in gathering followers that makes one a fascist, or the scale of brutality, but the choices themselves. We are all capable of fascism. Circumstances give us the opportunity, and our temperament determines the degree.

As fascists, we create the danger we seek to avoid. We convince ourselves that we are a victim despite our strength or blessings. This is very common in young adults, who blame all their troubles on their parents. They feel misunderstood and unloved, and channel their angst (and lack of money) into the pursuit of power. Once people have power, they tend to be confident and merciless. There are gradations of fascism everywhere, and almost universally, they are related to money and decision-making. The definition of power is almost synonymous with the love of wealth. Fascism is a self-centered view of the world that preaches the virtue of greed, security and obedience. Fascism can be religious, political or economic. The source of power has no bearing on how it is used or abused.

Commonwealth, in contrast, puts the love of money and power at arms length, and puts people first. Commonwealth is an idea based on equality, individual uniqueness, and responsibility. Commonwealth is an attempt at balance. It is the power of love in opposition to the love of power. Commonwealth is the light of the world where fascism is the darkness. Commonwealth recognizes that all men own the world. The fascist is only concerned with his share. Wealth generically, and money specifically, are where the ideas of commonwealth and fascism intersect. Sometimes they are hard to separate. Dissonance allows a person to be of two minds: selfless and selfish.

Being rich does not make one a fascist, and being poor does not make one wise. A small amount of power can be used wisely or unwisely, the same as a large amount of power.

### Who Owns The Money?

The question of who owns the money is more complicated than the question of who has possession or what body prints it. Owning money is like owning the sky. It is held in common. We are only able to use money because others are willing to accept it. A foreign currency will be rejected by a store for not being a part of the local society. Such money will be a valueless novelty.

The first act after signing the Declaration of Independence (1776) was to design another currency. It did not fare well. By the end of the war it was worthless. The shift from the Articles of Confederation (1781) to the Constitution (1789) was for the purpose of establishing a sovereign currency. Money is collectively held, the same as rights and liberty and freedom, or not at all. The Crown lost control of the colonies, in part, because Spanish dollars were commonly used instead of English pounds. Money is possible because of commonwealth, and a component of commonwealth.

Money is usually a government-issued commodity. Shockingly, it is not real. It is a belief. Money is an intellectual agreement based on our need to trade. An idea cannot be owned. Money gets used everyday, but it is completely unnecessary. We use it because we agreed to use it. The Constitution signifies an agreement to use a new form of money, just as the Euro of 1999 was a new currency in Europe.

In theory, money acts as a substitute for the bartering of goods or services between two parties. On the positive side, money generates mutual trust and convenience. On the negative side, it provides a commodity of nebulous value in the exchange. Both the good and the bad are amplified over time because of money's mathematical nature. The positive is the modern world: people busy at work advancing the quality of life. The negative is the modern world: people busy at work creating misery and wasting human and natural resources. As will be explained, money can automatically divide society between a group with too much and a group with too little. Fascism is not required. Math will divide the wealth!

Money makes the government omnipotent. It is a part of every transaction. When we buy and sell, the government collects a small percentage. When, where and how it takes that percentage may change, but government is always taking a percentage. Life is not free in the land of the free, under monarchy or democracy.

Money easily expands the number of players who can be involved in any transaction. They all take a small percentage. For example, in a home purchase, there are often three banks involved: the original mortgage bank, the

25

new mortgage bank, and the sellers' current bank where excess funds are deposited. An insurance company provides financial protection. A title company confirms that the deed is clear. Two lawyers are present advising and witnessing the transaction. There are usually two realtors and a home inspector involved in the sale. Local government seeks taxes and payment for any capital investments (sewers) and outstanding services (trash). All these hands take a percentage before the buyer steps over the threshold. Every transaction is a group of transactions. Money is synonymous with shared percentages. The final buyer is paying for everyone. The purchase amount gets disbursed into a whirlwind of different percentages. In the hopes of discovering something, many economists, managers, scientists and investors spend an inordinate amount of time studying these percentages. They miss both the tree and the forest.

Governments are tethered to other governments as money and goods trade hands worldwide. The local collective economy has the same characteristics as the international economy. Conversion rates represent the value of a nation. The farmer who was worried about the Futures value of his crop also needs to be worried about who will buy it. The money from different countries has a different value. As trade barriers come down, new levels of complexity are added. Everywhere you turn, there are nuanced discussions about percentages. America desires everyone to use the dollar because it gives an advantage. That advantage impinges upon the sovereignty of every nation, many of which are perpetually embroiled in civil war.

## Origins of Organizations

All organizations have founders who had the vision and put up (or borrowed) the original capital. By virtue of their ambition, they become the key decision-makers. This is the case with businesses, non-profits and governments. In America, the two key decision-makers regarding money were Benjamin Franklin and Robert Morris Jr. They overthrew the old government and created their own. One was more thoughtful than his peers, and the other was richest among his peers. We will discuss them more deeply in Chapter 14: What is Modern Finance?

Rebellions often turn out badly. The rebel becomes like the fascist leader who was replaced. In America's case, neither of these men were politically powerful. They did what they believed was right and worked primarily behind the scenes. The money problem is hard to solve, and our two heroes did not solve it. They repeated a very old and flawed habit: issue currency through debt, and use taxes to collect it back. This choice kicks off an illogical vicious cycle based on percentages. They lacked the imagination and empirical evidence to choose otherwise. The new democracy had all the same fiscal failings as the monarchy that preceded it.

The rallying cry of liberty was really 'taxation with representation.' Unfortunately, representation is not as critically important as the accuracy of the math. A government's act of taxation, at any percentage, for any purpose, has practical consequences. We can bring harm upon ourselves with a local decision just as easily as a decision from a far-away headquarters. How a decision is made is not as important as the quality of that decision.

The world has had wise kings and foolish kings, and now we struggle with wise democracies and foolish democracies. The claim was that democracy limits corruption, which was generally defined as people getting rich by cheating. Democracy has not prevented corruption. Even if it did, the wealth would still be divided. The laws of mathematics are stronger than majority rule.

Economic problems cause political problems. It is not political power creating economic problems, as many assume. Replacing the leaders and changing the laws does not address the root of the problem: our assumptions about money are incorrect.

The Founding Fathers rested their hopes on egalitarianism. If the King's failure was greed, then how could greed be benign to inform checks and balances? Their approach was naive and contradictory. Egalitarianism cannot limit greed. One presumes the opposite. The problem cannot be the solution.

## The Illusion of Choice

When Solon created democracy in Ancient Greece, Anarchus made two comments that continue to echo today. He said, *"the law was like a spider web; it could only capture the weak, while the strong would break right through."* In other words, laws would allow the strong to constrain the weak, but the weak would not be able to constrain the strong. His second comment was that it was a system where, *"the wise speak and the fools decide."* Laws have a habit of working for the benefit of one against the other, not equally for all.

People distrust the voter (voter ID laws), the clerks (rigged elections), and the process is partisan before it begins (party declaration is required). This highlights a larger issue: the wise do not need laws, and the unwise are incapable of making them or following them. The only way for democracy to work is for the majority to be wise. Dissonance, in all its forms, must be purged. When it comes to solving a problem, facts matter more than opinions.

## Checks and Balances

Checks and balances have never worked because the strong players battle one another and ignore the weak. 'Survival of the fittest' is survival of the most ruthless and merciless, but even that is a mischaracterization. Darwin described the fittest as those who would adapt and change to new conditions. Clinging to the past and tradition, as many are prone to do, should be characterized as unfit.

Solon was trying to solve an economic problem similar to what the colonies would experience at Benjamin Franklin's time. Solon failed, too. The local Chief of Police in a small city today is significantly more powerful than what the ancient Greeks regarded as a tyrant. We have more laws, and more fascism, than has ever existed in history. Progress comes from wisdom, not force.

Solon's example demonstrates that the best ideas of the wise can still be foolish. Economic history reveals that the problems are not greedy people, but a system that fails mathematically. There have always been people of goodwill, but egalitarianism is not a substitute for logic. There needs to be a better plan to put that goodwill into action.

Mathematical forces make some people rich and others poor. When we apply percentages, we take something from someone else, that they took from someone else, and so on. It is a very small edge that makes the world competitive rather than cooperative, but that small difference can compound to create a huge divide. A competitive system must have winners and losers. Only in a cooperative system can everyone win together.

Capitalism and democracy (economics and politics) form a macro-dissonance. The former assumes competition; the latter assumes cooperation. Both are carried out in the opposite manner. Trade is cooperative and elections are adversarial.

| **Macro Cognitive Dissonance** ||
| **CAPITALISM** | **DEMOCRACY** |
| *Competitive* | *Consensus* |
| **TRADE** | **ELECTIONS** |
| *Cooperative* | *Conflict* |

Using money implies a freedom of choice because of the circumstances of others willing to accept it, but the use of money can inhibit liberty as easily as it can enhance it. In sharing an agreement to accept money, we simultaneously accept an agreement not to share products or services freely. The rise of the Internet is a powerful example of sharing. TCP/IP (the connection), Linux (the operating system) and Google (the search engine) have transformed the world. The Internet is based on sharing. As a result, everyone is richer by a quality of life standard. No one has become poorer by the lack of money involved.

Money, in contrast, mimics a zero-sum game. The gain for one party is always a loss for another. My profit is your expense. We have hunger in the world because we sell food for money. If we shared food, no one would ever go hungry.

Only production generates wealth. Trade or sharing moves what was previously created from one party to the next, from the point of production to the point of final consumption. The movement of goods is a necessary service, but the application of percentages along the supply chain introduces volatility.

Many claim that desperation is a necessary incentive to increase productivity. This is false reasoning. Money is also a cause of great waste, too. It belies the fact that the high standard of living we enjoy has generated a tremendous amount of volunteer and non-profit efforts. Money is not the key motivator. A higher quality of life has always been the primary incentive. Money is only a means to an end. It is a distortion to use it as either a carrot or a stick. The goal is to unleash creative cooperation, not constrain it. Today money is an impediment to exchange and destructive of the Quality of Life. Desperation drives activity into non-productive endeavors, like people becoming day-traders for a living. Moving numbers through a maze of numbers is wasted labor.

Money creates new limitations. The government's claim to money expands as the number of transactions expands. The more active the economy, the more government is involved in settling disputes and creating and enforcing rules. Government grows as a result, and those who have nothing to do with a competitive conflict share this burden. The poor pay for the rich to squabble.

Government becomes a target of economic blame during fiscal difficulties. However, taxes and spending are not the real problem with government budgets and economic cycles. Revenue and expense problems are generic symptoms of any money system.

## Percentage Dissonance

| REPUBLICANS | DEMOCRATS |
|---|---|
| *High Profit %* | *Low Profit %* |
| *Low Tax %* | *High Tax %* |

The political parties argue over percentages, but not about the existence of the percentages themselves. Partisan politics often resemble the blind battling the blind. Opposing fascists both seek control and wealth. They blame each other rather than recognizing their own prejudices regarding percentages.

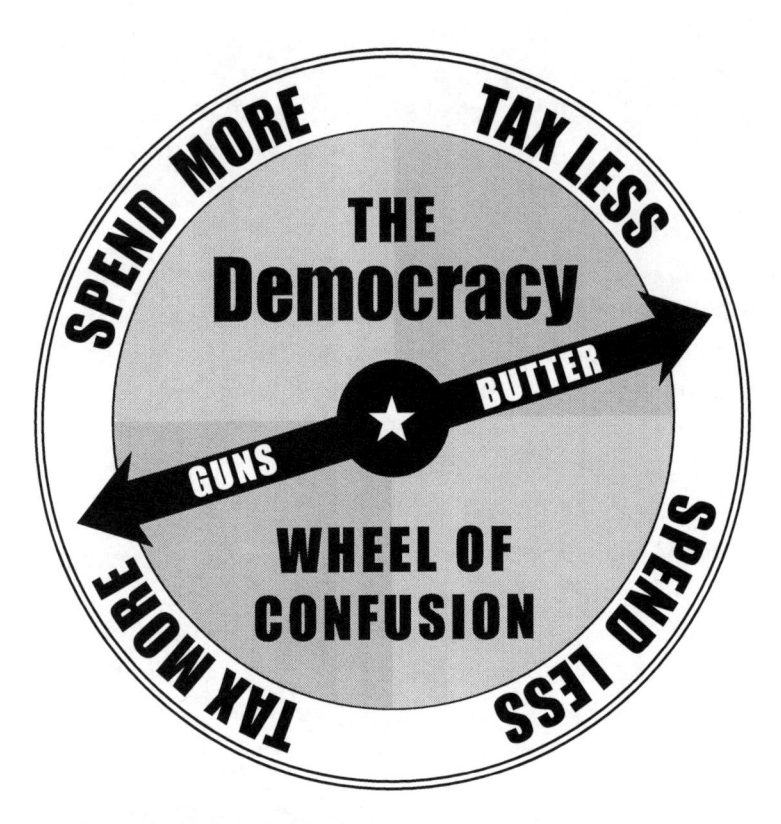

*THE Democracy WHEEL OF CONFUSION — SPEND MORE · TAX LESS · SPEND LESS · TAX MORE · GUNS · BUTTER*

### The Wheels of Confusion

There are only four choices for government: Spend More, Spend Less, Tax More, Tax Less. These choices constitute the Democracy Wheel of Confusion. Revenue and expense are the only variables. None of these choices will work. Businesses have a similar Wheel of Confusion: Increase Sales, Increase Overhead, Decrease Sales, and

Decrease Expenses. Overhead is increased in a bid to get more customers; sales are decreased to shed not-profitable-enough customers. Non-profits have their own configuration regarding who to ask for donations and how to spend it. Whether a person is taxing, selling or begging, a target and method for revenue must be chosen. The goal is always to have the revenue be greater than the expense. For the government, that is impossible. It starts off in debt and must remain there.

It does not matter how you combine the four choices. Inflation will continue unabated. As long as the application of percentages (2+2=5) is the norm, the system will remain volatile.

To make a meaningful change, the for-profit, non-profit, and government sectors must coordinate with individuals and other nations. This is not impossible. We cooperate to do the wrong things, we could just as easily cooperate to do the right things. Recognizing that we do not own the money is an important first step. Everybody could break-even at the same time. If there is profit, then there must be loss. Money is a misunderstood and mismanaged tool. Commonwealth eliminates both profit and loss, and only wealth remains.

Mathematically, wealth can exist only in the private sector. If money were a fixed object, like gold, of a limited amount, and the value of goods never changed, then it would be impossible to return more to the government that what it issued originally. The government can never cover its own expense. Imagine that the government has the world's only chicken, and eggs are the type of money. The government could only collect the eggs that it had previously spent. No other eggs exist. Any eggs currently in circulation would guarantee that the government be in debt for the same amount or more. Money is this magic egg, whether it is made from gold or paper. When the government is short funds, it borrows its eggs back in the form of bonds. It is impossible for government to withdraw all the eggs from the private sector and pay off the National Debt, without changing the value of the eggs or the goods. To avoid this mechanical problem, we have inflation and currency revaluation. The government prints more and more money, so there will be enough 'eggs' for everyone, including itself.

An annual budget surplus is a mathematical aberration. This sets the stage for larger deficits in the years that follow. It is a requirement of the underlying math. The Clinton boom was the Bush bust. Facts are few, but one fact is huge. There is currently a National Debt of $15 Trillion. If 2+2=5, then 2+2=$15,000,000,000,000. If you repeat more of the same behavior, then you get more of the same result. It will continue to compound, regardless of whom we elect.

A penny compounded fifty times is $5,629,499,534,213.12 ($5.6 Trillion dollars). The National Debt doubles approximately every five to eight years. It must or the currency will collapse. Every President will increase the Debt by the value of all the other Presidents combined. That is the nature of doubling.

Every day people create 'the need for money' as a byproduct of trading and consumption. Mathematically, we must generate a numerical profit so we have an excess that we can spend to consume and survive. It is illegal for people to print their own currency, although many have recognized that this is the shortest path to wealth. The government unconsciously recognizes the difference between creating a currency type and creating currency through profit, which is why it taxes revenue rather than arresting everyone for counterfeiting. Mathematically, however, recording profit (2+2=5) is the same as printing money. The buyer gives the seller permission to create money via the exchange. The buyer gets what he wants, the seller gets what he wants. Everyone else gets the inflation.

While we say the government creates money, it is more accurate to say that the government creates the debt that we consider to be money. In the private sector, we create profit, which the government eventually matches as increased National Debt.

There is a time lapse between the moments when the debt ceiling is raised. The interim is recognized as volatility or 'natural circumstances.' The change in perspective is usually based on how it directly affects oneself. In general, bad things are described as volatility, and somebody or something else is to blame, whereas natural occurrences are things that one can benefit from by being shrewd and managing properly. If it is expected gain, then it is natural, and if unexpected loss, than volatile. Economists often combine the two into an 'expected loss,' which is another version of cognitive dissonance.

Everyone and every organization follow a revenue and expense model. Criminal and non-profit activity are not mathematically different than for-profit activity. A broken oil burner is as big a nuisance for a church as a police-intercepted load of illegal contraband for a crime syndicate. Gain and loss are recorded the same everywhere. Nobody plans for a loss, despite what the economist expects.

## Debt

While governments are in perpetual debt, there are plenty of debtors in the private sector, too. The wealthy are good at generating profit, the poor and young are not, and are forced to borrow. Lenders get rich on other people's debt, which makes it easy for the rich to get richer, and the poor to get poorer. The criminal is best at getting wealthy because they buy lowest and sell highest. Stealing and then reselling can be easier than printing money because the income cannot be traced. The casinos provide an intersection for spending and gambling wealth, fencing stolen goods, and for laundering cash. Casinos are a lot like Congress, the Pentagon and Wall Street. However, the money flows with a lot of zeroes in the same pattern where there are few zeroes. The corruption at the top is a reflection of the troubles at the bottom. Everyone is seeking the easiest way to wealth. The more blazingly corrupt take the shortest path. If they get caught, then they can afford more lawyers to dissemble the truth.

Any action the government makes has a ripple effect, but the result will always be the same: more debt and more inflation. Someone spending more or less money at any particular moment, for any particular reason, is a constant phenomenon. The statistics can be massaged to say otherwise, but in the aggregate, no other result but inflation and debt are possible. Every transaction generates inflation. It does not matter who purchased what. Guns and butter are both inflationary. Mathematically, all spending is the same. The government debt must match the new inflation created by new transactions. This will be further explained in Chapter 4: What is Inflation?

Not surprisingly, every nation in the world is in debt. This is an important phenomenon. Government debt is the money that the private sector needs to function. Once the people accept their currency, the government needs to maintain it in constant supply. There is a direct mathematical relationship between public debt and the aggregate of private transactions. The government does not create debt in a vacuum. The debt limit is raised so the participants in the economy have enough money to be able to trade. The private sector and the public sector have a mutually parasitic relationship. The higher the government tax rate percentage, the higher the private sector profit percentage. Government is the largest debtor, employer, and customer in the economy. The more the private sector profits selling to the government and to each other, the more the government taxes the private sector. The constant shifting of percentages back and forth is a vicious cycle of mathematical confusion. People blindly study these variations. From a coupon-cutter to a hedge fund investor, they are looking for a hidden pattern from which to gain an advantage. What a waste of time! Survival for everyone is accomplished through cost shifting. It is mathematically impossible for everyone (public or private) to keep pace with inflation indefinitely. It is the nature of blowback that the day of reckoning will eventually arrive.

 The government is in the peculiar position of deriving its income from private-sector profit. That means when the economy is bad for the people and corporations, it is even worse for government. For example, a business can survive by breaking even. If the employees and the vendors get paid, and it shows no profit, the business pays no taxes and goes forward. It can cut overhead during lean times. Likewise, if the employees experience a pay cut or inflation, they can consume less and maybe pay fewer taxes, too. The people and businesses are significantly more nimble than the government. The government, however, must increase its spending during these slow periods. For them, if revenue is down, then there is also a pressure for their expenses to go up. Everyone wants to be in a state of profitability again. The states lobby the federal government for more cash to meet their own budgets. The federal government acts as the pressure release valve for inflation.

It is at these times that the federal government uses deficit financing to catch-up with private sector inflation. It is a regular occurrence in financial history. The debt limit is raised and large transfers are made to the state governments, which then attempt to pump cash into the local economy. Anybody who complains about the debt for the children is ignored. There is no mathematical alternative, only the frenzy of expediency. Unfortunately, this vicious cycle can never be stopped. The action and reaction are tied together. It is just a typical "*my expense is your profit*" transformation, but on a national scale. The roles have been reversed, just as they are in the private sector, when the seller becomes the buyer. The government becomes the giver rather than the taker.

When it comes to finance, the future is condemned by the past. Attempts to delay the debt, whether in public, corporate or private finance, are all based on the same logic: slow down the expenditures to give revenues a chance to increase. If only it were so easy. We are all connected in the commonwealth. Since my profit is your expense, cutting your expense cuts my profit, which is going to lead me to to cut my expense, which is someone else's profit. Every change will eventually work itself around. Death is the only escape. In fact, death is the only thing that keeps the system somewhat balanced. In death, the holdings of one generation must pass to the next generation, which is the impetus for the importance of inheritance. Every generation seems to enjoy a steadily increasing life expectancy, along with a population increase, which dulls the advantage for the next generation. There are more people waiting for what will be less money of less value.

## Societies

As a simple model, the economy is a distribution system. Everything originates from the Earth for free. Man must add his labor to fashion the natural resources into something useful. We work to produce what others consume, others work to produce what we consume. Because the Earth is large, certain resources are found in various places. The shifting of goods and services is both necessary and natural. Trade is in everyone's best interest, but what we are trading primarily is the labor to produce the goods, not the goods themselves.

We are exchanging local harvests, but as goods move, numbers move with them. It is the shifting within numerical ledgers that is the problem. Our needs are uniform. Everyone needs each other. Seldom do you hear a complaint that is production-related anymore. The struggle is always with the numbers.

The divide between the rich and the poor should be understood as a symptom of a mis-regulated currency. The rich are not necessarily greedy or fascist. They are fortunate within a fascist system. While some people are cleverer than others, and may work harder, those differences do not explain the wide discrepancy that exists.

The political process can give everyone a chance to vent their grievances, but we need a better analysis of the problem to solve it. There is no invisible hand. Science is based on explaining the result. A cause is either true or false. Treating the symptoms will never lead to a cure for the underlying disease. That is why it is important to recognize that we do not "own" money. It passes through our hands. We have a responsibility in regard to how we handle it.

The existence of government money masks the most important question in economics: What is value? How many eggs is one chicken worth? By continuously replacing one side of the barter exchange, the question of value is never addressed. We are hundreds of years late in holding this conversation. The island of Manhattan was exchanged for sixty Dutch guilders. The money had no meaning to the Native Americans. The island was a gift, not a sale. The Native Americans had a system based on sharing, not selling. There was no such thing as a hungry Native American until the white man arrived. When we celebrate Thanksgiving, it is to thank the Native Americans for sharing food. The Pilgrims and the Native Americans both understood the value of commonwealth. The genocide that followed was by the fascists who were more concerned with the Futures value of food, rather than its immediate benefit to feed everyone.

If Manhattan Island is worth $1 Trillion today, then the government must issue $1 trillion in currency. The government debt is always following the private economy, not leading. The United States government started off over $70 Million in debt, by using the private resources of people like Robert Morris Jr. To pay one citizen, government must take from another citizen. This could be sharing, but it is not. That is the critical difference between a selling system compared to a sharing system. The Native Americans could share an entire island and not feel any financial pain. We, on the other hand, suffer at our own hand. Selling is more painful than sharing.

Percentage variation is a ubiquitous problem. Because percentages have become accepted as a cultural norm, they are not recognized as the primary driver of volatility and inequity. It makes more sense to have a fixed percentage of zero, than to allow every transaction to be different. When we bargain over the percentage, nothing is accomplished. We are just poisoning the well. Commonwealth is common goals and common dignity. We all have a right to a measure of equality when we trade with each other. It is illegal to discriminate on the basis of race, gender and other criteria, but it is acceptable to discriminate for no reason at all.

If you go to a bank to borrow money, you get a different percentage rate for a car loan than you do for a mortgage. A new car has a different rate than an old car. A young person is charged a different rate than an old person. The same is true of the deposits. All these different percentage rates are forms of inequality that betray the concept of commonwealth and equality. It belies the fact that money is collectively owned, and creates classes that are favored or disfavored. This is not just a banking issue. It occurs throughout the economy. The same product is sold at different prices to different people by the same business.

Many cite an invisible hand as regulating the economy. Adam Smith (The Wealth of Nations, 1776) never said such a thing. On the contrary, what he said was that when we labor domestically for our own material security, it acts as an *invisible hand* strengthening our commonwealth. He was not a believer of free and reckless trade. In fact, he was writing in favor of tariffs. He was arguing against importing goods because it disrupted the commonwealth. It is unfortunate that people have misinterpreted his writing.

Adam Smith was correct regarding the importance of commonwealth, but incorrect about tariffs. Foreign trade is not a threat to a commonwealth, as long as it is done fairly. Any action can have either a good or bad effect. His cognitive dissonance was to suggest that selfishness within the commonwealth was acceptable. He evidently recognized that foreign goods might be acquired more cheaply. He should have asked, *'Why?'* The discrepancies in value between national currencies create the discrepancy in worker conditions, not vice-versa. Smith's attitude is a combination of might equals right with the ends will justify the means. It is a very narrow vision of society, and claims that good results can come from bad choices. This is the root of fascist indifference. The math, and history, proves him wrong. His entire line of thought is to flatter the merchant.

The invisible hand claim stems from an attitude that *"Whatever happens, is best."* This claim of amoral detachment was characterized by the foolish and bumbling Professor Pangloss in Voltaire's novel Candide (1759). Of course things will work themselves out, no matter how stupid we are. The end is pre-determined. We are all going to die eventually. The choice is in regard to how we want to live.

In general, there are three political factions in economics. The party of indifference is actually the largest party. Anything, by virtue of its existence, can be described as part of a natural balance, but that does not constitute scientific analysis of cause and effect or apply moral reasoning. At the time Adam Smith wrote his book, the economy was already off the rails. That was why political-economic discussions were regarded as important. The rise of the merchant-class was in full bloom; monarchy and the landed estates were waning.

The application of percentages had destroyed the economy. People were desperate, which was why rebellion was in the air. The same circumstances led to the writing of this book. The merchants of those days were convinced that they were wisest about economics because they handled money the most frequently. In fact, they were handling the money most improperly. Blaming the King is no longer a convenient excuse. Blaming the government is to repeat the original false claim. We the people have to confront our own dissonance.

Because we are all bound to the government, proxy binds us all to one another. We cannot escape the economy. We cannot escape commonwealth. The question is only, *'How well do we manage the resources of land and people?'* The answer is, *'Not very well, at present.'* We are all bound to the math, the progress and the trouble, equally. The word commonwealth recognizes that we are bound together.

## How do we share the bounty?

A competitive system drives man to want to be a master, rather than a slave. As master he can decide what to keep and what to share. In a world of extreme inequality (9:1), trusting equality is a radical idea. Those with an advantage fear that equality will become 1:9, not 5:5. The rich do not want to move down or trade places with anyone in the commonwealth. Rather, they would prefer that the poor move up. The rich often suggest following their own example: work hard, use variable percentages to your advantage, repeat. In other words, always take more than you give. Infomercials repeat the formula constantly. It is the foundation of buy-low sell-high.

Because we have created a numerical ladder, the only way to move up is for someone else to move down. This is broadly accomplished by someone's death or birth. A death adds free wealth into the system, a birth adds free labor. Somebody will benefit from every change. When the government issues more money, the entire ladder moves. People's relative inequality, however, remains the same.

We have few troubles with production and consumption. The challenge is that we need to be more skilled in both giving and receiving. It is our own hand that creates the desperation and volatility.

The issue is, *'How should we conduct ourselves in business and politics?'* It is difficult to separate the wheat from the chaff when we spend all our early years being brainwashed into the errors of history. We create heroes too quickly and let go of them too slowly. Slave-masters were the heroes of the American Revolution and the villains of the Civil War. Both battles were about merchants wanting to protect their variable percentages. All the wars, including the war of terrorism, have the same root.

The Democrats and Republicans are both claiming that 2+2=5. They differ on when and where a variable percentage should be applied. Neither taxes, nor profits, can resolve the numerical disparities. Taxes cannot create equality and profits cannot lift up the poor. Inflation is the problem, not the solution.

What we are experiencing is broken logic and a failed experiment. We need goods to survive. We must consume food, education, energy, and other things. As goods and services are consumed, their mathematical footprint remains. The mathematical percentage of taxes and profit, once created, can never expire. These percentages live on as debt and inflation. We are all chained to the past and each others' current transactions through the mutual currency. A peaceful coexistence with a mathematical absurdity is not possible.

It is easy to blame the rich for taking too much, or to blame the poor for not working hard enough, or to blame the government for incompetence or corruption, but none of those claims are wholly true. Percentages drive the inequality. We are all behaving the same way. There is plenty of blame to go around.

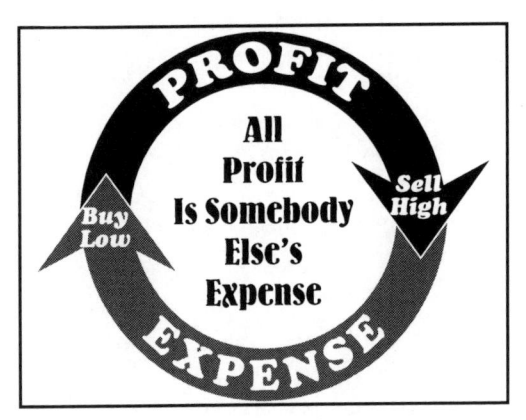

**PROFIT** — Buy Low — **All Profit Is Somebody Else's Expense** — Sell High — **EXPENSE**

It is important to follow the math, not just the totals. Most discussion, debate and disagreements are over totals, rather than analyzing the math being used. Percentages reveal both the problem and the solution. The problem is tiny. The challenge is that the wrong behavior is widespread.

When I sell to you, my profit is your expense. If I buy from you, my profit is not spent, rather it is transformed; my profit is now my expense and your profit. We are both engaged on both sides of a buy-low sell-high transaction. After the goods were consumed, the mark-up amounts created during both transactions remain within the economic system. All value, once created, can never disappear. This is why it is possible for every nation to be in debt and experiencing inflation. Both build incrementally. Every transaction involves a buy-low sell-high sequence. Even if selling at a loss, it still represents buy-low for the buyer. The percentage may change, and the winner may change, but not the underlying mathematical foundation. Any percentage is destructive of commonwealth.

The boom and bust cycle has two causes. One, the inability of the public debt to keep up with private sector inflation. Second, the concentration of wealth in the private sector, which generates unsustainable private debt elsewhere. Debt eventually collapses and ends the ability of others to maintain a growing rate of consumption, which the system depends upon. Larger percentages bring about disruption faster than smaller percentages. There is never a shortage of demand. There is a shortage of cash for those who have wants, and excessive cash hoards for those on the opposite side of the mathematical divide. The presence of great wealth and poverty marks the failure of commonwealth. It is not a sign of a healthy economy or progress. Percentages act like a cancer in the body commonwealth. Money is held in common, and how we handle it has consequences.

45

# 3. What is a Budget?

We live in a budget-driven society, because of the desire to control revenues and expenses. Man is capable of remembering the past and predicting the future, and we use that ability to think abstractly to create budgets. A budget measures our hopes and expectations. It provides a standard of skill, often a definition of success and failure, a roadmap, and a topic of much discussion. Budgets exist in local, state and federal governments and provide the entire framework for government. Nothing is accomplished that is not in the budget. The squeaky wheel that gets its grease is looking for favorable inclusion in the budget process. Corruption uses the budget for personal gain rather than for the commonwealth. If you are not in the budget, then you are invisible.

Budgets also exist in the private sector. Wall Street is myopic in terms of budget expectations. Stocks fluctuate based on meeting, exceeding or failing to meet expectations. The expectations can be provided by the company itself or by self-appointed analysts. Expectations are not uniform from one political party to another, or from business to business, or even from person to person. However, expectations themselves are held in common. The wise stockbroker, like the weatherman, is credited with predicting correctly 50% of the time something over which he has no control. He is superfluous but highly regarded, because he is involved in the art of prediction. They provide a false sense of control. The same is true of budgets. The clouds will blow regardless of the accuracy of a prediction, and the prediction will be as quickly forgotten as the clouds themselves. Budgets are like old weather reports and old newspapers. They require a lot of effort to create and are instantly out of date. They do a terrible job of predicting the future, but an excellent job of documenting failures of the past.

Budgeting exploded with the rise of computers and programs like Visi-Calc and Lotus 1-2-3. Today, custom programs build budgeting directly into the business operations. Much like the vital signs of a hospital patient, managers can closely nurse the health of their numbers. Much like the patient, the workers get no rest from the constant vigil of number watching. The definition of acceptable performance keeps moving.

Businesses and governments both seek totalitarian efficiency. Slave masters would like the slaves to run a marathon at the quick pace of a sprint. Everyone is expected to work harder and more efficiently, while inflation returns less reward for effort expended. This situation is reflected in the worries of the farmer who can feed others but not himself. The ability to collect data has fed the desire to predict and control data. Police-like states existed before computers, but they have blossomed with this new tool. The ability to measure is part of the corporate manager's demand for more results, even as the time spent measuring is a large component of inefficiency.

Managers set high standards for others, but low ones for themselves. Anything that they decide can be regarded as 'essential' for the competitive situation of the market. A million dollars will be spent on a one-minute television ad, while the workers in the warehouse are expected to increase their efficiency. The managers can waste money faster than the workers can create goods, the same way that lawmakers can spend money faster than it can be taxed.

Advertising agencies and marketing departments have similarly adopted any new technological developments, like social media, to harangue potential clients for more revenue. In the same way, governments resort to fees and new taxes. The spending is all planned out in the budget to meet the budget goals. What started out as a single page with simple calculations has compounded into volumes of nonsensical organizational priorities. The purpose of the organization becomes less defined over time, and so a mission statement is added to the list of budget items. The dissonance can compound in parallel with the budget.

While budgets are made from numbers, there is little analysis of the math. The process is based upon unreasonable expectations of disconnected numbers behaving uniformly. Seldom is the budget process itself regarded as the cause of unexpected consequences.

Budgets are used by businesses as a way to manage employees. Sales quotas, customer counts, client surveys, inventory turn-over, profit margins, gross and net sales, production rates, units sold, and cleanliness scores are just a few of the myriad of ways that the budget mentality is applied within a hierarchical business relationship. Anything that can be counted can be budgeted. Even things that cannot be counted, like quality, are subject to an attempt to be quantified.

In the classroom, children and their teachers are subject to similar demands with tests and score expectations. This has resulted in huge battles between elected officials and teacher unions over contract stipulations. The taxpayer funds both sides in these battles. The strong battle the strong, while claiming to defend the long-term interests of the weak.

Budget battles represent the dearth of commonwealth. Statistics are commonly used to prove a claim. The bell-curve is not an observation, but is often used as a blueprint for the expected results. Conformity to a statistical anomaly is considered a worthwhile goal. Depending upon what is being measured, and how, the bell curve itself can represent a great inequality. When statistical formulations serve as a self-validating budget framework, management becomes trite and fascist. The goal is lost.

The budget process moves from planning for the future, to predicting the future, and finally to creating goals. Numerical targets serve as an omnipotent idea. People are forced to obey the budget, even if it violates common sense. The budget has reduced entire organizations into slaves of numbers. Everyone becomes part of the supply, and the invented future is the demand. Man should be the master of his numbers, not its slave. Fear has replaced commonwealth. The banal has been elevated to the sacred.

Budgets also exist at the individual level. It is here that we can begin to understand the budget process as a mathematical phenomenon, rather than one of growing expectations. Personal budgets tend to be discussed as 1) a savings for a future expense, or 2) as an adjustment to ensure expenditures are less than income. For example, a small amount is saved from every paycheck and put into a separate envelope to be used 'when the time comes.' In the second approach, personal budgeting mimics governmental or business management. It is an effort to increase revenue and decrease expense. Cash flow concerns are at the heart of budgeting.

A personal budget does not require a consensus of unrelated players, obedience to authority, elaborate procedures to change your mind, or a constant chorus of blame or panic. These things only occur within organizations.

Risk is personally assumed, and it is not assigned, diverted or shifted onto others. There is no outside analyst comparing your management to an invented ideal. The only consequence and expectation is the will to survive. However, because all money is collectively owned, and flows from one party to another, personal habits get a lot of attention in both economic and business research. Consumption drives production in the standard economic model. The desire everywhere is for budgets to expand. More revenue and less expense is the universal ideal. When individuals are thriving, this is regarded as burgeoning trade.

All budgets are connected to other budgets. Budgets exist allegedly as a means to ensure the ability to consume. Yet, it seems that government is perpetually embroiled in a budget crisis. Over hundreds of years, there has been no improvement in management skill. A budget of a single year is considered a gargantuan accomplishment. In attempting to predict, plan and create the future according to a blueprint, we have introduced fear, panic and volatility. Spending and then cutting, building and then destroying, reorganizing, attempting to capitalize on brief opportunities, and responding to supposedly unexpected problems are all characteristics of the budget process. Chances are that some will claim that successful navigation of these events are due to the success of the budget process. In reality, it is the budget process itself that is creating some of these reputedly unpredictable incidents. Economics is not the study of scarcity or plenty; it is the study of the activity that creates scarcity and plenty.

Cause and effect should be a basic presumption of scientific economic analysis. If the economy is volatile, we created the volatility. If there is scarcity, then we have failed to expend our effort in the same hierarchy as our highest priorities, thus creating the scarcity. Budgets are not a cure, and are quite often the disease. Because of money, good ideas are abandoned; because of money, bad ideas are sustained.

Part of the problem with budgets is that all priorities are self-centered. They ignore the fact that we are part of a chain of transactions. Our revenue is someone else's expense. One group is underworked, overpaid and undercharged, while another group is overworked, underpaid and overcharged. This happens by design. While trade is cooperative, the mathematical relationship is fundamentally adversarial. Every transaction has a winner and a loser. Budgets set in place a plan to win in the aggregate, which means other groups must lose in the aggregate. Not surprisingly, when one group is highly satisfied, another group is suffering terribly. The employer has great profits, while the employees are struggling. One business advances while another suffers. Apple goes up while Microsoft goes down. Only expanding consumption can allow two competitors to rise together, which is why growth is viewed as the ideal.

While equality is a political ideal, there is no equality in the marketplace. Laws to provide equal treatment, equality under the law, or contract enforcement, only institutionalize the mathematical inequality of the marketplace. Laws act particularly unfavorably toward the coming generation. Given the central role of education in society, public and private budgets for education occupy a tremendous amount of budgetary resources. This is one of the best pieces of evidence that the budget process is a failure. Education should not be a burden for either the current generation or the next generation.

## The Basic Math of a Budget

As stated previously, money is an intellectual agreement. Value has no absolute definition. The question of how many eggs is one chicken worth cannot be answered conclusively. Nevertheless, trade has a mathematical root that we can study separate from how any particular values are applied. There are general mathematical laws regarding budgets.

A balanced budget is when revenues and expenses are the same. This can be expressed as R=E.

An imbalanced budget can be either a surplus or a deficit. A surplus is when revenue is greater than expenses: R>E or E<R. A deficit is when revenue is less than expenses: E>R or R<E. Like any mathematical formula, the budget formula can be read the same forward as backward. Like a glass half-full or half-empty, the language used to describe a budget is a personal preference. The amount of water does not change because of how it is described. There are three possible conditions for a budget (balanced, deficit or surplus), five ways to describe it (R>E, E<R, E>R, R<E, R=E) and two components (R and E). Like the weather, it is simple enough: sunny or rainy, hot or cold.

These budget formulas are missing the most important element: time. The government, organizations, businesses and individuals do not live in a stagnant model. The cash flow is constantly in flux. Revenues and expenses change for a myriad of reasons. Like a seesaw, the current state of the cash flow can be momentarily positive, negative or balanced.

The primary shortcoming of the budget approach is that it is an artificial logic; it attempts to enforce an unnatural rigidity on the natural process of life. Money is only a substitute for barter. Changes in values are driving one another's budgets, and our ability to trade freely. There is a qualitative difference between planning (which makes sense), and budgeting (which is nonsense).

For example, we can study the food purchases for a school cafeteria. Planning needs to reflect the school year, vacations, seasonal availability of fresh food, and the most difficult thing to predict: customer demand. Using historical data, we can get a sense of previous years' sales and expenses, but the more we attempt to fine-tune a budget using historical data, the more likely errors will be introduced.

One would not carry an umbrella today because it rained one year ago on this date. Adjusting our expectation to match better the previous calendar, for example, the same Monday of the same week of the same month, would fare no better. Rain is not determined by the calendar, but rather by the season. It does not repeat so precisely that any historical data is of any practical use. This inconsistency keeps weathermen employed. Yet, managers are constantly mining data in an attempt to find some hidden pattern upon which to claim a valid prediction. They think they are responding to new data when they make adjustments, when they are really adjusting to their own flawed assumptions.

The employees serving the food have the best sense of the buying habits of the students. The managers making the money decisions at the top are the most ignorant within the entire organization hierarchy. By trying to predict future cost and demand they are completely isolated from the present and the consequences of their decisions. It is an example of those having the knowledge and power having the least amount of understanding, and those with the understanding having the least power. This is tragic because the act of buying or selling is relatively simple.

If you miss the weather report, then chances are it will not have a significant impact on your day. With a modicum of planning, the budgeting process can be replaced. The imposition of a budget mentality within an organization creates more chaos than it avoids. The budget becomes the customer, not the client. The quality and selection of the school lunch is based on the budget, not based on the likes or needs of the students. Imagination is not being used to solve problems; it is being used to invent numbers which are the problem.

Corporate philosophies occasionally attempt to trust the front line to do their jobs properly. A resurgence of common sense occurs under the banner of buzz-words like *'employee empowerment.'* Unfortunately, the managers cannot resist their fears, and centralized financial control and decision-making quickly returns. The goal should only be the aggregate: R=E, but the means gets in the way of the goal. There is a desire to be better than the budget, which also reveals that the budget assumptions are suspect. The macro-mismanagement trickles down into a micro-mismanagement.

In general, the bigger the organization, the more poorly it is run. The huge revenue manages to cover up a lot of sins, which is yet another reason why growth is desired. The budget is an attempt at a self-fulfilling prophesy, but ends up being only a reflection of the assumptions, egos and emotions of those who craft it. Since the numbers are contrived, the budget can be used to bludgeon or reward the employees, at the will of the next manager up in the chain of command.

Budgets exist because there is a desire to control both sides of the equation. Revenue (R) is desired to be as high as possible, and expenses (E) are desired to be as low as possible. This is *'buy-low sell-high.'* The belief that money is real is the most ubiquitous idea in the world. The belief that money should be handled in a 'buy-low sell-high' manner is the second most ubiquitous idea in the world.

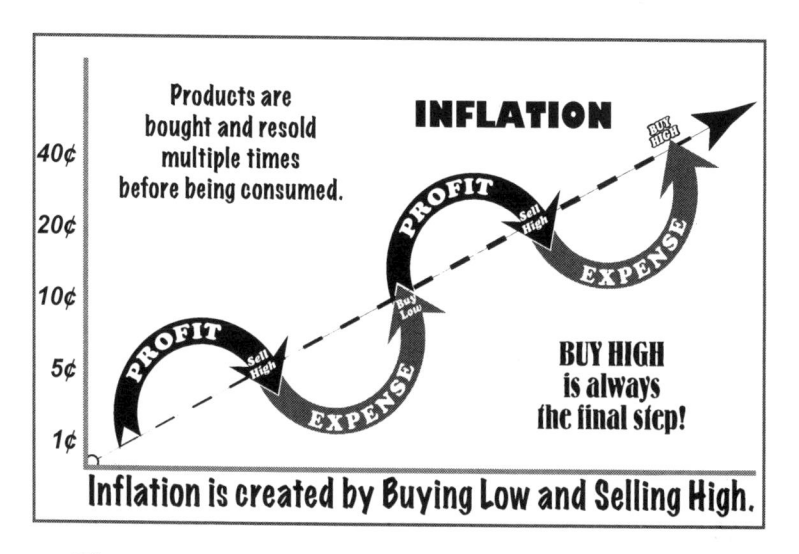

**Inflation is created by Buying Low and Selling High.**

    The greatest failure of the budget process is the drive to make the numbers happy while making the people miserable. Instead of many hands making light work, the budget seeks to have fewer people work harder. Budgets are diametrically opposed to all the goodness in commonwealth. They represent the worst type of planning and subtly destroy the quality of life.

    Money has exchanged hands the same *buy-low sell-high* way for thousands of years. Eliminating budgets will not eliminate the nature of the exchange.

    Planning is often appropriate. The problem with budgets is the attitude of the managers and their institutionalization of incorrect assumptions. The job of a manager is to make the work easier. Budgets are generally the reason work is harder. The managers want more from others, but have low standards for themselves. The budget gets used inappropriately to acclaim and condemn employees.

    If writing numbers down leads people to treat others badly, then it would be better to not write numbers down at all. After violence, budgets are the cruelest way that humans treat one another. They provide an excuse for the banality of indifference. A faith and fear of numbers takes precedence over reason and compassion. Customers, employees, citizens and vendors are the sources of revenue and expense, and there exists a perpetual attempt to squeeze more out of each group.

Budgeting would not be possible without the advent of double ledger accounting in the 15th century. Double entry accounting provides a snapshot in time of cash flow, assets and liabilities. It is a great historical and planning tool with or without the formalization of budgets. One would hope that with more information, there will be less chaos and more control. In practice, the chaos, greed and struggle are the same or worse, but they are better documented.

Cash flow problems are an unintended consequence of creating cash. Money, rather than solving problems, has become its own problem. Budgets are an unfortunate response to challenges caused by the Cost of Living within an inflationary spiral. To solve the problems that budgets are meant to solve, we need to get closer to the source of the problem: inflation.

# 4. What is Inflation?

Price is the point of contention between buy-low and sell-high. The settled price allegedly represents a negotiated compromise, but usually both parties are experiencing multiple pressures and would prefer something different. The past serves as the baseline for how we understand a price. Prices move due to fluctuating market conditions. Inflation is generally regarded as the sellers winning, and deflation is regarded as the buyers winning.

Inflation creates difficulties for budgets because the increased cost of any good requires either purchasing less of that good or less of some other good. It acts the same as revenue cut and lowers the Standard of Living. As a result, inflation gets scorned because it limits our appetite, and takes away our choices. For the same reason, deflation is welcomed when buying. It acts like a revenue increase, and allows for the buying of more goods.

### Price Dissonance

| BUYING | SELLING |
|---|---|
| *Inflation : Bad* | *Inflation : Good* |
| *Deflation : Good* | *Deflation : Bad* |

Our view of inflation and deflation is dependent on if we are buying and selling. It is its own dissonance. We are all buyers and sellers.

## Supply and Demand Theory

The most common explanations for inflation and deflation are one of four variants of Supply and Demand Theory: there are either too many or too few Buyers, Sellers, Products or Dollars (BSPD). All versions assume that the seller wants to sell-high and the buyer wants to buy-low. Nobody wants to pay-more, even if they are willing to charge-more. Deflation gets explained in the same way as inflation. It is a change in who wins or loses, but the underlying forces are the same.

Supply and Demand Theory claims that as the volume of BSPD fluctuates; the negotiated prices fluctuate in response. The macro-level condition determines the micro-level transaction.

**Conventional Theory of Inflation & Deflation**

**SUPPLY & DEMAND VARIATIONS**

Too Much or Too Little

- Too Many BUYERS / Too Few
- Too Few SELLERS / Too Many
- Too Much MONEY / Too Little
- Too Little PRODUCTS / Too Much
- INFLATION PRICES DEFLATION

As the quantities fluctuate the prices allegedly fluctuate.

A Buyer, a Seller, a Product and Money are necessary components of every transaction. Economic schools of thought have formed based on each part. These schools disagree on the specific cause, but agree regarding the process. For example, Supply-Siders suggest that the economy will run best by having more producers. According to their view, competition will increase choice and lower prices. They are pro-business, free-market advocates. Government regulations are unfair and unwise because they create advantages and disadvantages that the marketplace would not naturally provide. They accept that one business may come to dominate an industry because of skill and effort. That is okay, because the economy functions based on the survival of the fittest. A new business will eventually rise and challenge the leader. The analysis centers primarily on government regulations, which are interpreted as interference. This view is held primarily by those engaged in selling.

When it comes to the supply of money, there are two opposing versions. Libertarians focus on the amount of money available in the economy. They complain that the Federal Reserve and deficit spending have created a glut of money in the marketplace. Excess money allows prices to rise. They see the economy as a zero-sum game. Sellers charge according to what the buyers can afford. More money in the system means that buyer will pay more. The existence of inflation is considered proof of their claim. Curiously, more money does not allow people to buy more products; it only allows them to pay more for the same product.

In contrast, Keynesian economic arguments favor deficit spending by the government. They accept that competition will lower prices and increase efficiency, but the way to help sellers and create jobs is to infuse money into the economy and increase the number of buyers. When the economy is tight, it is because not enough buying is occurring, which makes the poor poorer, and businesses struggle. The rich do not need extra help. They are just another buyer who is not buying during lean times. In general, the Keynesian is more holistic, and takes into account the needs of the buyers and sellers.

Priming-the-pump allows people to buy more, not pay more. More buying will keep the producers busy, who will then hire more workers. This further increases consumption, production and a rising Standard of Living. Democrats propose getting more money into the hands of the poor and middle-class, because they will immediately spend it. For them, government spending is a positive thing.

Both Democrats and Republicans embrace Keynesian economics. They differ on where to direct government spending (guns or butter), but generally accept that deficit financing works the same way. The defense industry is sustained by government spending. Inflation and debt are of secondary importance to jobs and defense.

These different interpretations of how the economy functions are the constant fodder of political discussions. The goal is the same: peace and prosperity. Because they see the problem differently, they see the solution differently. The opposing strategies are constantly promoted and condemned.

Progressives, and those farther to the left, see economic problems rooted primarily in political privilege. They are outside of the free-market supply and demand belief system, and see trade more as a forced condition of survival. Given the history of monarchy, colonialism, slavery and despotism, there is some truth to their claims. Slaves would be fed just enough to be able to keep working. Power corrupts, and that corruption gets expressed in an economic manner. The laws favor corporate charters and their managers, rather than workers, even in a democracy.

Progressives are divided between two views. One is class struggle (the rich against the poor). The other is the living against an invented construct. Monarchy was an invented construct, supported by a claim of Divine Law. Corporate charters act the same way. Progressives embrace the idealistic freedom that all men were created equal, but believe the economy is rigged in favor of the Sellers. Free-market capitalists want more freedom to compete, progressives believe that they already have too much power, and competition generates waste, not efficiencies. Corporations were granted charters as a means to serve the people, but instead people are expected to serve the corporations.

Corporations, like governments, are driven by a budget mentality. Even when profitable, and holding large hoards of wealth, the mantra is always more. Their gain must come at the expense of someone else: customers, vendors, employees or the environment. Corporations, like monarchy, have an unfair advantage of age and size. In the progressive view, in a battle of survival of the fittest, the people must lose and corporations must win. They see the economy is a inflation or deflation, buyers versus sellers, winners versus losers conflict, but without the supply and demand explanation. It is the laws that give an unfair advantage. Their view is similar to the supply-siders, but without a trust of free-markets.

All schools of economic thought are trying to make sense of the nonsensical. Everybody recognizes similar problems. They attempt to use political power to apply their economic strategy.

Under the umbrella of Supply and Demand theory, the different factions agree on many points. Competition is regarded as good, and monopolies are bad. The Deficit is bad, but can be increased for a dire need of either guns or butter. The push and pull is whether there needs to be more buyers or more sellers, more money or less money. These competing explanations are more similar than different, and share a common weakness: the lack of a mathematical model to explain how inflation or deflation results. The assumptions are not properly tested.

Fluctuations in production and consumption are a part of the natural lifecycle of the planet. The marketplace is a reflection of this underlying condition. Man's habits are built around Earth's orbit of the Sun. Holiday calendars, the school year, harvests and season shifts impact the timing and volume of what gets consumed. Pricing, in contrast, is exclusively a man-made event. Whether prices are set higher or lower than previously, they have to be set by someone. Prices are a conscious choice.

The Supply and Demand theories attempt to establish a connection between the volumes of BSPD with pricing. It is tenuous. The cause and effect sequence is coincidental and anecdotal, not direct. Price changes are more frequent and volatile than the changes in the volume of buyers, sellers, products or dollars; nature is slow, steady and predictable, prices are not. Prices can be moving in opposite directions between competitors, even though they are both operating in the same environment. All these theories are based on using selective facts, not all of them.

To explain inflation and deflation, we should look at common behaviors of the participants, rather than at secondary conditions like the BSPD volume. A more accurate theory would accommodate any fluctuations in the four elements. Everyone is trying to buy-low and sell-high. We should study this common behavior more deeply to understand the mathematical results.

### What is inflation?

The act of *'buy-low sell-high'* is the applying of variable percentages to a price. This is what causes the price of goods to perpetually rise. The more people that touch the good, each adding their own small amount of profit, the more the good will eventually cost. The final consumer pays the profit for everyone who touched the good previously.

Deflation is only a change in what has become commonly accepted as the selling price. Deflation can be the result of sellers using a smaller percentage, or of buyers finding a more direct path to the good, thereby circumventing one or more middle-men's mark-up.

Inflation has NOTHING to do with supply or demand. Inflation is the mathematical consequence of percentages being applied on the path to being consumed. The problem is much more simple than what is often claimed. Our troubles have nothing to do with political privilege, although they can acerbate them. Everyone creates inflation. We are both the victim and the crime.

### The Inflation Sequence

We can understand inflation by following the trail of a single apple from a farmer's tree to the consumer's table. The farmer picks an apple and sells it. By the time a consumer eats it, it can have any price. In the examples to follow, the same apple can cost between 1.6 cents and 32 cents; a huge 20:1 difference. The pricing differences are unrelated to supply and demand. Prices are determined wholly by the mark-up percentages used.

A business will change their mark-up percentages for many reasons. A belief in Supply and Demand Theory undoubtedly plays a role, but inflation is a long-term mathematical phenomenon. We need to understand the math that the behavior is causing.

In our first example, a farmer picks an apple and sells it to the cooperative for one cent. The cooperative sells it to a wholesaler for two cents. The wholesaler sells it to a cold storage company for four cents. It is then sold to a distributor for eight cents. The supermarket buys it for sixteen cents. It is put on the shelf for the consumer at thirty-two cents. Everyone along the supply chain has enjoyed a 100% profit percentage. In cash money, however, their profit is very different: one cent for the farmer, one cent for the cooperative, two cents for the wholesaler, four cents for the cold storage, eight cents for the distributor and sixteen cents for the supermarket. (1+1+2+4+8+16=32) The eating of one apple has created 32 cents of money-value out of thin air.

Example 1 - 100%

| 100% Markup | Sell | Profit | Inflation Share |
|---|---|---|---|
| Farmer | 1¢ | 1¢ | 3.125% |
| Cooperative | 2¢ | 1¢ | 3.125% |
| Wholesaler | 4¢ | 2¢ | 6.250% |
| Cold Storage | 8¢ | 4¢ | 12.5 % |
| Distributor | 16¢ | 8¢ | 25.0 % |
| Supermarket | 32¢ | 16¢ | 50.0 % |

The second example is based on a 50% mark-up, rather than a 100% mark-up. The final cost of the apple drops significantly, from 32 cents to less than 8 cents. The farmer gets a larger share of the inflation that was created, but he did not change his original price of one cent. There is less income disparity. The inflation sharing is more level, with a low of 7.2% for the cooperative and a high of 33% for the supermarket. The spread is only 25.8 points, compared to the spread of 47 points at the 100% mark-up. A smaller mark-up results in lower prices and more equal earnings. The profit ranges from .5 cent to 2.5 cents, rather than from 1 cent to 16 cents.

Example 2 - 50%

| 50% Markup | Sell | Profit | Inflation Share |
|---|---|---|---|
| **Farmer** | 1.00 ¢ | 1.00 ¢ | 13.1 % |
| **Cooperative** | 1.50 ¢ | .50 ¢ | 7.2 % |
| **Wholesaler** | 2.25 ¢ | .75 ¢ | 9.8 % |
| **Cold Storage** | 3.38 ¢ | 1.15 ¢ | 15.1 % |
| **Distributor** | 5.06 ¢ | 1.70 ¢ | 22.4 % |
| **Supermarket** | 7.59 ¢ | 2.50 ¢ | 33.0 % |

The third example is based on a 10% mark-up. The final price of the apple is less than 2 cents! The farmer sold the apple for 1 cent in all three examples. This time, the apple was able to move from tree to table for less than twice its original cost. The farmer, at 62.1%, created the lion's share of inflation, whereas for others it varies only 3 points, from 6.21% to 9.32%. In the third example, everyone makes less than the farmer. In the other examples, with few exceptions, everyone was earning significantly more than the farmer.

| 10% Markup | Sell | Profit | Inflation Share |
|---|---|---|---|
| **Farmer** | 1.00 ¢ | 1.00 ¢ | 62.1 % |
| **Cooperative** | 1.10 ¢ | .10 ¢ | 6.21 % |
| **Wholesaler** | 1.21 ¢ | .11 ¢ | 6.83 % |
| **Cold Storage** | 1.33 ¢ | .12 ¢ | 7.45 % |
| **Distributor** | 1.46 ¢ | .13 ¢ | 8.07 % |
| **Supermarket** | 1.61 ¢ | .15 ¢ | 9.32 % |

Mark-up percentages reveal why it is possible for a farmer to feed thousands of people, but still have trouble feeding himself. When he goes to the supermarket, he must pay retail. The earnings on his apples are significantly less than what others enjoy. The next chart highlights the difference between what he earns and what he needs to spend on his own apple. When everyone works at a 10% mark-up, he can afford his apple. But at the higher percentages, he cannot afford to purchase his own output.

## Who or What Creates the Steep Curve of Inflation?

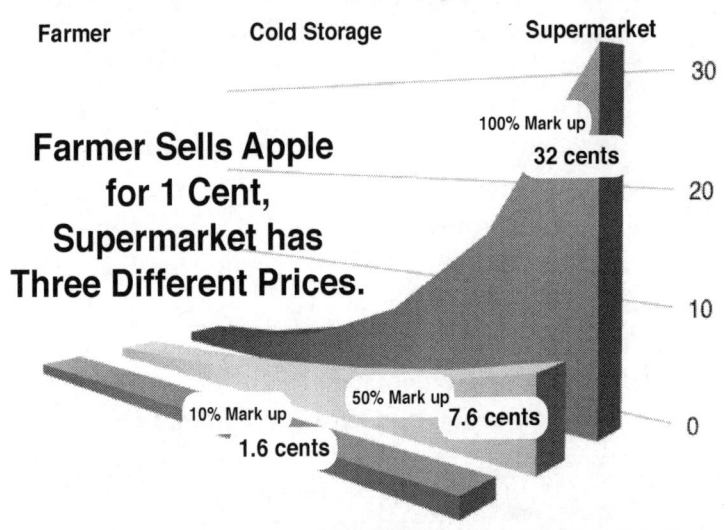

Farmer      Cold Storage      Supermarket

**Farmer Sells Apple for 1 Cent, Supermarket has Three Different Prices.**

100% Mark up — 32 cents
50% Mark up — 7.6 cents
10% Mark up — 1.6 cents

**FINAL HIGH COST IS CREATED BY EVERYONE USING A HIGH MARK UP PERCENTAGE, NOT BY NUMBER THAT TOUCH THE PRODUCT.**

We can learn quite a bit from this simple model. The sellers created the inflation, not the government. The volume of BSPD had no effect on the price. Inflation was created by the math being used. Each transaction is commonly dependent on the one immediately prior and after, but every transaction is unrelated and independent overall.

There is a very large disparity in income for the same labor of passing along the apple within the supply chain. A farmer has to sell thirty-two apples so he can afford to buy one apple at retail, but the distributor only has to sell four to earn enough to buy one apple. For a consumer to pay thirty-two cents, they must have earned enough profit from a similar chain of supply activity. Inflation is necessary to keep pace with inflation.

The apple was real; the value of the apple was invented by the habits of trade. Everyone involved in the transaction collectively created 32 cents of inflation. The chart below shows how price inflation occurs as goods move, the profit for each participant in the transaction, and their respective share of the creation of inflation. Notice that the farmer and the cooperative are getting the smallest share, and the last person to touch the apple has the most profit. The previous chart exposes the root cause of inflation, and the large disparity in income levels.

In our own way, we are all farmers. It is difficult for everyone to create more revenue than expenses, when the base mark-up is high. Budgets are a coping mechanism to a self-sustained problem.

The most common response to inflationary pressures is to charge-more and buy-less. Politicians, businesses and individuals seek to increase revenue and cut spending. This behavior worsens the collective condition with which we are struggling. The changes in the BSPD volume are the result, not the cause. The micro determines the macro. The alleged short-term solution compounds the long-term problem and drives the boom and bust cycles. The entire economy is teetering on the points of extreme profit. Huge gains quickly become huge losses. boom and bust cycles have reached a critical mass of too many crises, too fast and too deep, and the social fabric has disintegrated.

The boom and bust cycle represents the birth and death of communities, businesses and nations. Every war is either a civil war, or, following a trading route into a civil war. The rebels start by building domestic support and eventually reach out to the government's trading partners, or trading enemies. The new government begins indebted to whoever gave them support. When and if the old debt is forgiven, it usually arrives with new trade contracts.

It is a basic component of American foreign policy to build other nations in our image. Money grants and loans are distributed to governments in a manner similar to angel investors and venture capitalists funding the next big invention. The government then pays that money to American multi-national corporations to build airports, harbors, and roads. Other private companies arrive to invest more cash. They build infrastructure, factories and mining sites. The oil companies, especially, have a worldwide influence. If America begins to develop a trade imbalance with the country, then it can be partially corrected with armament sales and security training. The opposite situation, debt forgiveness, always comes with political concessions. Instead of being in debt to America, foreign nations are often in debt to American banks and corporations. This is possible because America represents all sides of the supply and demand equation. It is the largest buyer, the largest seller, has the most protected products and the most money. Despite having many advantages, it is not capable of maintaining a stable economy either for itself or the rest of the world. Foreign policy has all of the same gears as inflation (BSPD) in play.

Because of their high ideals of freedom and self-determination, Americans do not consider themselves imperialistic. They advocate free trade, freedom of speech, freedom of religion and freedom of assembly throughout the world. Free trade is only one component of many, yet it is invariably trade that generates the most trouble among all people.

Rebellion does not make a nation strong and wise; it often marks a point of weakness and stupidity. Some nations languish in this state for decades, if not centuries. The leader of one nation that was controlled by American influence described it as being held by two nooses. If the multinational pulls out, then their economy becomes even worse, but if they stay, the situation is untenable. Everyone around the world is trying to satisfy the budget conditions. No one has been successful. The sword has been as ineffective as the pen. The problem is with the numbers.

Even though it seems counter-intuitive, a lower mark-up percentage is best for everyone: workers, consumers, businesses and government. Inflation is not a mystery. It is the result of compounding percentages. We have been brainwashed to believe that profit is good and more is better. Budgeting offers no help. Measuring closely does not change what is being measured. Only a lower mark-up percentage can create a pricing equilibrium, reduce wage disparity, and reduce debt. The purpose of paper money was to support a cash economy. What we have today is a debt and inflation economy. Very little cash is in use.

# 5. What are Boom and Bust?

Boom and bust cycles are more than an economic event. The social, political and cultural fall-out has a significant impact on peoples lives and purpose. Dreams are either fulfilled or destroyed. At one extreme there is renaissance, and at the other civil war.

Boom and bust cycles are a consequence of inflation. The compounding of percentages slowly divides the wealth into two groups: the rich and the poor. We all need each other, but during a civil war, one side claims the other side is expendable. The ideal favors equality, and trading as equals. The reality develops into something quite different, even without factoring in generational differences.

At some point, the poor become too poor to continue paying their bills. This results in bankruptcies, foreclosures and business closings. Every such failure impacts others, directly or indirectly. The boom causes the bust. Deficit spending by government is the only possible remedy, which is why deficits have grown so large.

### Percentages & Compounding

Inflation has three sources. Profit is only one type of compounding percentages. The other two are taxes and interest. In general, businesses use profit, governments use taxes, whilst non-profits and individuals use interest. The different percentages are constantly compounding.

**Boom & Bust Drivers**

| REVENUE IS EXPENSE | GOVERNMENT | BUSINESS | BANKING |
|---|---|---|---|
| | \multicolumn{3}{c|}{**PERCENTAGES APPLIED**} |
| | Tax Rates | Profit Margins | Interest Rates |

**Three Ways of Creating Inflation**

A lot of inflation is hidden on the product side of the transaction. Smaller sizes and goods of lesser quality are sold at the same price as before. While the price did not change, inflation did occur. More goods can be produced faster. Manufacturing skill can sometimes mask an inflationary rise, which is why efficiencies are lauded. Another approach is to find cheaper labor, so the worker carries the burden of inflation rather than the customer.

Compounding percentages have deadly consequences. The disagreement over taxes is why the colonies revolted against the king. Complaints about taxes are common in history. *The Communist Manifesto* decried industrialism and the descent of men from serfs into paid wage laborers. It was an attack on private ambition and the quest for endless profit by corporations. Our complacency with interest was a main reason why America was attacked on 9/11. Osama bin Laden lays out this complaint in his *Letter to America* in October 2002. All three movements are responding to disparities created by the application of percentages.

Like the Supply and Demand Theory variants, revolutionaries tend to blame one sector of society, rather than examine how all the elements interact. Any percentage, no matter how small, or where applied, will eventually result in doubling. The rate of compounding is variable, but not the result. Nations develop massive inflation and debt values because of incremental cause and effect. Corporate and individual debt and wealth accumulate in the same manner.

Albert Einstein discovered *the Rule of 72*, which calculates the amount of time required to double the principal, based on the percentage rate of a loan. The same formula can be applied wherever percentages are used, not just to loans. A 10% markup doubles the value of an apple more slowly than a 50% markup, but the price will eventually compound. How we handle money and apply percentages has consequences. The difference between a pricing equilibrium and hyperinflation is the difference between renaissance and civil war.

## Monopoly

The best-known model of boom and bust cycles is the game *Monopoly*. Henry George was an economist of the late 19th century, and the game was meant to demonstrate his idea that increases in land values impoverish society. It was originally called The Landlord's Game, and was not intended to be a game for fun. People were supposed to learn how society creates the rich and poor as a byproduct of trade. Except for one person, everyone goes bankrupt. It reveals something anti-democratic in the economy. One person will gain all, and everyone else will lose all.

*Monopoly* is best understood as a generic mathematical model, rather than a land/rent exchange. It does not matter what good is being bought and sold. *Monopoly* demonstrates that inflation causes wealth to concentrate. Mathematical forces create the rich and poor, not political privilege, intelligence or hard work. The winners and the losers are all behaving the same way, so there is no reason to blame anyone specifically for the result. *We The People* are responsible.

The beginning of the game is the boom cycle. Everyone

appears to be getting richer together. This is the Keynesian approach, with the bank pumping more money into the game. Pent up demand is released, and buyers start buying. At this point, nobody owns any much property, so the players are equal. Slowly advantages form, as a result of luck with the dice roll. Eventually a tipping point is reached and the bust cycle begins. The bust cycle is not universal. There is the one person who is gaining from everyone else's losses, which serves as 'proof' that the boom cycle is not dead. The data is being misread. The bust cycle is when the rich get richer, and the poor get poorer. It sets the stage for civil war and revolution, not just the end of a game.

The rags to riches phenomenon is considered to be a strength of democratic-capitalism. It is actually a symptom of dysfunctionalism. Rising to the top is not freedom; it is the process of desperation. Volatility causes the rich to fall and the poor to rise. Neither extreme would exist in a properly managed commonwealth.

Probably unwittingly, *Monopoly* is a model of two allegedly different economic systems: capitalism and socialism. It is capitalistic because everyone is free to buy and sell in an entrepreneurial way. It is socialist because everyone is paid the same amount: $200 for passing GO.

*Monopoly* is a perfect democratic model, too. People start equally. There is no graft, vice or corruption, or advantages for wealth, power, tradition or age. There is no emotional manipulation or advertising. People do not age or die, or increase or decrease their buying habits. It is a stable and predictable economic environment. Fellow players are honest. There is no government or overhead of checks and balances. It is a free population with one simple need, randomly chosen by the roll of dice. Despite this simplicity and utopian beginning, it is not long before the wealth divides and the economy collapses.

The compounding of profit for one player is the compounding of loss for other players. It is the buy-low sell-high cycle that is being compounded. The conclusion is inevitable: inflation and debt. We are following a path of mutually assured destruction through competition, rather than mutually assured production and consumption through cooperation. The Game *Monopoly* demonstrates a mathematical phenomenon that we ignore at our peril.

### Capitalism & Socialism

Historically, we have seen capitalist systems move towards socialism, and, socialist systems move towards capitalism. This is not a coincidence; both systems are more similar than different. They start at opposite extremes in terms of private ownership of property. Capitalists want to liberate greed, whereas the socialists seek to restrain greed. In capitalism there is limited planning; under socialism there is an abundance of planning. Planning and budgeting is akin to controlling what numbers can be thrown on the dice. It does not change the mathematical formula of the game. It only impacts the arrival date of the inevitable outcome. The capitalists move toward more planning and more regulations, the communists move toward less planning and less regulations. Both are copying failure. Neither regulations, nor the lack of them, can work. The math is incorrect.

### Regulated Economies

*Monopoly* splits the difference between a regulated and unregulated economy. There is a diversity of rents from inexpensive to expensive. It uses a fixed price model so inflation is limited. Once the properties are developed to include hotels, all inflation stops. The steps to arrive at that point, however, are more than enough to determine the outcome. The players need a lot more than $200 for passing GO to survive, especially if they lack ownership of a property group. That is the situation for every new generation.

In a game without property groups, it is important to recognize the condition of the bank. If the property were to be equally distributed and undeveloped, no players will go bankrupt, but the bank would eventually collapse. Agrarian societies represent a slower model with fewer land transactions and smaller populations, but old monarchs failed financially the same way as modern governments and large societies.

Once money is considered to be more than a chit, and has its own value, collapse is inevitable. The three sectors of the economy, government, businesses and private individuals, are each powerful enough on their own to destroy the economy. Everyone is connected to whatever debt exists, the struggle against inflation, and the looming bust cycle. Freedom can only work if everybody follows the same Golden Rule.

Our society, like *Monopoly*, guarantees few winners and many losers. This is not a logical way for any nation to be organized. The ideal of commonwealth is peace and prosperity for all members of society. To give the next generation a better world than the one we were given, then we must change the rules of the game. We need to teach something better than what we were taught, and change our accounting habits.

## Revolutions

Revolutions are successful civil wars. Unsuccessful civil wars are regarded as uprisings. Both sides feel strongly that their way is the best way.

Civil wars are generally an attack by the middle-class against the upper class. An up-and-coming leader seeks recruits who aspire to have more. The young get involved because they have the most energy, nothing to lose, and the most to gain. They are also the easiest to sway with a lie, the cheapest to bribe, and, being young, lack self-awareness.

The poor seldom get involved in revolutionary politics. They do not have the luxury of time, wealth or education to organize.

Revolutionary leaders rise to power using violence, and by following the same habits of the people they seek to overthrow. Violence is never enlightened, whether from above or below. It does, however, mark the point where the problems caused by inflation are no longer sustainable. The boom and bust cycles have reached a critical mass of too many crises, too fast and too deep, and the social fabric has disintegrated.

*Monopoly* demonstrates that the economy will be the same no matter who is in charge. An economy with profits, interest or taxes will constantly struggle. All compounding percentages are critically important. All revolutions have sought a more just society, and have been for naught because of a lack of mathematical clarity.

# 6. What is the Cost of Living?

Changes to the Cost of Living wreak havoc with budgets. If advance planning could fix expenses and revenues, then the self-fulfilling prophesy that a budget attempts would be easily accomplished. Economics is the study of success and failure because budget expectations, formalized or not, fall victim to inflationary pressures.

The Cost of Living can be expressed as Revenue over Expenses: $R/E=CL$. When $R/E$ is greater than 1, there is a budget surplus and a rising Standard of Living. When $R/E$ is a fraction, there is a budget shortfall and a declining Standard of Living. Strictly speaking, however, $E=CL$. Expenses are the Cost of Living. R (revenue) is how you pay for it.

The Cost of Living is a mathematical formula with political or social consequences. It is the divide between the rich and the poor, getting ahead or falling behind, the good times and the tough times. It concerns the ability to live within ones means and the quality of life. It is psychological, mathematical and material. For some, happiness is getting what they want, whereas for others, it is wanting what they have. Life can be a perpetual hunger or a state of contentment, regardless of the material circumstances.

The Cost of Living (CL) is intimately related to the Standard of Living (SL). One of the odd things about this relationship is that there can be an inverse correlation to the budget goal. For example, living beyond the budget (carrying a deficit by borrowing) can increase the Standard of Living. To adapt the old cliché, one may not be a millionaire, but one can live like one by borrowing and then spending a million dollars.

Most economic theory claims that increased revenue increases the Standard of Living. This is the motivation behind *'priming the pump,' 'stimulus packages,'* and getting a professional degree. Materially and emotionally, there is an expectation that bigger numbers mean more happiness. Yet, many with fame and fortune are miserable, as the tabloids are quick to document. Greater revenue ensures that one can spend more, but happiness cannot be easily quantified. Statistics imply an increase in material wealth with an increase in revenue. The higher the income, the more one can purchase. Unfortunately, however, the cost of what one purchases changes over time, too. A small and steady increase in revenue may or may not keep pace with inflation or fixed expenses. Larger revenue does not guarantee that you can purchase more, only that you will spend more.

When analyzing the Cost of Living, the amount of dollars is secondary. What matters more is the ratio between revenue and expense. The ratio indicates whether one is 1) breaking even, 2) flush with cash, or 3) losing money. The spending and revenue can vary wildly from individual to individual or from organization to organization, but their comfort or discomfort with money is based on ratios. Everyone has a unique mathematical relationship with money, and it is driven by ratios. Being unable to meet a mortgage payment is stressful, regardless of the size of the bill or value of the home. Failed budgets are painful.

When expenses are greater than revenue, that person is living fractionally. For example, $50,000 in expenses, but only $40,000 in revenue: 40000/50000 = 4/5, which is .8, or less than 1. Any fraction is a negative ratio. When revenues are greater than expenses, that person is living at or above 1. For example, $40,000 in expenses with $50,000 in revenue. 50000/40000 = 5/4, which is greater than one: 1.25. Any whole number is a positive ratio. A negative ratio is only possible with borrowing.

## The Cost Of Living Ratio

|  | REVENUE | EXPENSE | RATIO |
|---|---|---|---|
| NEGATIVE | $40,000 | $50,000 | 4/5 or .8 — |
| POSITIVE | $50,000 | $40,000 | 5/4 or 1.25 + |

A Negative Ratio Is Only Possible With Borrowing.

For someone who is living fractionally, or nominally at a whole number 1, their expenses are always tight with their revenue. They have to be careful from day to day, and change their spending, eating and travel habits based on cash flow. They may splurge when feeling flush, and then contract as necessary. For them, inflation and unanticipated expenses are a perpetual challenge. The more that is spent on any one object, then the less money is available to spend on another product. It is a zero-sum-game existence, especially when credit is not available. This lifestyle represents the majority of people and businesses. While some people have amassed huge hoards of wealth, or inherited wealth, few people live without any concern for money. Those who have become wealthy usually struggled with a fractional ratio at some point in their life. The struggle of businesses and for personal advancement shares a similar fate.

For those living fractionally, budget adjustments are a constant way of life, not a formalized procedure. If the cost of gasoline rises, then they may change their food spending to compensate. Businesses and individuals, in general, respond to inflationary pressures better than governments. Governments fix their budgets and are slow to deviate from them. Administrators are sure to spend their budgets for fear they will get cut in the one that follows. A lot of political wrangling stems from the fact that the government, by design, sets a long-term budget that locks itself into a fractional position. While the budget is passed as balanced, it almost always includes a component of borrowing, and assumptions that will not be true. Even when spending equals what was earned, a financial angst exists. Inflation is constantly nipping at their heels.

The challenge is always to get revenue to be greater than expenses. Fiscal changes can be quite significant, negatively and positively, but yesterday is always a difficult baseline to maintain today. Pressure does not stop once one gets ahead.

## Ability to Respond

|  | PACE | SCALE |
|---|---|---|
| GOVERNMENT | *Slow* | *Huge* |
| BUSINESS | *Medium* | *Limited* |
| INDIVIDUAL | *Fast* | *Small* |

Everyone has fixed expenses that they cannot change quickly or easily. This generates the tension between the Cost of Living and the Standard of Living. Using debt as a solution to maintain a Standard of Living has brought both the great and small to their knees. Those with a higher Standard of Living can be poorer than those with a lower

Standard of Living, if they are living on borrowed money. The seemingly rich can be trapped in a negative ratio, having borrowed more than can ever be repaid. This comes to light in bankruptcy proceedings where businesses or individuals are millions and billions of dollars in debt. Their wealth was all borrowed. Similarly, America is the richest nation in the world by being the world's largest debtor.

### Standard Of Living Pressure

|  | REVENUE | EXPENSE |
|---|---|---|
| RISING STANDARD | *Increasing* | *Decreasing* |
| FALLING STANDARD | *Decreasing* | *Increasing* |

Revenue and expense can only move up or down.
There are no other possibilities.
The same issues as the Wheel of Confusion
and budget planning.

In general, the middle-class experiences a negative ratio until late in life, after they have paid off their home mortgage. They struggle to keep cash flow revenue ahead of expenses, and do not live extravagantly. The poor are constantly on the line between a positive and negative cash flow. Lack of access to credit, or access only to expensive credit, keeps them at a perpetual mathematical and material disadvantage.

Success is determined primarily by access to cheap credit. Almost all wealthy individuals have control of a business that has borrowed heavily. A public corporation is an indebted business. The original founder gets rich, and stocks form a barrier of protection between his personal wealth and the collective wealth of joint ownership.

Some poverty is a result of being a victim of a financial crime, some is the result of institutionalized bigotry, but on the whole, poverty is primarily a result of risks taken within the system, rather than a characteristic of the economic system itself. That may sound like a contradiction to the previous claim that every transaction is imbalanced and therefore the whole must be imbalanced. It is the same logic extended. All risk is collectively shared, just as all money is collectively owned. Trading with profit creates an imbalance, but investments (borrowing and spending) create its own cascade of imbalance. Banks, government and wealthy individuals (those living well in excess of 1) cater to risk-takers, because that is where new revenue will be generated.

When there is a borrowing of a billion dollars, there must be a corresponding pressure elsewhere. The most egregious example of this speculation is at Wall Street, which must create a vacuum at Main Street. Wall Street is entirely based on a fractional Cost of Living formula. All the money that drives the system is borrowed, which is then lent out again and again in a cascade of debt and inflation driven by the attempt to derive profits via interest payments. Individuals and institutions siphon off the investments, and the interest revenue, to maintain their Cost of Living advantage. Wall Street does not manufacture anything. It attempts to master small percentage changes. The entire system is constantly at risk, and there are frequent collapses because of the inherent weakness of the fractional equation.

Borrowing introduces more instability to the problem of imbalanced trade and increases the struggle for a positive Cost of Living equation for everyone, not just for the borrower and the lender. Everyone's actions have an impact on everyone else's Cost of Living equation. Just as my profit is your expense, and your profit my expense, so too is your risk my risk, and my risk your risk. Risk-taking fuels the inflation that changes the Cost of Living ratio and challenges everyone's budget. Whatever product is being sold, the profit must increase by a margin large enough to cover the expense of the borrowed money. The lender, or investor, are essentially implementing his or her own tax on the business, and by proxy, upon everyone associated with the business. They supply money to the business in the same way that the government supplies money to the country.

A normal business, with a stable overhead and productive capacity is at risk with or without borrowed money. Borrowing, however, is a warning bell. Borrowing increases overhead for a business. If there is any interruption in the revenue stream, because of competition or consumer preferences, then the business can fall deeper in its fractional position. They are always borrowing from near a fractional position to start. The borrowing event is a willingness on the part of the entrepreneur to shift from a positive ratio to a negative ratio, because otherwise there would be no need to borrow. Banks oftentimes expect collateral or a shared burden before they lend, so the old surplus gets spent. The business becomes fractional after the expansion and new equipment is installed for which the funds were borrowed. Consider what this means: Wall Street firms are living off borrowed money and lending to businesses that are living off borrowed money. Should collapse of these houses of cards ever be a surprise? More borrowing *'to stay afloat'* is to make the negative ratio larger.

Interest payments reflect a double jeopardy. They increase expenses and mark a consumption of surplus. Risk is a mathematical phenomenon, just like the Cost of Living and the Standard of Living, and it has a long-term effect on budgets. Everyone is at risk of poverty. Ill intent or mismanagement are not required. The volatile system impacts governments, businesses and individuals. Risk-taking to solve the revenue problem increases the difficulty of the Cost of Living equation. The same actions that push revenues up also push expenses up.

When there is trade, money is exchanged for a new commodity. With interest, money is exchanged for something purchased long ago. The original object was purchased with time, not money. It is a contract of servitude. Interest and principle become a permanent inflexible component of the Cost of Living expense, which means that current consumption must be adjusted because of yesterday's consumption. Once in a negative ratio, the individual or organization is stuck in their past, and enslaved for the future. That describes the majority of businesses and home-owning individuals. The 30-year mortgage is an institutionalized system of risk-taking. The ability to borrow allows people to buy houses beyond their means, and for the values of houses to rise. People become trapped in their houses. They can sell-high, but new living quarters require them to buy-high. The only way to establish a positive ratio is to put others in a negative ratio. The entire system is based on cost shifting. Inflation is the result and the cause for more cost shifting.

Poverty occurs without regard to political structure (monarchy, democracy, communism or tyranny) or technology (agrarian or industrial). In the case of natural disasters or crop failures, hunger is a nature-caused phenomenon. In the absence of those things, hunger and poverty are a mathematical phenomenon.

Poverty is when expenses are greater than Revenue (E>R). Wealth is when revenue is greater than expenses (R>E). 'Living within ones means,' the goal of a budget process, and the Standard of Living depends upon ones starting point and the ability to adapt to changes in income or expenses. Pain is felt when the Standard of Living is dropping, regardless of the previous status It can be as painful to cut from a $10 Million budget as it is from a $10,000 budget. Nobody wants to reverse course.

Acute poverty is when a reasonable Cost of Living cannot be maintained. This is the condition of homelessness, hunger and the lack of healthcare and educational opportunities that many in the nation and the world suffer. America, and the world, has a lot of acute poverty.

Poverty is a process that unfolds in different ways at different ages for different people. Depending upon revenue and expenses, people and organizations can move in and out of positive and negative ratios. When someone is young, they are undercapitalized for living on their own. They may borrow for an education or to purchase a car. A young couple may borrow to buy a house, and need to borrow again as the family grows. Borrowing may occur because of an unexpected expense (broken furnace, car accident, health bills, job loss). Borrowing may occur because of too large an appetite (vacation, furniture, second house). Businesses and governments have a similar lifecycle and struggle with being undercapitalized. One of the primary reasons for new borrowing is to pay the debts of old borrowing. Banks constantly advertise loan consolidation and more borrowing.

**Wealth Profiles**

We each experience a different economy. Let's take a look at how expenses and revenue values can adjust within a Cost of Living/Standard of Living framework. For the sake of simplicity, these ratios contain a doubling or tripling from a previous point. In reality, the increase or decrease could be any percentage. These formulas will help to expose what people experience with numbers. Everyone has an economic profile that is in constant flux.

The basic equation was Revenue over Expense equals the Cost of Living. (R/E=CL).

If there is an increase in the revenue, but the cost of goods rises to match, ones standard of living is stagnant while their income is rising (R*2/E*2=CL). This is the condition that the working poor or lower middle class experience. They cannot get ahead.

If a person is on a fixed income, and the cost of goods is rising, then their Standard of Living is dropping. Reducing consumption is not a long-term defense against inflation because the cost of goods consumed will continue to rise. The equation is R/E*2. This is the poverty that many elderly experience.

If you increase the amount of money a person has, and the cost of goods is rising and/or the need for more goods is increasing, then the increase in revenue may or may not be enough to keep up with increases in expenses. The equation is R*2/E*3. This is the most common experience. It is usually the face of 'making it,' and can evolve from stage to stage in succession. It fits a young couple with a new home, the same couple with a growing family and childcare expenses, and the extra costs of sending a child off to college. It is also the standard experience for expanding and growing a business. There is usually some fluctuation R*3/E*2, R*4/E*3, etc.

Because of savings, the wealthy can temporarily insulate themselves from the effects of rising expenses to maintain their Standard of Living. They may also have more options to either reduce expenses or increase income, but their experience of financial worry is the same as everyone else. This helps to explain why the battles against tax increases by those 'who can seemly afford it easiest' are fought with the same intensity as the poor who fight for mercy from high-priced goods and low wages.

Every tax increase is an increase in expense, regardless of one's income level. It makes sense to donate money fighting a tax increase because it is a one-time expense, whereas if the Bill passes the new expense becomes permanent. Rich or poor, everyone wants to increase revenue and lower expenses. Seldom do people argue that they should pay more taxes. If they support a tax increase, it is usually so someone else is paying more. This correlates to the buy-low sell-high philosophy of traditional economics. Everyone seeks an improved ratio for himself or herself.

The Cost of Living is a simple mathematical formula, but the psychology can be quite complex. Some people can never be happy. Money has obliterated their perspective of life. That was what Charles Dickens was trying to get across in his story The Christmas Carol. The character of Scrooge was based on common attitudes regarding money.

Money can endanger people's well-being. The hungry robber may be driven by desperation, but what drives the white-collar criminal? Those with money are afraid, too. Money creates security fears, either immediately or as a future projection. Fear can win easily on both sides of the Cost of Living divide. Managers in control of budgets are in charge of a system of caution, which is what makes the risk-takers stand out. They are not necessarily cleverer; they are usually more desperate or confused. Part of genius is madness.

There are practical consequences to our decisions and the numbers we put to paper. If we are going to use money, then we need to understand it better. Dissonance is the most common characteristic. There is an on-going battle for the hearts and minds of the next generation. On the one side are those who teach greed as a virtue; on the other side are those who teach greed as a vice. The same person embraces opposite points of view. Get rich and be charitable is the most common lesson that children hear. It is an echo of the maximize revenue and control expenses approach.

For people to avoid a negative ratio, everyone in society needs to live closer to 1, rather than by high multiples. To eliminate extremes of poverty, there must be the self-restraint to prevent extremes of wealth. A stable system that provides for everyone is possible, and easy to accomplish, if everyone views money as a tool and recognizes the consequences of its misuse. Everyone needs to feel safe. Like freedom and liberty, safety is something that the community provides. The existence of homelessness and hunger means that we have failed. Money is false security. The same formula that creates the poor will eventually ensnare the rich. Volatility is a man-made event.

# 7. The Politics of Money

The game *Monopoly* demonstrates that wealth divides automatically because of the rules of mathematics. This is a non-political phenomenon. Boom is bust. At the beginning of the game, everyone is getting rich as the bank gets poorer. Then, the Law of Diminishing Returns takes over. The bank sinks deeper into debt, and the players begin to run out of money, too. For all but one player, the expenses become greater than revenue.

In the real world, nobody can control what other players charge them, or, if other players will buy their wares. *Monopoly* guarantees one winner; reality is more complex. Animosities develop as events unfold.

History has shown a tendency by the poor to blame the rich for winning, but the rich have no control over their good fortune. They win because of how the dice fall, and the luck of being in the right place at the right time. A small advantage can compound. If the majority of your transactions are advantageous, then you gain. If not, then you bleed. Everyone is playing by the same rules, and trying to make only advantageous transactions. A seemingly invincible position of success is not perpetually sustainable. Time makes all men equal. Blaming the rich for winning is an intellectual dead-end.

History has also revealed a tendency by the rich to blame the poor for losing. Some suggest that the poor are lazy or stupid. Others create schools of business and write books on personal finance. They seek to teach the poor what they did to get rich. Bookstores and infomercials promulgate this alleged wisdom. Both blame and evangelization is an intellectual dead-end. Copying success is to copy failure in development. For example, investing in real estate during a boom market accelerates the arrival of the bust market. The good times are temporary. The system is too volatile.

Nobody is too big to fail. Once expenses get ahead of revenue, any size hoard of wealth can slowly bleed away. Both publicly and privately, deficit financing and then additional borrowing are used to sustain old debts and future consumption. Borrowing is an accommodation to a fiscal engineering failure. We have bad laws and bad habits. Treating the symptoms, and blaming one another, are a political dead-end.

At any one moment, the economy is a zero-sum game. If you manage to get more money from the other players, than they get from you, then they go bankrupt instead of you. Why we have rich and poor is not be a mystery. Money is man-made, and we bring trouble onto one another by the manner in which we trade.

A lot of effort gets expended trying to counteract the concentration of wealth. People are generally egalitarian and use their powers to help others. Poor individuals use charity, rich individuals use philanthropy, businesses use profit sharing and establish charitable foundations, and governments use taxes, grants and subsidies. Regardless of efficiency, compassion for the misfortunate should always be encouraged. Unfortunately, the laws of mathematics are strong and unyielding. What gets redistributed as a result of compassion cannot counteract the overwhelming number of man-hours spent generating inflation. Where money comes from is as important as where it goes. If we use better math, then we can produce and consume without dividing society into separate classes of winners and losers.

## Religion

Religious thought has entered the politics of money debate. There are efforts to buy or sell redemption, as if it were a product like any other product.

Some claim that the rich are God's Will. Because they are righteous, they deserve and are granted material rewards. It is true that a virtuous society will reap the rewards of virtue. It is not true that wealth alone is a sign of virtue. The existence of poverty in a society indicates a dearth of virtue. In a commonwealth, no one should suffer.

Others wear poverty as a badge of God's honor. They believe it is better to be poor than rich, because one can only become rich through unjust methods. Both positions confuse the means and the ends. Virtue or righteousness are not based on possessions, but based on beliefs and behaviors. Possessions are the result, not the cause.

Atheists, like Karl Marx, have implored the poor workers to unite, and to rise up and attack the powerful owners. He wisely spoke against poverty, but unwisely spoke against peace. Marxists misunderstand religion. A brotherhood of comrades requires the same enlightenment as a brotherhood of the faithful. There can be no communism without community. Civil war destroys a society. For economics to work, the means are the ends must be in balance. Animosity is not insight.

Marx's economic analysis bears a strong resemblance to Adam Smith's ideas of capital. They differed politically, particularly in who they regarded as a savage. Smith viewed Native Americans as savages; Marx viewed industrialists,

Robber Barons and slave-masters as savages. Their definition of the word savage diverges. Smith was describing the pre-industrial material conditions of how they lived. For Marx, savage was a pejorative term regarding how owners were treating workers. One definition was physical; the other was social. There are many misjudgments where money and culture are concerned. Unclear or contradictory definitions are common. This is part of the challenge of understanding history. Present-day dissonance is compounded with yesteryear dissonance. Smith saw strength as a weakness, and a weakness as strength. Native Americans had a culture that was equal to or superior to the Europeans in many ways, especially regarding economics. Marx was right that violence is savage, but it is savage regardless of the target.

The Bible is full of apparently mixed messages. In one passage we are to *turn our plowshares into swords* (Joel 3:10). In another, *turn our swords into plowshares* (Isaiah 2:4). The Bible can say whatever people we want to hear. Winners and losers, owners and laborers, rulers and subjects, all claim that they deserve the rewards of their labor and inheritance. The rich and the poor can both claim to be holier than the other, but that does not explain the history of how or why wealth divided.

### Rights and Revolutions

Free market proponents claim that entrepreneurs get rich because of the chances they took. Risk is used as its own moral justification: winner takes all. Unfortunately, the need or willingness to risk marks the previous failure of commonwealth. It is not logical for a community to risk some members for the good of others. It is like tossing virgins into the mouth of the volcano to appease the mountain god. By a more logical arrangement we all could be safe and satisfied. Planning should be avoiding risk, not encouraging risks. Rights claim a protection from harm, not the freedom to inflict harm. A willingness to suffer individual loss puts all of society in jeopardy.

Revolutionaries justify killing the rich as a means to an end. Those in power have justified killing as a means of retaining power and maintaining order. Violence is a method for both plunder and control. Unfortunately, economic imbalances are caused by our accounting methods. Violence cannot change the math. A left wing or right wing police state increases the overhead of waste and lowers the Standard of Living and Quality of Life. Everyone is to blame equally because money is handled the same way by all. The bloodshed of history is one colossal mistake. To eliminate winners and losers, the rules of the game need to be changed at a much more fundamental level.

Every war is a civil war for control of the purse in the wake of the divide of wealth. The mathematical divide becomes personalized, stereotypes develop, and blame eventually overshadows analysis. Bigotry, prejudice and violence all mark the failure of commonwealth.

America overthrew the evil empire of its day, and quickly evolved into a new empire. Just as the poor become rich, and become the person that previously disappointed them, so too do nations and businesses follow the same path. The British Empire came to be as overextended as the Roman Empire. Apple is now as monolithic as Microsoft and IBM had been. Power may trade hands, but the concentration of power remains. To defeat an enemy, one needs to become as large and as ruthless as the enemy. The merciless prevail in a competitive system, not the egalitarian.

## The Role of Government

There is no escape from the law of diminishing returns. New leaders face old problems and are just as helpless in solving them. The laws of mathematics are stronger than either an autocratic leader or majority rule. Mathematics needs to be respected. Power alone is ineffective against inflation. The populace needs to be as wise as their literacy implies.

The global *Monopoly* board eventually reaches a financial crisis. At some point the banks and government are helpless. Buyers stop purchasing and the revenue streams collapse. The system is unsustainable politically and mathematically.

Government is a primary agent in the economy because it coins the money. It also has the impossible task of trying to placate two people who are fighting over money, and expects a share of their money through taxation. The situation is fraught with fear. Both sides can unite and turn against the government, which is common when someone enters a fray between two combatants. Political coalitions commonly defeat incumbents and challenge the rulers of the status quo.

To exert authority, the government resorts to mind control (public education), force (police) and bribery. It is impossible for the government to keep all the people happy all the time, under a volatile system. There are too many contradictions. As power changes hands, the problems continue. False analysis and false accusations offer false hope.

Unlike the game *Monopoly*, the government constantly shifts sides and changes the rules. Every privilege for one person, corporation, industry, or party is a burden for another. Everyone is struggling and lobbying, trying to cause the wealth to divide in a way that benefits themselves, especially after the tide has moved against them. Every political victory is pyrrhic. Economic volatility provides a perpetual fodder for disagreement. New faces engage in old arguments, old solutions are applied anew and fail again.

The ongoing fights over money divide, unite and confuse people. Unlike the rigid stratification of a caste system, in the modern world we are a part of many different social groups. The division of labor has created a division of loyalties.

At the same time, we have created a shared experience of consumption and mass knowledge. Co-dependency and literacy has made us more empathetic. The ubiquity of money has made us all financially connected. Technology has closed the physical gap of separation. Yet, there are bitter differences regarding money, which are built on untested clichés.

As humans, we all have the same needs as our ancestors. We experience the same joys and sorrows, and aspire to a common liberty. There are many forces driving us together. Primarily, the only thing driving us apart is the financial system.

**Transactional Economics**

Transactional Economics is a term for describing the process of how wealth separates. The Cost of Living formula defined wealth and poverty as a mathematical ratio; transactional economics explains why some players win and others lose. It is based on the same math.

As noted previously, every transaction is imbalanced because of the buy-low sell-high habit. We are all buyers and sellers and consumers. Our revenue is the result of selling (labor for wages, selling products, or lending money); our expenses are what we consume to survive and thrive (food, housing, healthcare, education, business equipment and supplies, etc.). There is no mathematical difference between micro and macroeconomics, inflation, budget crises, and boom and bust cycles. The same mathematical event drives them all.

We all need to make transactions to survive. We need to produce to consume. That reality is impossible to alter. In the game *Monopoly*, everyone takes turns, and everyone has the same number of transactions. In reality, the number of players and the number of transactions per player can vary widely.

Transactional economics unmasks some of the volatility of the marketplace that the *Monopoly* model implies. What follows are rough numbers to demonstrate the relative differences that players experience. For simplicity, transactions are counted as an aggregate. Multiple payments from or to the same source are treated as one transaction.

A wage earner has only one transaction for revenue. It is with their employer. They take a job at a set rate of pay, report to work and get paid at a fixed interval. They use their revenue to pay a multitude of expenses (rent, food, auto). Their formula could be something like R=1 E=40. One transaction of revenue; forty transactions of expense.

For the business that hires the wage earner, that salary is one of many expenses. The business derives its revenue from sales. Their formula could be R=500 (clients) E=100 (vendors and employees). E could be divided into groups like wages, supplies, fixed overhead, advertising, R&D, etc.

Businesses come in different sizes. A small business might be R500 E100, a larger business could be R50000 E1000. A business that makes a huge item (airplanes, airports, steel mills) but has few clients would have a different profile: R30, E20000. A government contractor might be R1 E150. A banking entity like Master Card could be R100,000,000 and E1000. A small child would be R0 E0. A retired pensioner could be R1 E30, living frugally on Social Security.

The number of transactions makes a difference in how people experience the economy. Imagine playing a game of *Monopoly* with four players, where one of the players gets to roll four times more than everyone else. At the beginning of the game, during the boom cycle, this would offer a tremendous advantage. They would be buying up all the property in advance of everyone else. Everybody that followed would be forced to pay rent. This disadvantage is what every new generation experiences when they transition away from R0 E0 and enter the workforce as R1 E+. Our luck in the lottery of birth may give us some temporary advantages, but we are all born into the same system.

Having more turns also changes how one can respond to inflation. A business with a lot of expenses has a lot of areas to cut or renegotiate pricing. The individual must pay the cost of gasoline or not travel, or cut something else. The individual has less control over both revenue and expense. They can request a pay increase, but they cannot control either revenue or expense easily.

Everyone is connected. The government can raise taxes and pay public employees more, but that increase becomes a pay cut for private sector employees. Similarly, a pay increase in the private sector must increase the price of the goods being sold, and that inflation works the same as a pay cut for those outside of the company. The divide between rich and poor, advantage and disadvantage, is constantly shifting. Having more turns while losing money on each transaction is a huge disadvantage, and can bring about bankruptcy quickly. There is no safe haven when risk has become institutionalized. That is the key difference between a commonwealth and competitive capitalism.

When voters trust a business-person as a politician, and expect them to take charge of the economy, the business leader has experienced a different economy than most of the voters. For him, the solution is to maximize profits and suppress wages. The voters want good jobs, and are usually divided between the desire to earn more and for goods to cost less. Neither of these ideas are in a typical business-person's toolkit. Even if the candidate's employees were paid well, it was accomplished by charging customers more. There is no escape from this triangularization.

## Transactional Economics
**The economic experience is different for everyone.**

|  | Sources of Revenue | # of Expenses |
|---|---|---|
| CHILD | 0 | 0 |
| SINGLE WAGE EARNER | 1 | 40 |
| YOUNG COUPLE | 2 | 100 |
| COUPLE WITH CHILDREN | 1 or 2 | 250 |
| RETIREE | 1 | 30 |
| SMALL BUSINESS | 500+ | 100 |
| GOVERNMENT CONTRACTOR | 1 | 150 |
| BIG BOX RETAILER | 1 Million | 10,000 |
| UTILITY | 10+ Million | 1500 |
| AIRPLANE MANUFACTURER | 50 | 5000 |
| AIRLINE | 10+ Million | 1000 |
| CREDIT CARD COMPANY | 100+ Million | 1000 |
| LOCAL BANK | 2500+ | 250 |
| NATIONAL BANK | 10+ Million | 1000 |

"We The People" Have Fewer Transactions In The Game, Compared To The Organizations That We Buy From And That Employ Us.

There are many political factions concerning economics, and they are all right and wrong in their own way. More revenue will fix any budget, but it will do so by negatively impacting someone else's budget. Unions want higher wages, but the cost is borne by the consumer or the taxpayer. More profits for businesses are borne by vendors, employees, consumers and taxpayers who are overworked, underpaid and overcharged.

Economic and political theory calls for the government to act as an impartial arbitrator, but how can people be treated equally when their roles and experiences are so radically different? Any one size fits all tax code would not fit anyone properly. A complicated tax code, which attempts to do favors for certain players, would automatically be unfair to or exclude someone else. There is a blurry line between rights and privileges. Since all numbers are connected, and every transaction imbalanced, any help for one player must put many other players at a disadvantage.

The use of fiat money and the nature of inflation ensure that the economy is not a zero sum game, but it does share one important aspect of a zero sum situation: my revenue is your expense. Obviously, consumption is good and necessary. Long term, however, the mathematical echo of every transaction is to our collective disadvantage. It is impossible for individuals or organizations to be balanced and fair in a structurally unbalanced and perpetually volatile system. Empathy cannot counterbalance the laws of mathematics that we are experiencing. We need smarter rules, not a blind faith in egalitarianism or invisible hands.

Transactional analysis explains why wealth divides in the game *Monopoly* and in real life. A business is profitable when it makes more profitable transactions than non-profitable transactions. The more transactions it makes, the potential exists for both great wealth and great loss. In general, it takes a huge expense to generate huge revenue. A small business or an individual cannot make enough profitable transactions to accumulate the wealth of a large corporation. Nor do they receive enough credit to lose as much as a large corporation.

Large businesses get more turns in the game. Size becomes its own advantage. Size also makes it possible to negotiate down the cost of expenses, wages and to set the terms of the sale. This introduces more imbalances into the system.

Large businesses themselves create winners and loser. Two businesses competing head to head with the same product for the same buyer, can be receiving different prices from a shared vendor. A different markup percentage is applied for preferred clients. An example of size difference is Wal-Mart. They can purchase multiple truckloads of a product and get a price that is significantly less than their competitors. The competitor is buying higher and must either sell higher or work on a smaller profit percentage than Wal-Mart.

One price is not the complete picture. The pay of the employees, the cost of benefits, tax breaks, utility costs, etc., all fall into the aggregate of expenses. Both Wal-Mart and the local store are attempting to buy-low sell-high. It is as fair a competition as David versus Goliath. Size does not necessarily win. What matters is the underlying mathematical ratio: are revenues greater than expenses? They can co-exist peacefully if consumers have enough demand, but we know that demand will fluctuate.

If the vendor sold to both companies at the same price, the local company might be able to compete more easily with Wal-Mart. Should the vendor favor one over the other? Whichever choice it makes is right or wrong, fair or unfair, to somebody. The government cannot set a logical rule. Like the trade of eggs for chickens, there is no right answer as to if volume warrants a different rate. It is a common practice, of course, but as a matter of policy, should it be encouraged or discouraged? Will the vendor lose Wal-Mart as a client if they offer them the same price as as the local company?

There are moral, ethical, and political clouds that surround every financial transaction. Everyone is equally worried about revenue and expenses and inflation. The government will be considered incompetent or adversarial, no matter what choice it makes. We should allow mathematical realities to inform our choices, not our fears and prejudices.

Free-market advocates claim that any choice a business makes is best, and all choices the government makes are wrong. This claim is as illogical as monarchy, just reversed. What is important is the quality of the decision, not who makes it.

**What is Fair?**

It is difficult for anyone to keep revenue larger than expenses. While expenses can be controlled to some extent, there is even less control over revenue. People cannot be forced to buy something. Thoreau writes in *Walden* of an Indian Chief who was reduced to making baskets. When he solicits at the local lawyer's house, they refuse to purchase anything. He walks away complaining that they are starving him to death. After thousands of generations living in balance with nature, he was among the first Native Americans to know hunger brought on by the comfort of modern commerce. The civilized man introduced a savage system when it came to the issue of distribution.

Wal-Mart is generally profitable, but other large businesses have not fared as well. Some auto manufactures have had an overhead that greatly exceeded their revenues. Wal-Mart is a middleman. Auto manufactures start from the ground up. First they engineer a product, and then assemble parts from a variety of sources. They sell directly to the consumer through a dealer franchise system. At Wal-Mart, employee wages are low and the products are generally inexpensive. Auto manufacturing employees are unionized and paid well. The higher cost of those wages and benefits is reflected in the price of the automobile. The union advantage for the worker becomes a disadvantage for the consumer. This is generically why America seeks to import goods made with cheaper labor, whether it is cars or the products on the Wal-Mart shelf.

The fact that we cannot pay ourselves to manufacture the goods we consume is a sign that the system is in deep disarray. If we are more advanced socially and technologically, then we should be able to produce what we consume more easily. Instead, we have made it harder.

Auto manufacturers have fewer sales than Wal-Mart, but at a considerably higher price point per sale. Both make many more transactions than small businesses or an individual. Today, the majority of the population are employees. When the country was founded, the majority of people were self-employed. By the time of the Civil War, that number dropped in half. For most people, their revenue is wholly dependent on one transaction.

Wal-Mart, the auto manufacturers, and many other corporations are Goliath's. They have the capacity to lose money in the same process that allows them to make money. Because we must consume to survive, nobody has the ability to stand still for long. The game must be played. The percentages must battle against one another. This is the consequence of a money-driven economy.

Two farmers could barter eggs for milk forever. In fact, all farmers could trade food forever, regardless of how items were valued. Money changes the nature of trade. The purpose of trade is only to make sure we have what we need when we need it. The money system guarantees that trade will be difficult, when the intention was to make it easier.

The wealth divides because once one gains an advantage, it can easily compound. Similarly, once one is placed at a disadvantage, that disadvantage can compound. The *Monopoly* game demonstrates the consequences of inflation and compounding. Even with the same amount of turns per player, and equal rules for everyone, the wealth divides. Our reality is that some players have many more transactions than other players.

It is currently impossible to formulate a level playing field between small and large businesses, or between union and non-union workers, or between American made and foreign made goods, and especially between the young and the old.

The budget formula reveals the mathematical mechanics. The rich take more than they give. The poor give more than they take. The rich are experiencing 2+2=5 in the aggregate of their transactions. The poor are experiencing 5=2+2. The former expand their consumption whereas the latter must restrict consumption and fall into debt. The harder the disadvantaged work, the more the advantaged gain. We are a commonwealth, whether we want to be or not. The choice is the degree of imbalance that we will tolerate.

Work can sustain people from day to day, but making a lot of transactions allows profit beyond subsistence needs, and that gives the person or business a powerful advantage. It is accurate to say that the rich create the poor. The usual method is to combine a positive balance and a lot of transactions. However, the *Monopoly* game demonstrates that you can become rich even when making the same number of transactions as everyone else.

It is mathematically impossible for everyone to become fiscally rich simultaneously. John Kennedy claimed that a rising tide would lift all boats. What is true for water is not true for finances. We can grow materially rich, however. America's primary advantage in the global economy is the long lapse since our Civil War. Our productive wealth has been allowed to compound, rather than being destroyed by bombs. However, as we migrate towards a mathematically dysfunctional police state, the sheer volume of non-productive activity, combined with intentionally manufacturing obsolescence, will have the same effect as many bombs. The invisible hand of fiscal habit blights areas of society.

Not all transactions are a brief exchange of goods for money. Many involve a long-term contract. The most important of these are loans. There is no lending in *Monopoly*. The game ends when everyone goes broke. In reality, we keep the game going by using credit and issuing debt. Every new government is the first party involved in long-term contracts. It accepted loans that form the basis of its currency, which made their own currency acceptable in international trade. Money stems from the intellectual agreement to accept credit. One party has nothing to trade except for a promise. The trade of promissory notes eventually became money.

**The Rat Race**

Because of mathematical contradictions, a central currency acts like a doomsday machine. The government is in debt because it cannot collect more than what it spent for long. Drawing money out of the system, as both President Coolidge and President Clinton did, will create a depression. The spike in stock prices is the boom before the bust.

Inflation has tragic social consequences. Within the context of the political economy, the inflation phenomenon needs a release. The mathematical aggregate is that all price inflation (profit) is the National Debt. This math drives all politics. One man's profit becomes another man's debt (the creditor vs debtor conflict.) Debt and inflation drive the demand for bigger profits and bigger wages (the owner vs worker conflict). Productivity gains and higher selling prices are the survival responses of those who produce goods (the Cost of Living increases with productivity gains). Debt and increasing overhead costs drive sales and marketing at a frantic pace. Any action that creates a profit can be justified (it takes money to make money, or slash costs - assume more debt or cut jobs). The results become either a big success or a big failure. Moral and environmental consequences of economic activity become secondary when the choice is to survive or perish. Those who manage to accumulate a surplus then invest (loan at compound interest) in response to inflation, thus driving the inflationary pressures they are hoping to escape. The existence of surplus creates the illusion of excessive wealth (the rich vs poor conflict).

With each step in the inflation progression, the values get bigger. Because money and time are linked, time becomes a liability rather than an asset. The Rat Race is the process of chasing moving numbers, but nobody can outrun inflation. The numbers grow at too fast a pace, eventually resulting in political unrest. Everyone is a loser when the social fabric tears, but the big numbers mask the real problem: inflation eats everyone alive. Interest makes the trouble with inflation worse. While a loan will help the borrower today, it makes everything worse tomorrow. Lending should never be regarded as a solution to escape inflation or to stimulate the economy.

The problems are rooted deep in the history of every nation. Debt is necessary to create money. Taxes create a need for profit. Profit creates inflation. Inflation divides the wealth, which creates the need for more lending. Debt is a secondary symptom of taxation. A central currency cannot logically be taxed. It is important to get the sequence of events correct. When politicians want businesses and government to return to profitability (surplus budgets), they are really saying that they want to return to the conditions that created the problem. They fail to recognize how the boom causes the bust. What we want is equilibrium. For the people to be free and equal, the math must be in balance (2+2=4). Everyone needs to be debt-free, and stay debt-free, including the next generation. People need to be more important than numbers. All animosity is false reasoning.

# 8. What is the GDP/GNP?

The Gross Domestic Product (GDP) and the Gross National Product (GNP) are aggregate numbers. There is a slight difference in the methodology used, but generically they are the measure of macro economic output in dollars. These numbers are considered to be important because they reflect how busy we are producing goods and services for each other's consumption. Politicians economists and pundits regularly use them to imply a rising or falling standard of living and/or quality of life. It is believed that GDP/GNP are a key indicator of economic health and policy success or failure.

There are a number of problems with relying on these figures. Anything that is not a financial transaction is not counted. For example, if someone volunteers their time, paints their own house, or does a car repair for a friend, it is not recorded in the official output of the nation. Self-sufficiency is a measuring liability. The purchase of the paint or auto parts would be counted, but not the value of the labor to use the materials. Other off-market transactions include under-the-counter, illegal activities (gambling, drugs, prostitution), and cash second-hand sales.

It is guesstimated that these off-market transactions could be between 5% and 30% of the GDP/GNP total. If true, then small changes in the GDP/GNP could be easily offset by larger changes in the off-market aggregate. One aggregate could move up while the other aggregate moves down. They could both be moving in the same direction simultaneously, too.

Another problem with these calculations are they cannot make any qualitative reading. There is no way to account for planned obsolescence, losses due to catastrophe, or the generic quality of the dollar output. Pawning your possessions has the same value as buying them, as a measure economic activity. An entire town or a way of life could be destroyed and the numbers would reflect nothing of it.

*What are these economists doing, and how does it affect policy?*

GDP/GNP measures 'government aware' transactions. These are the transactions that the government attempts to influence through taxes and legislation. The off-market transactions are usually illegal specifically because they are untaxed and unregulated. Many states have legalized formerly illicit activities in the hopes of closing a budget shortage. Gambling is legal when the State runs the lottery and taxes the winnings and the labor involved. When organized crime manages gambling, and fails to pay taxes, the exact same behavior is illegal. Legal gambling is measured as economic output, even though nothing is produced.

Governments act on the false assumption that the budget approach is working. By making the local (counted) economy larger, they expect to be able to balance revenue and expenses more easily. Everyone acts similarly. Businesses try to grow sales. Non-profits attempt to raise more funds. Wage earners seek richer compensation. It is commonly believed that growth can solve the problem of shortage. Unfortunately, the problems scale up in size as well. The ratio does not change favorably automatically. It is possible that waste will increase, thereby making the ratio worse. The false belief that growth can solve problems is why the GDP/GNP gets so much attention.

A corollary to the idea that growth can solve problems is the idea that having centralized control makes things easier to manage. Somehow, having one person doing ten things simultaneously is better than having ten people each doing one thing well. This was the argument in favor of The Constitution, which took thirteen small problems and centralized them into one big problem. Had they been able to solve the money problem on a small scale, then they would have been able to solve it on a large scale. In fact, all they did was make the money problem larger. They did not have a grasp of the situation.

Both the growth and the centralization approaches ignore the importance of the R/E ratio. Centralization requires more regulation. The more the state regulates, the more its expenses will rise. Not only do problems scale, but they can compound at a different rate than the useful economic activity. This is the failure of the last 230 years of American government. We have created an economic prison. All of the solutions, combined with the expansion of the nation, have made the original problems worse. We now have multiple layers of false solutions.

The most troubling aspect of the GDP/GNP is that all it measures is the fiction of inflation. Inflation is a microeconomics transaction, caused by the application of percentages, in a buy-low sell-high sequence. The GDP/GNP is just the aggregate of these reported transactions. The growth in the GDP/GNP is not a growth in productive output; it is a growth in the value applied. It is painfully common to hear it claimed that a growth in the GDP/GNP will help relieve poverty. One Prime Minister recently reported that both the GDP/GNP and inflation were expected to increase at 7.5%. He did not recognize that the totality of the alleged growth in the GDP/GNP was just the increase in inflation. The twin increases were not going to relieve anything. He viewed the increase in GDP/GNP as good news, and the increase in inflation as bad news. He did not recognize the connection. His economic advisors were expressing cognitive dissonance. The GDP/GNP, like inflation, is commonly discussed and poorly understood.

The best way to understand the link between inflation and the GDP/GNP is to see it in action. Let's again use the example of an apple moving from tree to table, and being touched by five different businesses on its way. In the previous model, the farmer picked the apple and sold it to the cooperative, which sold it to the wholesaler, who sold it to the cold storage company, who sold it to the distributor, who sold it to the supermarket, who sold it to the consumer. Using a 50% profit margin, the apple cost 7.6 cents. Using a 100% profit margin, the same apple would cost 32 cents.

The difference between an economist an an entrepreneur is that an economist adds up all the totals, whereas the entrepreneur inflates their purchase price into a selling price. If we multiply our single apple by 100 million apples, the gross revenue for each business is one million dollars times the selling price. For example, in an economy with a one-cent apple and a 50% mark-up the GDP/GNP is $20.78 Million (1+1.5+2.25+3.38+5.06+7.59=20.78). Using a 100% mark-up, the GDP/GNP is $63 Million (1+2+4+8+16+32=63).

The GDP/GNP is a reflection of the mark-up used and the original cost of the apple. An economist adds up the gross sales for each business to arrive at the GDP/GNP. There is no practical difference between a $63 million GDP/GNP and a $20.78 Million GDP/GNP. The only difference is the numbers that people write down. The same exact numbers of apples are moving from tree to table. Whether it is one apple

109

or 100 million, the math is exactly the same. The only thing that grew was the numbers, not the physical output.

## Total of Gross Sales by Sector = GDP

| INDUSTRY | COUNTRY A | COUNTRY B | COUNTRY C |
|---|---|---|---|
| Farmers | $1,000,000 | $1,000,000 | $1,000,000 |
| Cooperatives | $2,000,000 | $1,500,000 | $1,100,000 |
| Wholesalers | $4,000,000 | $2,250,000 | $1,210,000 |
| Cold Storages | $8,000,000 | $3,380,000 | $1,330,000 |
| Distributors | $16,000,000 | $5,060,000 | $1,460,000 |
| Supermarkets | $32,000,000 | $7,590,000 | $1,610,000 |
| **GDP:** | $63 Million | $20.7 Million | $7.7 Million |

Problem: The GDP is only measuring inflation.

| 100% Markup | 50% Markup | 10% Markup |

*This is still one apple moving from tree to table.*

(Examples presented on pages 64-65 are mirrored above: The micro is the macro.)

There is another odd flaw in the economist's GDP/GNP methodology. The total is based on revenues, but not every business is profitable. A business that is losing money must borrow. That borrowing is counted as a sale for the bank. Banks have a unique revenue/expense ratio. They purchase the depositors money with interest, and sell the depositors money as a loan. This is unlike other forms of barter. Money is being exchanged for money. This double counting inflates the GDP/GNP because losses are never recorded, the same as planned obsolescence, destructive losses, and unregulated transactions. Gambling and financial services move money from one hand to another, yet it is counted as a sale. For example, when a non-profit foundation gives money to a non-profit organization. The movement is counted as expense and revenue. Every transaction of money that is 'government aware' gets counted, even when no product is being produced or consumed. The government has centralized the measuring of data, but like budgets, it is measuring its own false assumptions.

Banking and the creation of paper money have allowed both debt and inflation to become infinite. Measuring and misunderstanding the GDP/GNP is a common. The national debt and annual budget can be a very high percentage of the alleged GDP/GNP output. In some countries, the budget deficit is greater than the measured GDP/GNP, which is proof that the measure is meaningless.

If one man goes hungry, then all men share the shame. The hunger needs to be dealt with directly and immediately by the collective. Looking at numbers can be mind-numbing if you do not understand how they were created. Policy, and policy analysis, should not be based on such nonsensical numbers. You do not need a spread sheet to understand that the system is not working, and a spread sheet is not proof that it is working.

# 9. The National Debt is the Inverse of Inflation

A Balance Sheet attempts to summarize an entity's financial condition. It documents assets, liability and equity. Equity is the difference between assets and liabilities. Much like a budget, equity is either a positive or a negative, rich or poor. On a traditional balance sheet, equity is the value of property, and would be referred to as 'owner equity.' He 'owns' the business, and equity reflects what the business is worth after all bills are paid.

Trade is the exchange of goods for money. The Balance Sheet reflects both sides of the exchange, and our role as both buyer and seller. It contains what is owned and what are owed, as mathematical amounts. As such, the existence of a chicken coop, chickens and eggs must be transposed into a dollar value. Given what we know about inflation, the value is almost meaningless. It can be any number and describe the same thing. The interest in a Balance Sheet, like a budget, stems from a concern about ratios.

Just as a business has a Balance Sheet, a nation also has a macro Balance Sheet. For a nation, equity is the people and its infrastructure, both the physical and the spiritual. The entirety of National Equity cannot be valued mathematically, but it is obvious in the Quality of Life of the people. The extremes of civil war or renaissance are both possible. Spiritual equity is as volatile as any set of numbers, as waves of trust or mistrust spread across the people. The physical equity varies from place to place. There are poor towns and rich towns, poor states and rich states. America, compared to some parts of the world, has accumulated a lot of wealth after years of building and manufacturing.

In the National Balance Sheet, the difference between the private and public sectors is the difference between assets and liabilities. Regardless of how things are valued, the math needs to balance. If the nation is $16 Trillion in debt, then there needs to be $16 trillion in assets and equity in the private sector.

The GDP/GNP measures the inflation of goods as they are moved and consumed. It is an annual snapshot that summarizes the transactions for one year. The National Debt reflects the same activity, but is the summary total for many years. The National Debt measures all inflation since the origin of the nation. Money is man-made, and there is nothing to measure that is not inflation.

The formula for the National Balance Sheet is: the National Debt is the inverse of private sector created inflation (ND=I).

Any revenue generated in the private sector corresponds to the debt of the federal government. This explains why the debt increments continually. It illuminates why 'priming the pump' is necessary, and why a stimulus works before it fails.

Inflation is being recorded as both an asset and a liability. Money begins with government and to government inflation must return.

The ND=I formula can be expressed in other ways: debt equals profit (D=P); public sector debt is the inverse of private sector wealth (ND=PW); taxes equal inflation

(T=I); profit equals taxes (P=T). We know that revenue equals inflation (R=I). Every transaction generates inflation. It does not matter if the transaction is 'government aware' or not. Reselling your goods at a yard sale, the local school bake sale, and sales by a non-profit all generate inflation. All activity has a mathematical footprint if money is involved.

The baseline of trade is that any revenue for one is an expense for another. On the grander scale, the revenue for the private sector is the debt of the government.

The exchange of inflation makes consumption fiscally possible. Inflation and debt are the consequence of whatever percentage is used. Governments, businesses, non-profits and individuals are all full participants in the buy-low sell-high cycle. Everyone is equally responsible for the troubles with money, past and present.

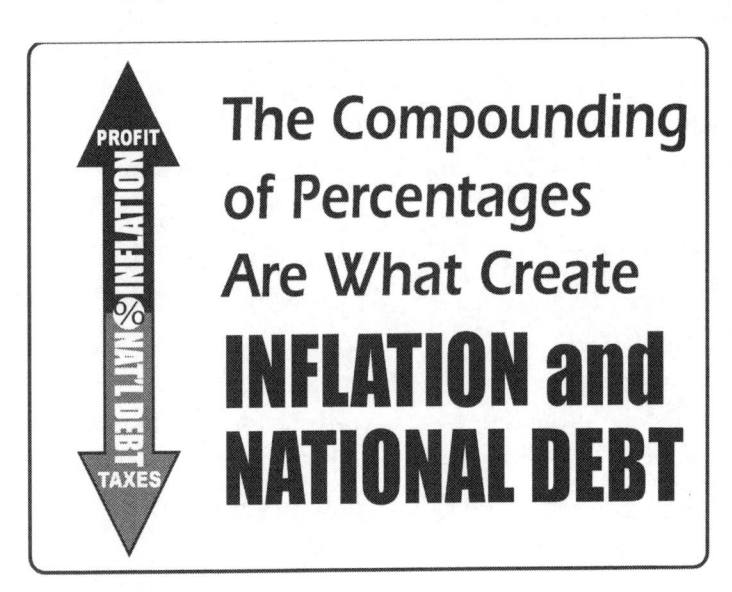

**The Compounding of Percentages Are What Create INFLATION and NATIONAL DEBT**

Before money was common, taxes were paid as a share of the harvest. Government taxes to support itself. Taxing food probably did not result in hunger, but taxing money unleashed a mathematical phenomenon: inflation and debt. For taxes to be paid with money, then buying and selling must take place using the government's currency. It is a dramatic shift away from a barter economy to an accounting-ledger economy.

Money has been a problem throughout history for the government, traders, and city dwellers, but not for the self-sufficient. Money becomes more important with trade, mobility and divisions of labor. Industrialism was a dramatic change in all three. There is no going back to a barter economy. We need to find the stability that self-sufficiency offered in a co-dependent system. Cooperative labor has many advantageous. The fiscal issues are because there is a problem with the math. The Balance Sheet reveals the problem.

Economic theory dominates the modern world. Disputes regarding the proper role, use and distribution of money and resources are common. Politically we are divided, almost globally, between Democrats (liberals) and Republicans (conservatives). If the nation were a business, then they both want to run it as they see fit using their primary tool of either taxes or profits. In trying to cope with the inflationary forces that divide the wealth, raising either profit or tax percentages will further increase the divide. Either choice will drive inflation and debt.

Profit percentages must be large enough to cover taxes; tax percentages must be large enough to cover expenses. There is a mathematical arms race between profits and taxes. Increasing one percentage will force an increase to the other. A better choice is to lower both percentages. Inflation and debt will continue if the rate is not zero, but at a slower rate; the larger the percentage, the faster and greater the volatility.

Religious, ethnic, or national boundaries are secondary to economics. Liberals generally claim that taxes and regulation will distribute our resources to the proper place at the proper time. Conservatives generally claim that profits and unregulated markets will accomplish the same. Few believe a King, Pope or President is right because of their position. All opinions, on all matters, are subject to debate. That is a good thing, but only if we challenge our own beliefs with the same vigor that we challenge the beliefs of others.

The ND=I (National Debt equals Inflation) theory proposes that profits and taxes are mathematical equivalents. Liberals and conservatives are both creating inflation; they just use a different method to create it. Both sides in the dominant political divide are wrong, which is why progress is so difficult and success so fleeting. We are witnessing a battle between two different versions of dissonance. A third version of economic dissonance is the worldwide terrorist movement. A forth would be the waning ideas of communism. In all cases, there is a disconnect between cause and effect. If any of these factions had absolute power, they would be an absolute failure. Math is not on their side.

Money has always involved a difficult moral choice. How do we treat our brother? The economic debate is centuries old. Despite being billed as Enlightenment, removing religion and monarchy from the state has not helped to solve the money problem. It has always been easier to recognize the sins of another than our own. We forgive our own choices, and blame others for the macro trends, rather than recognizing how our own behavior is part of the problem. Blaming government was easy before democracy, and blaming the other party was easy after democracy.

It is important to recognize that inflation starts in the private sector. *Monopoly* demonstrates that conclusively, there is no government overhead in the game. Poverty is the responsibility of the citizens, not the government, as a consequence of inflation.

Even in a barter economy, the possibility of inflation still exists. Either side could demand more eggs or more milk in the exchange. Money is not the original source of inflation, but its use does guarantee that inflation will occur and compound. It is impossible to pay taxes and break-even without creating some inflation.

When we handle something that others value, and demand something in the exchange, we will create inflation. Because money is mathematical, it is more easily recognizable and recorded, and inflation becomes a larger problem as time passes.

Inflation exists whenever there is an agreement to trade quid pro quo, rather than to share. Wanting or expecting something in return is a moral equation. How can we attain political equality when we treat our time, skills, products and misfortunes unequally in a mathematically imbalanced generational caste system? Every egg we crack has an ancestry of thousands of years. Nobody can claim ownership of the egg or the chicken that we trade. We are all just visitors passing through. We cooperate based on the depth or shallowness of our wisdom.

The residual problem with money and inflation can be described as a mathematical echo. The goods are consumed, the two parties are satisfied, but a mathematical footprint remains. A National Debt is always the inverse of inflation. Eliminate inflation, and you eliminate the National Debt. We can trade fairly using cash, but we need to understand how to trade. Just like driving a car, there needs to be standards of behavior.

When a government creates money, there needs to be an important debate: For whose purpose does the money exist? Does money exist to facilitate trade within the private sector, or does it exist as a way for the government to tax the resources of the people? Unfortunately, history reveals that George Washington supported the central bank because it allowed the executive to wage a war without the need to garner support from the citizens. He could act without restraint. In *Commonsense*, Thomas Paine decried the ability of a monarchy to wage war on his own whim. The central banking system of the United Kingdom was resurrected in the United States with the adoption of the Constitution. George Washington was a new face with a new title, but he came with the old habits of power and privilege. Any head of government can pursue endless war with access a central bank, regardless of how they came to power.

The promise of democracy was that it would usher in an epoch of peace. War has been as bad in modern times as any time of history. The reason to abandon monarchy was because of how the King abused power. Power today is being wielded the same way as before. While more egalitarian and far-sighted than some of their contemporaries, Washington, Jefferson and Madison had more in common with the Pharaoh than with Moses. Their alleged enlightenment contained a large measure of dissonance. Revolutionaries are always willing to crack eggs, but only because they want to claim ownership of the eggs. They are willing to destroy what they cannot possess. Violence adds to the misery of inflation. To have a peaceful society, debt and inflation need to be controlled or eliminated.

It is no more possible to pay off the National Debt than it is possible to live without consumption. While there is a huge discrepancy between the wealth of different individuals and organizations, we all fit under the umbrella of our nation's debt. If we take our personal wealth to another country, we may enjoy a substantial short-term advantage. This is why individuals and corporations migrate to new financial opportunities. Long term, every nation is in debt and suffers from the same modern dysfunction that paper money created: infinite debt and infinite inflation.

We cannot escape the consequences of our own actions. When money was a specie like gold or silver, it was believed that more money would solve economic problems. This led to hundreds of years of experiments trying to turn lead into gold. When that failed, the powers of Europe sought gold and silver on new continents. While they found plenty of gold and silver, it did not solve any problems.

History reveals that money has been a problem regardless of its material; regardless of its quantity, and regardless of how many forms of it exist. The problem is mathematical in nature, and has to do with how we count.

The Debt Limit needs to be raised constantly to keep up with the inflation created in the private sector. All banks can be thought of as a franchise of the Federal Reserve. If a bank gets in trouble, then a nation's central bank, with access to the debt limit and the printing press, can bail them out. A bank can borrow to support its borrowing, the same as a business. Recently we have seen the banks of different nations go to the World Bank, which is a conglomerate of national banks, for a bail out. Our mathematical problems cannot be solved with the same habits that created them.

Ironically, our multi-trillion dollar debt reflects our humanity. Revolutions are economically inspired. Recreating a new currency, in the aftermath of war, allows for a fresh start but at a tremendous expense to humanity. America has experienced a long period of domestic peace since the Civil War. As a result, the numbers have not been reset back to zero, and each generation is incrementally more compressed with financial angst. America desperately needs a new economic theory and a break from tradition. Democracy is socially enlightened. That enlightenment needs to spread to economics.

How we buy and sell is at the root of our social society. Those who criticize the central bank, like elements of the

Tea Party and libertarians, ignore that it was the private sector that created the government, not vice-versa. While governments have failed to solve some problems, and have created new ones, it is not the sole source of our troubles. Money is collectively owned no matter who coins it.

The problems are in our personal accounting procedures. That is where the math we use is being recorded. The government, in coining the first penny, reflects that personal behavior, and by virtue of that authority owns all the debt. We have a system based on ponzi mathematics. The belief that 2+2=5 has been institutionalized. Inflation is the asset of the private sector. National Debt is the liability of the public sector. The National Debt being the inverse of inflation describes the long-term macro problem.

2+2=5 is what caused the problem. We are all part of the problem, and therefore, we all must be part of the solution. The promise of democracy is that the majority would do the right thing. To be debt-free and inflation-free, we should start from the assumption that 2+2=4.

# 10. What is a Ponzi Scheme?

A ponzi scheme operates on the expectation that someone can give back to you more than what you gave them originally. Rather than two people working cooperatively to create something new, one person makes a claim that the other person believes. It is a *'con'* or *'confidence game'* because the victim has faith in the false promises of the operator. It shifts the focus from doing something physically productive to creating wealth via accounting methods.

The victim of a ponzi scheme is not without fault. They expect to gain something without laboring. Common sense requires that if you can gain without working, then someone must be laboring without getting paid. There is no such thing as a free lunch, but they are seduced by their greed. The investors convince themselves that they are the ones at risk, not that they plan to take advantage of others. It is always a bitter surprise when they discover that they were the one getting squeezed. They should have been suspicious of fraud, but they blindly accepted the miraculous: 2+2 can equal 5.

A ponzi scheme mimics traditional business practices. That is what makes them so believable. The nut of the problem, of course, is that our traditional business practices mimic a ponzi scheme. This is the problem we need to fix.

We teach 2+2=4 in math class, and 2+2=5 in business class. We have been conditioned to believe that adding percentages to values is a normal way to count, and the larger the percentage, the better. Business accounting was an intellectual fraud before it became purposeful fraud.

What makes a ponzi scheme successful is the number of witnesses that testify to its validity. Everyone who has experienced the early boom is a firm believer that what he or she has witnessed is true, and not an illusion. Unfortunately, an equation is false wherever it is applied. If 2+2=5 is wrong in math class, then it needs to be wrong in business class, too. If we operate on the assumption that 2+2=5, then eventually 5=2+2. This boom then bust sequence applies to more than illegitimate ponzi schemes. The cycle occurs in every game of *Monopoly*. There does not need to be intentional fraud for a scheme to collapse, there only needs to be a flawed mathematical assumption at the outset. The laws of mathematics must balance: (2+2=5) = (5=2+2). Boom = Bust.

The term ponzi originates from the antics of Charles Ponzi (1882-1949), but he was not the first person to engage in skimming while performing a service that involves redistributing the wealth of others. A bank does the same thing when it pays interest on a deposit. In a traditional business, money goes out and product comes in, then product goes out and money comes in. Banking and ponzi schemes have no products. Money goes out and money comes in.

The difference between the ponzi scheme and banking is that in banking the borrower pays the bank back plus interest. In a ponzi scheme, the new money coming in is believed to being treated the same as a bank deposit. In fact, the alleged interest being paid to a previous investor comes from a new investor.

Today, most banks offer investment services, clouding the difference between legitimate and illegitimate business. When someone loses money in a ponzi scheme, it is because they are being treated like a borrower. The roles have been unexpectedly reversed. Instead of investors living off the debtors, early investors are living off of later investors. It is a betrayal of the financial caste system.

People have become conditioned to embrace a double standard. They do not want to be treated the same way that they have been treating others. Investors are willing to inflict pain on others; they are reluctant to feel that pain themselves. They have been convinced that risk-taking is normal, and that rather than harming others, they are helping the economy, planning for the future and helping others who need credit. They do not see all the consequences of the math.

Interest acts as a revenue generator for the banker and the investor, the same as the profit percentage applied to a product in a business generates revenue. Banks also offer a lot of services for free, unlike traditional businesses. The crux of the problem is that any applied percentage is false. Whether we are on the gaining end or losing end initially is irrelevant. What goes around must come around. No gain can be free or effortless. It has to be taken from somebody else through deception.

Fraud is a potential trap in any transaction. In the trade of a chicken for eggs, the chicken could be sickly or the eggs rotten. A ponzi scheme operates as a mathematical fraud, rather than as a fraudulent exchange of goods, but disappointments are a consequence of forming unreasonable expectations. Expecting 2+2 to equal 5 is to set oneself up for regret. We must all trade to survive, and we must all produce if we are to consume. The gap between our ability to recognize and execute our needs is the opportunity for greed and stupidity to supplant common sense.

It is the nature of all monetary transactions, whether by a government, a bank, a business or a ponzi scheme, to claim that the exchange is for the benefit of everyone involved. Everything is promoted as a win-win situation. Ponzi mathematics exists wherever there is money present. Governments are also engaged in promising to deliver more than what it receives.

These claims seem plausible because inflation has generated mathematical growth (2+2=5). The problem is that the new growth is not sustainable. The same inflation eventually meets 5=2+2. What was gained gets lost, and the new inflation spiral has set a higher bar for survival. The eventual lose-lose is much more bitter than the initial win-win. Poverty compounds as inflation compounds.

When combined with the population boom, there are probably more people living a miserable existence today than at any other time in history. The modern world is not the crown of creation. Not only are the poor miserable, but even those that are doing well struggle. America no longer has an economy based on manufacturing and trade. Many people are employed in ponzi schemes, where they must accept a lie as the truth, and continuously promote false expectations in others. This is a core requirement in advertising, insurance, and the financial services industry. Lies are also part of politics and government, and generically a part of all competitive sales. The only way to sell anything is to raise people's expectations of why they should buy from you rather than from someone else.

A ponzi scheme offers larger returns than what the bank offers. *"It is the best deal."* Investing is another variant of buy-low sell-high, only people are selling their money rather than an apple. Once people are conditioned to believe that money can *'grow,'* one lie can always be bigger than the previous lie, and therefore more attractive. There is a constant pressure for one-upmanship, and to improve on whatever new standard was accomplished yesterday. Just as inflation and debt have no logical limit, neither do expectations.

In general, a ponzi scheme refers to an activity that is outright fraud. A pyramid or multi-line marketing structure is usually involved in providing an actual product, but mathematically these systems all share the same characteristics. Moving a product helps to masquerade the numerical truth.

A ponzi scheme operates by paying interest (or profit) to early investors with the proceeds from later investors. As long as new money comes into the system, it can work. If there is an interruption in the revenue stream, however, then the whole thing quickly collapses. Given the boom and bust nature of the economy, it is difficult to maintain both the illusion and the math of perpetual growth. The advantage that ponzi schemes have is that as traditional business seems to be too risky, more people turn to financial services. This allows financial firms to seemingly thrive when the real economy is suffering, but eventually the math catches up.

Recent changes in the world economy revealed a large number of old and huge ponzi schemes. Bernie Madoff was running the largest one in history, but there are probably larger ones yet to be recognized. There are endowment and pension funds that do not move very frequently, or pay out a significantly large percentage of the fund to reveal the paucity. It is withdrawals that cause the scheme to collapse. This should not be a surprise. Banks do not hold onto their deposits either. If there were a run on a bank, they could not return their depositors' cash any easier than a ponzi scheme. A ponzi scheme hides under the same regulations that govern banking.

Ponzi schemes, banks and traditional business all operate under budgetary pressures to maintain positive revenue over expenses ratio. For the person running the ponzi scheme, however, there is a huge and different problem. The more people that join in, the bigger the lie becomes, and the more difficult it is to maintain. There is a desire for ever larger returns from the clients. Low returns will cause investors to flee, exposing the fraud. If new investors are barred from joining the scheme, the system will collapse without new money. There is no workable equilibrium for the number of clients or investment size in a ponzi scheme. It is in a state of permanent crisis until it collapses. Wall Street is conglomeration of ponzi schemes, which is why it is engulfed in a perpetual sense of urgency.

Because greed has grown so ubiquitous, and oversight so complacent, we now know that fraud can be as tall as a skyscraper and still be invisible to many people. For the truth to set people free, they must overcome their own denial. Bernie Madoff knew he was a fraud. He told people what they wanted to hear. The tragedy was not the lost funds, the travesty was the denial by the investors and regulators. If somebody can become rich without working, then somebody must be working without getting paid. Investing is a slave system by proxy. Just as we abolished slavery, we need to abolish unearned income.

In modern times, people own stocks in the companies that employ them. They have essentially become slaves of themselves, earning unearned income from their own underpaid labor. The mathematical dissonance of modern finance is startling. People believe what they are told, no matter how illogical the claim. Once people have been brainwashed to accept 2+2=5, they will believe any lie or deny any truth regarding money. Investors have lost their moral conscience.

We have been indoctrinated to accept what should be unacceptable. Insurance companies are a ponzi scheme that are able to survive because what is paid out is rigorously controlled. With insurance, the premium is always a percentage of the thing being insured, and the item being insured has a fixed value. There is limited exposure. The risk is divided between everyone who buys insurance. People who have made a successful insurance claim provide the same positive testimony as the early clients in a fraud-based ponzi scheme.

Insurance has a shorter cash cycle than a typical ponzi scheme. Therefore, adding or losing clients is less of a problem. An investor in a Madoff-type scheme may be a client for years, without ever adding new funds. With insurance, new funds are required to be paid annually. If the company loses money, it just increases its premiums the next year. Insurance is a ponzi scheme because one still expects to receive more than they put in. Any funds received must come from other clients.

The bulk of an insurance payment goes towards salespeople and overhead. The difference between insurance and a ponzi scheme is the money is handled slightly more transparently. Mathematically it is the same. In most states, the purchase of insurance is mandatory for different activities. The industry enjoys a captive customer. The allegedly competitive industry is an oligarchy, rather than a monopoly, but the same abuses occur. Many court cases have been brought against the insurance industry because of fraud, neglect, malfeasance, and deception. The same is true of the banking industry, which is a cozy partner in keeping people in debt and afraid. The insurance industry has managed to cultivate a client with low expectations. The client in a ponzi scheme, in contrast, has high expectations. Banks operate between these two extremes.

In the aftermath of 9/11, the first bill passed by Congress was a bailout for the insurance companies. This is because insurance cannot work. Insurance is cost shifting, and all costs must shift back to the National debt. Today there are many different types of insurance. We have insurance for insurance, and insurance purchasing insurance. For example, we have health insurance paying the doctor who is required to have malpractice insurance. Where a ponzi scheme must collapse, the insurance scheme can keep adding new layers. We can now buy insurance on cell phones, televisions and other minor purchases. Insurance is the most lucrative business in the world, and produces nothing.

It is commonly believed that the government can regulate the financial industries. It is impossible. Dishonest businesses have the same framework as the legitimate ones. A ponzi scheme cannot be regulated. The math will not allow it. There is no way to punish an insurance company. Million dollar fines work their way back into the next round of insurance premium increases.

Insurance spikes overhead, and is a major reason why the revenue over expense ratio of budgets is difficult to maintain. Insurance victimizes everyone, yet people believe it helps someone, including themselves.

Insurance acts as a shadow government, trying to provide the safety net that the government fails to provide. This is because taxes are themselves a ponzi scheme. Insurance is outsourcing by the government, which is why the government often requires it. For example, the government could provide free healthcare, adopt a single-payer model, and completely eliminate the health insurance industry. The battle over requiring healthcare insurance would be seen as minor compared to a bill outlawing insurance completely.

People mistakenly believe that they cannot live without insurance. While banking serves some purpose as a gatekeeper in helping the flow of labor and products, insurance offers little.

We should be questioning why any purchase or repair can not be easily afforded. Where is the return from industrialism, efficiency and population growth? We have been conditioned to accept inflation and the values that are applied to goods and services as absolute. Because of our historical inability to think about trade differently, and our callous acceptance of greed as a virtue, ponzi mathematics are the dominant feature of the global economy.

Everyone is working for the ponzi scheme apparatus, either directly or indirectly. Practical problems have become difficult to solve because we accept 2+2=5 and have enshrined this flawed formula in all of our major institutions: government, business, banking, insurance and real estate.

# 11. Big History: The Anatomy of Ideas

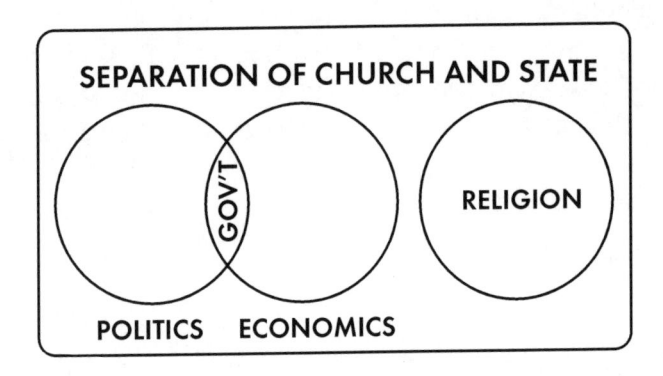

**SEPARATION OF CHURCH AND STATE**

GOV'T — RELIGION

POLITICS   ECONOMICS

It is better to recognize that ideas rule the world, not men, because men can change what they believe, but ideas themselves are unchangeable. Ideas exist in their own separate and pure state, and we give them life by accepting them. We are both observers and participants in an epic clash of ideas.

A Venn diagram is represented by overlapping circles: one black, the other white, and the overlap is grey. The combination generally represents a 'sweet spot' of balance, but it can also be the source of dissonance. The circles themselves can represent opposite or complimentary things. Each circle is extreme, one-dimensional, or pure, depending upon your perspective. The overlap implies integration. The yin-yang symbol represents a similar concept, and the belief that ideas and power are constantly shifting.

The Big History model is a Venn diagram using three circles stacked to form a pyramid. Each circle overlaps on two of its sides, which forms three unique combinations. There is a fourth area, in the center, where all three circles overlap.

The circles represent three types of ideas: religious, political and economic. These topics correspond to our human experience: abstract, social and physical. This trinity repeats often: our brain, our heart and our hands, or, our thoughts, feelings and actions. All of human existence falls into these three categories.

Ideas form our perception. The ideas of any one person are a group of ideas, just as an economic transaction is a group or chain of transactions. There are always connections between the one and the many. This model helps to explain why people understand the same data differently.

| CATEGORY | THEORY | EMPIRE | ORGANIZATION |
|---|---|---|---|
| *Religion* | *Abstract* → | *Non-Profit* | *Church/Univ.* |
| *Politics* | *Social* → | *Non-Religious* | *Governments* |
| *Economics* | *Physical* → | *Non-Political* | *Businesses* |

Where two ideas overlap, the empires of government, business and churches (non-profits) have formed. The balance they represent is achieved by excluding the remaining category of thought. This indicates that each empire is uniquely incomplete. The empires are non-political (Business), non-religious (Government) and non-profit (Churches). For example, Economics + Religion = Business, and excludes Politics.

Within these empires of Church, State, and Business are many individual organizations. They exist to satisfy our needs, and are formed based upon a combination of secondary ideas. People who agree on one set of ideas form an entity, and those who disagree form a separate entity. Intellectually, the separation of Church and State and Business is a completely natural event, and mimics the division of labor and the separate parts of us. Our three main institutions reflect specialization.

However, we exist as individuals separate from the main categories, empires, and organizations. Our primary unit is the family. In the model, we occupy the center, and need to balance with everything and everyone. We struggle amongst contradictory perceptions and purpose. The center reflects why and how dissonance becomes part of the human experience. It is not healthy for individuals or organizations to be working at cross-purposes. All men want balance between the one and the many. We have inadvertently institutionalized perpetual conflict.

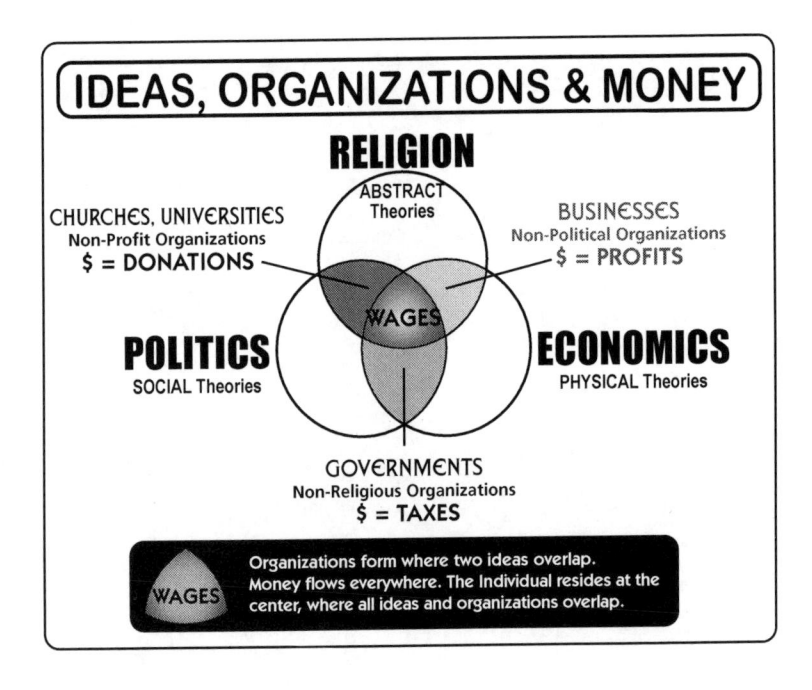

## IDEAS, ORGANIZATIONS & MONEY

**RELIGION**
ABSTRACT Theories

CHURCHES, UNIVERSITIES
Non-Profit Organizations
$ = DONATIONS

BUSINESSES
Non-Political Organizations
$ = PROFITS

WAGES

**POLITICS**
SOCIAL Theories

**ECONOMICS**
PHYSICAL Theories

GOVERNMENTS
Non-Religious Organizations
$ = TAXES

WAGES — Organizations form where two ideas overlap. Money flows everywhere. The Individual resides at the center, where all ideas and organizations overlap.

The Big History labels should not be taken too literally. The Religion realm and Church empire includes atheism, humanism and secular organizations. Whether or not God exists is an abstract question, so it falls under the abstract theory category. Similarly, both socialism and capitalism fall under economics. They are theories about how to best organize the physical world. All ideas fit into a category type. The purpose of the model is to explore how categories of thought interact with one another.

Change can be represented by shifting the discs towards the center, or by layering the discs in a different order. The ascendency of one category of thought can exert an influence on other categories and organizations. For example, when politics rises in importance, there are political changes. The democratic ideals that challenged monarchial government marked the ascendency of political theories.

New ideas in one realm can impact ideas in other realms. For example, socialism was a new idea in the economic realm (mid 1800's). Yet, Marx's view of capital is remarkably similar to Adam Smith's theory written in 1776. The difference is that Marx's analysis is infused with democratic political ideals. The rights of the worker replaced the rights of the citizen. The laborer and the owner were to be considered equal, the same as the citizen and the king.

During the American and French Revolutions, economic theories were used to support a political view. As the idea of socialism spread a century later, economic theories became more contentious, and political ideas were used to support the economic view. The priority of belief shifted. Islamic revolutions represent an ascendency of religious ideas.

**WHICH IDEA IS ON TOP?**

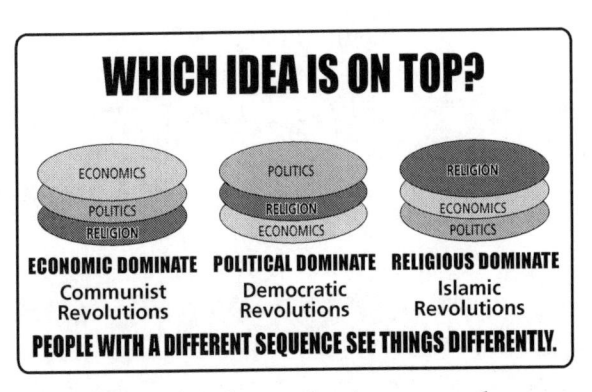

| ECONOMICS | POLITICS | RELIGION |
| POLITICS | RELIGION | ECONOMICS |
| RELIGION | ECONOMICS | POLITICS |
| **ECONOMIC DOMINATE** | **POLITICAL DOMINATE** | **RELIGIOUS DOMINATE** |
| Communist Revolutions | Democratic Revolutions | Islamic Revolutions |

**PEOPLE WITH A DIFFERENT SEQUENCE SEE THINGS DIFFERENTLY.**

Philosophies, empires and organizations may change quickly or slowly, regress or progress, but they all endure. Our needs are fixed and unchanging, and we plow through different combinations of ideas in a search for improvement and balance between the one and the many. In the same manner as generations passing through the cycles of life, important ideas get lost and rediscovered. Within organizations, the vision of leadership changes with different occupants. We see that acutely in presidential elections. Traditions can change with new people (liberalism), or be reattempted as a new solution (conservatism). Change is a constant battle between new ideas and a reprise of old ideas.

Peace and prosperity is a universal goal. The question is *How?* People who disagree cannot accomplish anything. We need to produce to consume, so the results of wrong and right choices eventually present themselves. We suffer or thrive primarily by our own hand. Do we want peace or war? Are we attempting to enslave one another or trying to work cooperatively? The differences between what, why and how we do things can be quite stark. Dissonance adds many layers of hypocrisy and confusion.

Money is common to all. This book argues that inflation and debt are the primary source of trouble. There are other issues, however, which this chapter and the next two will explore. How we think is as important as what we think.

## What is the priority?

The three empires, and the separate organizations within them, must form a hierarchy of priorities. Within the overlap area, one idea category must take precedence over the other. For example, in government, should rights or economic policy be the priority in decision-making? Whose rights, and which economic priority? Since government is the social realm, it is automatically taking sides.

In churches, should the truth or peaceful coexistence with non-members be the priority? Should we love others or judge others?

In businesses, should personal, employer, investor, community or the environmental conditions be the priority? Which mouths should be fed first?

Every organization is providing a service to society, but a hierarchy of values effects the Quality of Life for everyone. Decisions must be made between competing values.

## Competing Values Within & Between Organizations

| ORGANIZATION | COMBINATION | VALUES | FOCUS |
|---|---|---|---|
| CHURCHES & UNIVERSITIES | ABSTRACT & SOCIAL | TRUTH OR PEACE? | FUTURE |
| GOVERNMENT | SOCIAL & PHYSICAL | RIGHTS OR PRODUCTION? | PAST |
| BUSINESS | PHYSICAL & ABSTRACT | SURVIVAL OR COOPERATION? | TODAY |

## Comparing religion within revolutionary movements

Because of dissonance, things are not always as they seem. This is true on a personal level as well as on a grander scale. For example, America has long been embroiled in a great-alleged battle between capitalism and socialism, but both the American and Russian revolutions overthrew monarchy. Their roots are more alike than different.

In Russia, the Church and State were nearly synonymous. In America, religion was autonomous. There was no national religion, but regions of the country were religiously affiliated. All monarchs claimed that they ruled through divine law. God was on their side, and they either tolerated or persecuted different religious beliefs. Freedom of religion was part of some monarchies.

*The Declaration of Independence* claimed that God saw all men as equal. This was an extension of the idea that all religions are equal. Ideas migrate. Both the rebels and the monarch were claiming that God was on their side. The meaning of Divine Law had changed.

Communists opposed religion because it made people too passive. According to Marx, the faithful would not revolt and overthrow their economic oppressors. In America, however, the historical view was that religion was too inflammatory and aggressive. Through completely opposite reasoning, both separated church from state. In a relatively short time, God went from being the dominant idea to being secularized or suppressed, even though the revolutionary arguments were morally based.

Violent Islamic jihadists, in contrast, are fueled by the desire to have religion more involved in politics. Conservative Christian movements have the same goal. Elements of both tend to be the most paranoid about the other, because they see the world more similarly. Splitting hairs is like splitting the atom. The smaller the differences, the more explosive the passions.

Revolutionaries make claim to some form of divine law, either by God or by Nature. For the atheist communist, it was the marketplace of history. According to the Hegelian dialectic, ideas battle and combine to form new ideas. It is akin to the theory of evolution and competitive capitalism. The law of the jungle is that might is right, and only the most fit survive. Ideas have their battleground, too. The Marxists were arguing that because they had the new idea, it was automatically the best idea.

All Revolutionaries claim providence to an idea that is the best for the many. They would deny being motivated by personal greed. They see greed and abuse of power by others as the main obstacle to a just society. They are willing to sacrifice themselves, and the life of their self-defined enemy, for the greater good. Killing represents a well-reasoned choice, like removing a cancerous tumor. Afterwards, presumably, the body will heal and be strong, pure and happy once again, but they need to be in charge, first. Their lust for power mirrors the lust of those in power. Every crime has a motive. History is a crime of complex interpretations of simple motives by similar criminals.

Dissonance is holding two contradictory ideas simultaneously. To see only good in oneself, and only the bad in another, is a characteristic of dissonance. Wherever there is violence, there is a triumph of dissonance.

Digging further into history, we discover that The American Revolution would not have happened without the support of the churches. The teachers of Divine Law changed their mind. The Great Awakening (1730-1750) marked the idea of individual redemption and played a part in the individualistic self-determination of democracy. War marks the death of commonwealth. Taxes were the cause célèbre in the 1770's. Here we are, hundreds of years after monarchy ended, still arguing over taxes. Dissonance can easily survive the battlefield victory.

In the case of the American Civil War, religion was used to argue both in favor of and against slavery. Some claimed that God made negroes inferior to whites. The Declaration of Independence, in contrast, made the claim that all men were equals. The Southerners claimed a right to separate from the Union using the same document that argued against their position. The tension between principles and policies has thousands of nuances. Logic and consistency are hard to find in history. We are all, to some extent, both the victim and the crime.

### Cognitive Dissonance

Believing that 2+2=4 in math class, and believing that 2+2=5 in business class, is cognitive dissonance. Another way to understand cognitive dissonance is as the lack of comparative analysis. Contradictory ideas exist simultaneously in the same mind or institution because they are never compared with one another. Similar to the left hand not knowing what the right hand is doing, cognitive dissonance is an internal house divided: a mind. Emotional dissonance is simultaneous feelings of love and hate. Physical dissonance is laboring to destroy.

People do not want to be wrong. In fact, once they realize that they are wrong, they can never accept what was wrong again. External pressures may force them to mask what they know, but once they know a new truth, they can never consciously reject it.

The book *1984*, by George Orwell, is the study of a man who comes to believe the opposite of what he once believed. Society attempts to force him to believe the old lie again. History is full of the failures of authority that attempted to impose a dogmatic belief. Because of their own denial, authority attempts to use force to make truth submissive. It can never work for long. A house can no more be divided than the person. The truth cannot be suppressed indefinitely. Dissonance creates too many problems to maintain itself.

Progress and enlightenment are the letting go of false ideas and the embracing of better ideas. Looking back over history, we can recognize that what we consider to be very crazy ideas was once the norm. That is a warning to us. Our epiphanies are a stop on a journey, not the final destination. The battle against dissonance is perpetual, and we should not rest on the laurels of previous generations.

Orwell described dissonance as *doublethink*, and there were three primary versions: War is Peace. Freedom is Slavery. Ignorance is Strength. Wrapping them together was an acceptance that 2+2=5. Orwell's novel included multiple countries locked into a state of perpetual war, each believing a unique combination of lies, which made them mutually incompatible.

His novel described both domestic and international politics. People who accept the same combinations of half-truths all get along. Progress, however, is based on people agreeing on a truth that actually is the truth, and rejecting formerly held half-truths. In this case, the truth is that war is war, peace is peace, freedom is freedom, slavery is slavery, ignorance is ignorance, strength is strength, and 2+2=4. These are seemingly obvious equations, but they are not in practice. The opposite of dissonance is virtue and consistency.

## Comparative Analysis

The mind is very good at comparative analysis. If you cut a piece of cake in half, one can instantly recognize which side is bigger. Comparative analysis goes beyond quantifiable things. We can recognize superiority in a musical performance, the weather of a particular day, the flavor of a cake. All of our senses are capable of comparative analysis. The more we use all our senses, including logic and morality, and make comparisons, then the more certain we can be of our conclusion.

Metaphysics is a term that roughly means, *'the knowledge of how we know.'* It is a *'thinking about thinking'* line of inquiry. How do we know anything? Why is 2+2=4 right, and 2+2=5 wrong, at least in math class? We can use other numerical computations to test our first numerical computation (4-2=2). In the same way, we can test all the ideas we believe. They do not need to be quantifiable. Quality can be recognized by a level of consistency. For example, treating others the way that you want to be treated is consistent. Treating people badly, but expecting to be treated well, is inconsistent. Comparative analysis helps us to recognize consistency, and thus avoid or purge our dissonance. That is the vigorous process of metaphysics. It is difficult because it is not about accepting, rejecting, blaming or changing others, it is about accepting or rejecting our own positions. A willingness to change oneself is the first step in enlightenment.

Using comparative analysis to sift through a number of points should allow one to reach a conclusion that is consciously chosen, rather than implanted through habit or indoctrination. No matter who we are, where or when we were born, our initial experience in the world indoctrinates us to a certain set of untested beliefs or prejudices.

Our willingness and ability to study beliefs objectively requires a measure of maturity and intellectual detachment. Denial is emotional, and a roadblock to progress. It is easier to deny inconsistencies than to straighten them. Nevertheless, it is hard to deny the evidence of our own life once it comes into focus. We know our own mistakes better than anyone else, which is why people find different value in the same book, movie, or conversation. The words may be the same, but they impact the receiver differently. We each have our own unique dissonance to purge.

The battling of ideas is at the root of man and society. Beliefs are constantly in flux as new information and experience impact our previous indoctrination. At all times, there are people at different stages of a similar journey. As a result, progress appears slow, but shifts are occurring constantly. The question is always, *"Which direction is right?"*

Being wise about topic A does not make one wise about topic B. People are not right because of their position in society or because of tradition. They are right if what they think is true. The most powerful in society are often the least informed. They are indoctrinated as a condition of acceptance into their position and isolated from contrary voices. Nevertheless, what is *more true* eventually reaches their ears. Institutions can change their thinking, albeit more slowly than those outside. They are often the last to know which makes them the last to act.

**False Choices**

People who are wrong make mistakes. We all make mistakes because everyone is human. The need for freedom of speech and freedom of religion are directly related to authority imposing a mistaken interpretation. The abuse of power usually stems from the hesitation to admit a mistake. The Bill of Rights provides people with the space in which to make mistakes, but the primary goal is to limit the abuse of power. It recognizes that it is impossible to compel somebody to believe something they reject, and that authority should not be isolated from criticism. Of course, people who just had that same experience created the Bill of Rights. They overthrew their belief in hereditary and divine authority before they overthrew the King. Letting go of mistakes is hard for everyone. Power, education and wealth make it difficult, but so too does ignorance and inexperience. Everyone is comfortable in whatever lies they accept. The promise of consensus politics is that people high and low can convince one another to let go of the old lies and embrace new thinking. Mutual respect is the first step in solving problems, and disrespect the first act of creating them.

Using force to compel obedience is both spiritually and intellectually bankrupt, and usually results in ruin. This is as true in a domestic relationship as it is in business negotiations or political diplomacy. Violence is proof of failure. There is always a time before violence breaks out that peaceful reform is possible, but one or both sides does not seize it. Often by the time an authority comes to recognize legitimate complaints, the complainant no longer recognizes the authority.

One argument in favor of democracy is that one man cannot thwart the will of the majority. Unfortunately, there is nothing to prevent a democracy from splitting into multiple political parties that maintain mutually exclusive versions of dissonance. That was what Orwell was suggesting in 1984. It does not follow that when two sides are locked into an epic battle, that one side is right, and the other side is wrong. It is equally possible that both sides are wrong.

This book challenges the party of profits (Republicans) and the party of taxes (Democrats), the free-market Libertarians, and the many theological movements that accept violence as a necessity of freedom and piety. From my point of view, they all have cognitive dissonance. The only thing they agree on is obviously wrong: 2+2=5.

There are two enemies. One is inflation, and the other, as Pogo suggested, is ourselves. Inflation cannot be satisfied. It is a silent demon that drives many troubles. Our dissonance regarding basic arithmetic hampers the success of modern man.

The errors of history are because people have failed to put separate pieces of information together properly. We become more right when we put more compatible ideas together. A wrong or incomplete conclusion is the result of not testing what we believe. Progress is a vigorous self-test. Excuses, justifications, lies and errors can easily be substituted for truth, reason and fact. We refuse our mirror, not the messenger. Diplomacy is required to attain peace between two parties, but the principle cause of difficulty is the refusal to self-examine by either or both parties. Self-examination is not a negotiated compromise.

## Wisdom versus Truth

There is a conventional wisdom, which is a consensus of tradition, but not a conventional truth. Wisdom is a description of usually knowing what is right or true. It is primarily habit. Truth, in contrast to wisdom, does not bend to peer pressure, consensus or tradition. Truth exists, and it is for man to discover. It is lost because even the best indoctrination is a poor substitute for experience. The teacher can teach, students can learn, but it takes experience to understand. There is no way to skip from birth to wisdom without some struggle, and truth is beyond wisdom. Truth is so clear and transparent that man has trouble seeing it. Sometimes it is so bright that it blinds us and we close our eyes. Man has trouble recognizing the truth, yet it always surrounds us. We must continually train our senses to recognize it.

Thomas Jefferson wrote, *"We hold these truths to be self-evident."* If that were literally true, there would have been no need to make the claim. What he meant was that the conventional wisdom regarding the divine and hereditary superiority of the King was false. A new conventional wisdom was developing: the Creator, if he existed, was impartial, and all men were equal.

*The Declaration of Independence* declared war on the King. He was the only one to whom this new idea applied, but many people accepted the king's place in society as God's will. History, however, shows that a king's rise to power was based on popular opinion. He was 'elected,' the same as a president.

In *Commonsense*, Thomas Paine describes the biblical story of Gideon. Gideon was a victorious general, and in the aftermath of war, the grateful people wanted him to be their king. He declined, and said, *'THE LORD SHALL RULE OVER YOU.'* Paine uses this story to explain that any king is illegitimate. A god-fearing leader would choose as Gideon did, and would favor equality and individual enlightenment, rather than a top-down hierarchy. A god-fearing man would reject the opportunity to be king.

Compare that to Mao in 20th century China, who claimed that all *'political power grows out of the barrel of a gun,'* and God did not exist. He considered himself to be the best choice for running a strong central government. Morality is still defined as equality, but it is combined with *'might is right.'* Not surprisingly, he had a gun in his hand. In his other hand, there was a piece of paper. That sacred text, self-written or not, becomes the permission to use violence. Both fascists and the non-violent use a sacred text to justify their actions.

People embrace those who protect them from their fears, which is why generals become presidents and politicians lay claim to their veteran status. Whether the divide is within a country or across borders, to be a hero one first needs to make an enemy.

Washington and Jefferson were just as much fascist rebels as King George was a fascist ruler. *The Declaration of Independence* reads, "Enemies in War; in Peace Friends." Osama bin Laden's *Letter to America* (November 2002) reads exactly the same way. Peace is only deemed possible after victory. President Nixon made a career of anti-communism, only to make peace with Russia and China once he became president. A position of strength over ones enemy is the only acceptable 'equality' that dissonance allows. It is neither peace nor equality. Slaves want to trade places with the slave-master. Ending slavery requires everyone to be truely equal; the low rise and the high come down.

Had Jefferson written, '*We hold this wisdom to be best: all men should be treated as equals,*' he would have done far better. Jefferson, and a great many others, did not act on what they claimed. They were the middle-class: subjects to the King and slave-masters of their human 'property.' Their dissonance is self-evident. They demanded equality from their superior immediately, but they were slow to grant the same favor to their inferiors. It is easier to blame others for their lack of virtue, than to set an example of virtue. Violence is always hypocritical, since it sets a higher standard for others than for oneself. Imbalances begin with small acts of disrespect, pride and jealousy.

## Dissonance of Means and Ends: Equality or Inequality?

Equality, and inequality, are both regarded as a necessary means to an ends. Organizations generally have someone at the head to make decisions. How they wield that power and the choices they make have consequences. The truth is equally good for everyone. The objective of the rebel and the King are similar. Neither wants to bring violence upon themselves, but act out of a belief of what is best for society. Political violence is believed to be a response to a provocation. The challenge is, how do we organization a society for the benefit of all, so violent opposition does not occur?

Long after Gideon, Solon created democracy in Greece. Men would rule over men by consensus. Solon came to power because he was trusted by both the rich and the poor to solve their economic problems. Unfortunately, he never really looked at what caused the economic issues. He focused on repurchasing and freeing those sold into slavery. After that, he focused on settling disagreements through compromise. He eventually limited free speech on contentious issues, like war, where no agreement was possible. He came to regret the law against free speech, and eventually broke it himself. Respect alone cannot solve a problem. It only provides the setting for having a discussion.

Socrates arrived 100 years later. He tested many people by asking simple questions about their beliefs. He found the unwise in all ranks. He recognized that wisdom was a consequence of virtue and consistency, not education or position or tradition. He stated: *"The difficulty, my friends, is not in avoiding death, but in avoiding unrighteousness; for that runs faster than death."*

Socrates died at the hands of the Sophists, who were willing to silence criticism. The topic of their disagreement still resonates today.

The Sophists, like Solon, believed everyone should be paid for their labor, and slavery was wrong. Socrates, in contrast, questioned the value of what was paid. He believed that expensive teachers taught people what they wanted to hear, rather than the truth. Socrates challenged both their livelihood and their teachings. Like Solon, Socrates felt that the truth and righteousness were more important than money. The sophists, in contrast, loved money, and had their self-esteem tied to it.

Socrates was the teacher of Plato. Plato believed in inequality for the purpose of having a ruling elite, and felt that non-natives should be slaves. Much like Hitler, Plato felt his Athenians were superior, and others were barbarians.

Plato was the teacher of Aristotle. Aristotle also argued in favor of slavery, maintaining that it was a natural balance for society for some to serve and others to be served. His belief was echoed by American slave-masters and the proponents of free market theories where might is right and superior.

Chances are, Socrates would have rejected the claims of Aristotle. It is doubtful he would have agreed with Plato, either. Unfortunately, everything we know of Socrates is based on what Plato wrote. The student is both recalling and arguing with his teacher.

## Ideas Rule

Nobody rules in a vacuum. Conventional wisdom is democratically held, whether the belief is monarchy or democracy or something else. Jim Crow was perfectly normal in the South, because the people accepted their cultural conditioning. The whites applied the threat of violence, and the non-whites chose to tolerate it until leaders arose that challenged it. Whites objected too. Changes are not complete until there is enough internal and external peer pressure to make certain behaviors unacceptable.

Jesus arrived 350 years after Aristotle, thousands of years after Moses, yet slavery continued until the 19th century. It is still found in some parts of the world. History is a window and reveals many of the same problems that we are struggling with today: Who should be in charge, how should people be treated, how does the wealth of society get distributed?

The American Founders were more similar to Aristotle than to Socrates. The western world is built on sophism (anti-slavery and pro-greed) with protections for free speech. We are all students and teachers. We need to be sure that what we teach and learn is true. We need to move beyond sophism.

### Influence of Teachers

|  | GREED | SLAVERY |
|---|---|---|
| SOLON | Anti | Anti |
| SOCRATES | Anti | Anti |
| SOPHISTS | Pro | Anti |
| PLATO | Anti | Pro |
| ARISTOTLE | Pro | Natural |
| JESUS | Anti | Anti |

Teachers: Good (aware of truth) / Bad (unaware of truth)

Students

Solon, Socrates and Jesus were in agreement.

147

If anyone is suffering, and/or people are driven to attacking the government, or a particular group, then the administration of the public trust, and our fulfillment of personal duty has failed the commonwealth. All conflict involves ignorance regarding something. When bad ideas have become better rooted than good ideas, trouble escalates. It is an unfortunate thing that people often argue against the truth and equality. They want power, glory, wealth, and worst of all, revenge. A lot of what people call justice is a masquerade for retribution, and the petty need to silence criticism.

The truth will always rattle our bones because it requires letting go of some falsehood that we hold dearly. Mercy is a crazy idea for the merciless. Sharing is a crazy idea for the greedy. It is pride that dies the hardest. We grip most dearly a high opinion of ourselves. Any straw will do. We are superior because of where we were born, our ethnicity, religion, a particular skill or our wealth. The list is endless. People need self-esteem and confidence, but they need humility as well. The mirror is not half as scary as it is comical. The ability to laugh at oneself is one of the great joys in life. Pride takes small achievements too seriously.

A government of the people, by the people and for the people requires one essential ingredient: people of virtue. Virtue is when one gives more than they take, love rather than hate, forgive rather than punish. Virtue is the opposite of conventional business and finance practices. The sophist methodology is not the best choice for society. Trade for profit is certainly preferable to slavery, but profit is a variation of slavery. Trade is an equal exchange, whereas profit is always an unequal exchange.

Like with Thomas Jefferson, for all people there is a tension between what we claim to believe and how we act. We progress and regress simultaneously. His belief in equality preceded his practice of equality. That is natural. Nevertheless, he could have freed his own slaves before revolting against the king. Holding two contradictory ideas is the primary characteristic of dissonance. Rulers with dissonance create coalitions based on mutually incompatible half-truths. While they may die, their example endures. The Big History model makes it easier to separate the virtue from the dissonance. The beliefs of any specific person are unimportant. We need to defend virtue, not reputations.

**Virtue is Consistent**

To believe in equality while judging others to be inferior, to start violence and call it fighting for peace, are inconsistencies. Similar to the cost of living revenue-expense ratio, there is a wisdom ratio where our personal and public values can be at cross-purposes. We are not always thinking, feeling and acting clearly and consistently. We repeat the bad habits we encounter in others, believing we do not have them ourselves. Wisdom and virtue are non-exclusive to age, education, reputation or status. It is a struggle for everyone to think and act consistently with their motives and goals.

We have a choice regarding in which direction we want to move before deciding the merit of any question. Intellectually, we either choose to improve the future, or choose to cling to the past; to protect our gains or to share and help others. We set our own example as leaders and followers. Dissonance exists when we fill our roles inconsistently. For everyone to be happy and free, we must be consistent within and across our relationships. How we respond to any challenge is the example we teach. Ideally, children will be taught to think about the truth, and not indoctrinated into lies and untested prejudices.

Life is a cooperative endeavor. The more we produce, the more we can consume. Part of that cycle is distributive. The more that is produced, the more easily the non-productive children and elderly can survive, and we with them. More production and less destruction raise the Standard of Living. Less profit, taxes and interest lowers the Cost of Living. Both choices improve equality and commonwealth. More virtue means there will be less suffering, less conflict and less waste.

A true revolution is when a gentle hand reforms the harsh hand. A faux revolution is when a harsh hand replaces a harsh hand. Non-violent revolutions are becoming more common, which is a sign that virtue is gaining in the world.

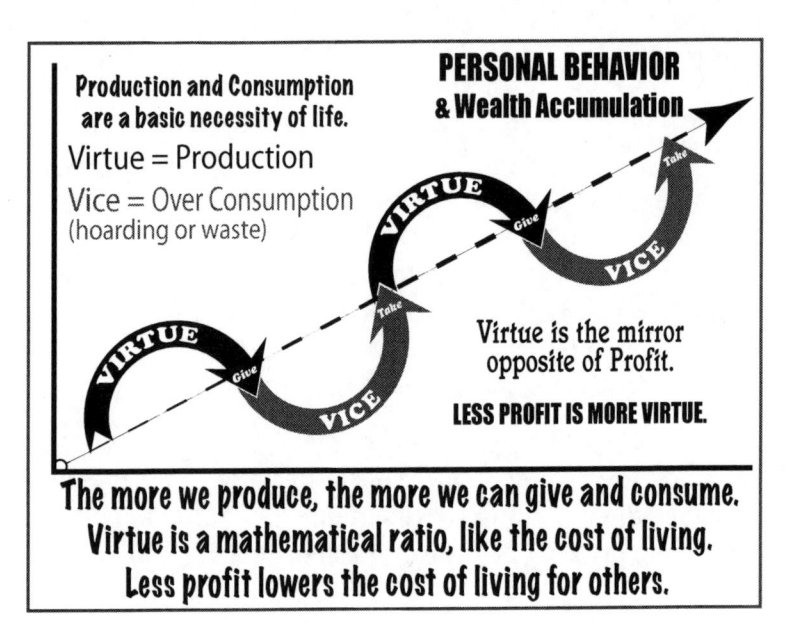

---

**PERSONAL BEHAVIOR & Wealth Accumulation**

Production and Consumption are a basic necessity of life.

Virtue = Production

Vice = Over Consumption (hoarding or waste)

Virtue is the mirror opposite of Profit.

**LESS PROFIT IS MORE VIRTUE.**

**The more we produce, the more we can give and consume. Virtue is a mathematical ratio, like the cost of living. Less profit lowers the cost of living for others.**

---

### History is a Mess

The American Civil War was a battle over states rights and slavery, allegedly. In reality, every organization had their own motivation. There was something about the past that they wanted to preserve or change, and something about the future they wanted to control.

Bankers and industrialists in the North were playing a different game of *Monopoly* than the agrarian South. Northern churches were opposed to slavery, and not surprisingly, slavery had already ended there. The same was true in the South. Southern churches defended slavery, and slavery was an acceptable practice in Southern economic theory. Politically, religion had been adapted to make the whites superior, just as divine law had previously made the monarch superior. The main ideas of society form a complimentary set, regardless of internal contradictions.

Ideas are always a double-edged sword. The North freed their slaves through a series of intellectual approaches, most of which used religion to validate the concept of equality. Some would preach peaceful resistance to slavery as consistent in end and means with God's will. Others would preach war making the same claims, using the example of Moses. The doctrinal divides can be very odd when looked at objectively. Similar goals can have opposite strategies.

During the Civil War, the South was battling for the economic status quo wrapped up in states rights. The North was fighting from a religious-predominate perspective, that coincided with the North's belief in economic theory. The sophist industrialists opposed slavery because they felt it was an unfair competitive advantage. Lincoln, however, was fighting from a government-predominate perspective. For him the priority was the preservation of the government, not right from wrong, or economic conditions. Lincoln, like the King in the past and the Tsar of the future, was interested in preserving his empire, with the church and the businesses as its subjects. His heroes were the Founding Fathers, who risked civil war for power. He did the same as his heroes, or so he thought.

The Big History model can demonstrate how quickly and easily a truth or dissonance can spread and effect other institutions of society. Lincoln, like King George, did everything possible to consolidate the role of government and his position at its head. Yet, he believed he was following the vision of the original rebels. Even if the Union split, there was no danger of a monarchy returning. He was not defending democracy, he was defending the United States in the same way the British king defended the United Kingdom. Lincoln was neither a hero, nor a villain, but just another confused individual with too much power.

Deposed leaders like Saddam Hussein in Iraq, and Muammar Gaddafi in Libya, made the same attempt to defend their union and their supremacy. Tyrants are never fighting for tyranny. They believe themselves to be responsible for the order and success of society. For them to lose power is for chaos to bloom. The unfolding resistance and civil war affirms their prejudice.

Those in power mistakenly believe that their organization and interpretations of history are superior. They fail to see themselves as equal partner with others in society, and often cast a group or individuals as evil. Equality is not common sense, but a truly difficult concept to grasp. To love your enemy, as Jesus preached, remains the most radical idea of all. Self-awareness and self-restraint are skills which must be developed.

While the concept of equality fuels revolutions, the revolution itself marks the inability to practice equality on both sides of the divide. Dominant ideas get attacked because of a lack of balance in society. Most commonly, the coming generation attacks the older generation. Some of them are more acutely aware of the gap between rhetoric and reality.

For Americans, equality has often been interpreted as a political issue, not an economic one. The battles for woman's suffrage, civil and minority rights, mixed and gay marriage were considered political issues. The rise of the unions and the Occupy Wall Street movement were challenges to economic habits, but the economic conditions themselves are viewed primarily as a result of political inequality. Challenges focus on regulations and abuses of power, not established economic theory orthodoxy.

America has been at war with communists and Islamists who have a different view of history. We debate economic theory from within a very narrow perspective, and as a result, the shouting over taxes has gone for hundreds of years. Our belief in politics lacks balance, in the same way as the communists focus on ownership lacks balance, or the violent jihadist focus on religion lacks balance.

In modern times, the big change was that democracies were now at war with one another, rather than monarchies. The assembly line brought industrialism and war on a global scale. Production was used to develop mutually assured destruction.

The church, which had once ruled the world, has been irreverently compartmentalized. Hitler, who was responsible for the worst war, was focused on religious destruction and Aryan superiority. He was well outside the norm for his time. Old lies are rediscovered and readapted. The blood of the monarch was no longer divine, but had been democratized in all Aryans. He was repeating the claims of the American slave-masters. The ideas that constitute fascism are common. The belief that only one religion is true, and only those followers can get into heaven, is the same lie migrating.

History is full of individuals with different ideas. Their ideas need to be tested. As we can see with the ancient Greeks, small nuances can be a significant difference. We should not copy dissonance. Rather, we should try to understand how dissonance develops. We cannot change the past, but if we are wise, then we can create a better future by cleaning the rubbish out of our heads.

The Big History model works as an intellectual and organizational map of every person and organization, and as a timeline. Every person is his or her own unique combination of ideas. Every nation is experiencing its own similarly patterned history. The common goal is the balance of ideas, feelings and actions. If we are to find the peace and prosperity that virtue promises, then we need to study dissonance more deeply.

# 12. The Anatomy of Contradictory Ideas

Man is very good at both creating problems and solving them. Unfortunately, we do not discover that our solutions are making things worse until after the fact. We are a creative species as a necessity of survival. We try to solve problems as we understand them, but can we solve them better? Our solutions form a court of public opinion, or conventional wisdom, which becomes our working definition of virtue. Every generation prepares the next generation for the role of responsibility. We teach the virtues we believe.

There are, of course, huge debates over various issues. One would like to believe that after thousands of years clever people have solved all of the world's challenges, but we all know that is not the case. We conquer old problems and new ones arrive. Children must learn virtue anew, and what they learn is often inaccurate.

The Big History model encompasses all of the shifts of human understanding and action, and can be applied to any dispute or agreement or philosophical perspective. It helps to reveal the power of ideas. While a big idea about big ideas, it fits at the micro level, too. It scales from the individual person, up to individual organizations, and onward to schools of thought and the entire history of mankind. The micro is the macro. It can help us discern consistencies and inconsistencies. Inconsistencies are at the root of all conflicts and failures. Emerson wrote that a *"foolish consistency is the hobgoblin of little minds."* It follows then, that a wise consistency is the foundation of progress.

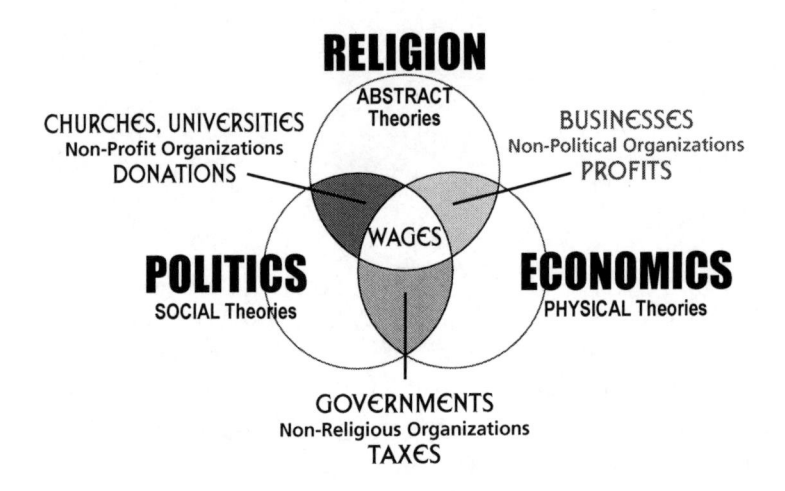

```
                        RELIGION
                       ABSTRACT
CHURCHES, UNIVERSITIES  Theories    BUSINESSES
 Non-Profit Organizations        Non-Political Organizations
    DONATIONS                          PROFITS
                        WAGES
    POLITICS                        ECONOMICS
   SOCIAL Theories                 PHYSICAL Theories

                      GOVERNMENTS
                 Non-Religious Organizations
                          TAXES
```

The Big History model is dynamic. The cultural gears are in constant motion, and everyone is a unique evolutionary machine. We can plot our own virtue and prejudices and how others arrive at theirs. The Big History model might be a map for success. The hope is once we can see our strengths and weaknesses that we can then separate them.

To accomplish our needs, we have formed goal-focused organizations that represent empire types. These empires are represented by the elements that overlap. Governments combine social and physical, and exclude the abstract; for-profit businesses combine the physical and abstract, and exclude the social; non-profit organizations combine abstract and social, and exclude the physical. At the center, all the circles overlap. Here resides the individual.

We all work for and promote the empires. Directly or indirectly, we are the connecting force between all ideas, organizations and actions. We fill our roles based on how we combine the various philosophies and opportunities. We have some freedom to choose which empires and which beliefs we will subscribe to, but we are impacted by all of them, regardless of our personal beliefs.

The Big History model is a system of opposites. Each empire combines two ideas and excludes a third. That makes each empire unique, and each has the potential to be an ally or an adversary with the other empires. However, the elements that create the empires are not homogenous. The larger circles independently represent a body of thought regarding the contentious topics of religion, politics and economics. There are literally millions of nuances among competing religious, political and economic theories. For example, Christianity is just one of many religions, and there are thousands of sects within it. There may be commonality on one issue and hard disagreement on another.

Organizations and sub-organizations form within the empires based on a unique combination of different prejudices. For example, the empire of government has three levels (federal, state and local) and within each level there are thousands of departments and agencies. Outside of government there are watchdog and lobbyist groups, supporters and detractors, manipulators and consultants, suppliers and opportunists. Every point of view can be considered a prejudice, not because of a desire to be hurtful to others, but because most beliefs, as the model implies, are incomplete.

There are no shortages of opinions. Every goal, action, problem, and procedure are being viewed differently. One person will be bragging about what another finds shameful. There are opposites everywhere, and comparative analysis can help survey how our ideas, emotions and actions interact. The following chart details some of the assumptions behind our prejudices and virtues. The assumptions of each realm are similar but have different nuances. An appreciation for subtlety is how we solve problems.

| RELIGION | POLITICS | ECONOMICS |
|---|---|---|
| ABSTRACT | SOCIAL | PHYSICAL |
| NON-PROFIT | NON-RELIGIOUS | NON-POLITICAL |
| IDEAS | EMOTIONS | ACTIONS |
| REASON | FEELINGS | PROCEDURES |
| RELATED/UNRELATED | MORAL/IMMORAL | CAUSE & EFFECT |
| RIGHT or WRONG | GOOD or BAD | TRUE or FALSE |
| MORALITY | JUSTICE | AMORAL |
| TRUST or FEAR | LOVE or HATE | GIVE or TAKE |
| LOGICAL | SPIRITUAL | MECHANICAL |
| DISCERNMENT | AGREEMENT | SCIENTIFIC PRACTICE |

You may be surprised to see Spiritual listed under the social heading, rather than under the abstract or religious heading. The spirit refers to social connections, whether it is between God and man, a married couple, family, friends or co-workers. It is the lack of spirit that brings on a social crisis. God is a person, just like everyone else. Atheists reject a spiritual connection with God that believers accept. When a spiritual connection is lacking, a member of one political party can easily scorn another party, or one religion another religion. Love and hate are spiritual conditions based upon emotions. Similarly, you may be surprised to see reason and logic under religion. People tend to think of science one-dimensionally. Science has ideas, emotional and action components. Science can be divided into scientific method, scientific goals, and scientific practice. All reason and logic fall under abstract thinking. Science follows the abstract, social and physical paradigm.

There is no natural conflict between religion and reason. Atheists reason that God does not exist; believers reason that He does exist. The history of what certain individuals do with political power notwithstanding, religion is of the abstract realm along with scientific inquiry.

Reason explores cause and effect. The theories of evolution and the Big Bang are studies of cause and effect. If you believe a lightening bolt hitting a primordial pool created life, there is still the question of what created the lightening bolt? *What was before the Big Bang? What is at the edge of the universe?* Questions never end, like the question, *'Who created God?' Are two events related or not?* All big questions involving cause and effect eventually meet an unsolvable mystery. We can learn a lot during the process.

We know more than our ancestors, but knowledge makes the mystery larger, not smaller. We use reason to form a hypothesis, formulate experiments and search for evidence to support our logic. Reason is scientific method, regardless of the conclusion. The abstract category refers to thinking.

Emotions, in contrast, deal with the result. Is what we have good or bad? Politics is the social category and refers to feelings. Emotions do not ask how something arrived, but only register pleasure or pain. Is it something to keep and cultivate, or something to avoid and prevent? The political realm is where those goals are debated and determined. The social realm is subjective and problematic, because what one person enjoys may be suffering for another person. If people are at emotional opposites, then they can be working for an opposing result. Should the government conduct stem cell research? Should the government defend or abolish slavery?

Emotions determine the scientific goal. Hitler, for example, wanted to use genetics to prove that whites were superior to satisfy his emotional need.

Action falls under the physical category. This is scientific practice. Applied science tests the causality that reason develops, and discovery is then applied for its best impact: to bring pleasure and avoid pain. Unity and consensus are important for scientific goals, but scientific action tests for accuracy. Is something true or false? Can we build a machine that works as intended?

Balance and accuracy are critical in all areas. If we mistakenly believe a falsehood, then good can result only by accident. The best choices are balanced and will result in more balance. Balance is understanding cause and effect, choosing good over bad, and true over false.

When Jesse Owens won the 1936 Olympics, it shattered Hitler's claim that non-whites were inferior. Not only did Germany fail, but all Aryans failed, too. Hitler twisted scientific reasoning and goals. In the death camps, he would go on to twist scientific action. It was absurd to tattoo numbers onto people that you intended to kill. What was the purpose of all the record keeping? His distorted spiritual connection, an extreme self-love and hatred of others, led to many distorted scientific practices, including where humans were cruelly used as test subjects. He was unique because of his success in leading a nation into an extreme misdirection, but the paths he traveled to get there are well worn. False reasoning and emotional separation create scapegoats. Every realm also has a matching virtue and vice. In politics, they are humility and pride. The results speak for themselves.

Ideas (abstract realm) and emotions (social realm) are both self-centered phenomenon. Science cannot 'prove' what is right or good. It can only test for true or false. Many questions are beyond the boundaries for science to test. In the hierarchy of the human condition, religion should be at the top. If we fail to respect cause and effect, then we believe a lie. Unfortunately, how we feel effects what we reason. This is a subtle but important condition when it comes to recognizing dissonance in ourselves. When our emotions mis-register reality, there is an opportunity for error. The error can be as huge as World War II, or as local as a disagreement with a friend.

Theories, empires and organizations are just like the people that created them. Ideas, emotions and actions are inseparable. Balance can only be achieved through consistency. The world is a reflection of humanity's success or failure to think, feel and act in harmony. Balance is in everyone's interest.

**Heroes and Villains**

The myriad of personal choices and opportunities are overwhelming. A hierarchy of priority is developed based on the role we occupy. For a parent it may be family; for the breadwinner, their job; for a student, their studies; for a church, the services; for government, the laws; for a business, sales. We are all familiar with these roles. The only way to fully understand any choice is to make it. Once we do, we are able to define heroes and villains based on how they interact with our roles. We enjoy our supporters and are displeased by our detractors. Cause and effect, good and bad, true and false all combine when we make a judgement.

Our choices are our ambition, and ambition is a double-edged sword. People discover that it is lonely at the top, if they manage to make it. Others lose their desire, want to get off the path they chose, but are stuck. Whatever next choice we make has all the same issues. We cannot escape the human condition. Life is too brief to experiment with many choices. What people need most is balance, but that is difficult to achieve in a system that is structurally imbalanced. Economic volatility intrudes upon everyone, and sets off many conflicts.

As a result of faulty reasoning and unfortunate experiences, some people develop one-dimensional personalities. They become full of hate, rage and anger and live life on the offensive. For them, the fault of history can only be the one target to which they have dedicated themselves to oppose. This blame can fall on anything. It can be a person, a business type, a political party, an organization, a belief, a skin color, a nationality or an ethnicity. In a world of tremendous size, diversity and activity, there are plenty of opportunities to rage against straw men, near or far. We follow our misjudgements as far as we can go, and when we get to the end, we embrace a change that we previously felt was impossible or ridiculous. Epiphanies are fair-weather friends.

Sometimes the one-dimensional personality can be the emotional opposite of anger. They are not full of hate and rage, but of concern and sympathy for a specific group of people that they wish to help. The target group may suffer from illness, ignorance, injustice or a social condition.

The one-dimensional person can be an extreme pessimist or an extreme optimist, a demagogue or a prophet, a destroyer or a philanthropist. Given the nature of dissonance, there are often elements of both. One person's hero is another's villain, but more importantly, creating a victim requires a hero and a villain. We elevate ourselves as we condemn others. Triangularizations are common.

The best epiphanies are when the right hand and the left hand discover what each other are doing. The hand that loves heroes discovers the hand that hates villains. Suddenly, scapegoats and straw men are not the enemy, but our own faulty reasoning. What somebody loves and hates defines how they understand the world. We create our heroes and our villains based on how we interpret roles and ideas. When we discover that our heroes and villains share the same characteristics, then we discover ourselves. That is the central idea that the Big History model hopes to illuminate. The drawing is a mirror of our prejudices and experience.

## Mapping Anger

All anger can be mapped within the Big History diagram. For example, when an employee who is angry at his boss over wages. The disagreement is located within the for-profit business empire. The boss is at the top of the pyramid, and the employee is at the bottom. The complaint is that the boss is being unfair or greedy, which is a complaint with moral right/wrong intonations (which falls under the abstract/religion realm), but the boss is making decisions for the business empire, where profit is the defined virtue. His job is to keep expenses down, not make people happy. Fairness may be the virtue in politics or religion, but not in business. A fair business is open to overlap. An unfair business is not.

On the personal level, the boss is trying to maximize the revenue, the same as the employee. The conflict is because they are similar, not because they are different. Two dogs are fighting over the same bone. In this case the bone is money, but it could be power, respect, perks, job duties, God's favor or something else. People who are similar fight, because the same thing is important to both of them. While the conflict takes place within one empire, the other realms inform it. Fairness is a political concept, not a business concept.

Courts in the political realm attempt to adjudicate business disputes. An accusation of unfairness is not necessarily true. The worker may be greedy and self-aggrandizing. Disputes can rise to the point of being a legal issue. Lawmakers create laws that reflect the side which they support. The recent disputes between bankers and consumers, and the attempt at new financial regulations, is an example of how the two realms collide and change. Most disputes in court are related to business, including organized crime, which is just illegal business. The reason for a jury of peers, rather than a jury by superiors or victims, is that our peers are most likely to share the same experiences as ourselves. We are more willing to accept the judgement of an equal than of an enemy or a superior.

Balance is the ideal because theoretically there would be no conflict, no trial, no jury, no court. The thicker the book of laws, the greater the lack of balance in society. In America's case, the imbalance has been institutionalized into a dissonance called 'checks and balances.' Ironic, since there is no balance, except in name and claim. The structure breeds conflict.

The worker versus employer conflict is an up-down divide within a business organization. Capitalism versus socialism is a left-right conflict within economic theory. There are many conflict combinations, including diagonal. Karl Marx blamed the religious leaders, thereby crossing from the bottom of economics to the top of religion. Workers can blame government for protecting abusive employers. The businesses can blame government for both taxes and regulations. It is common for someone at the top of one empire to complain about the choices made in another empire. For example, a music celebrity speaks out against politicians. There is plenty of hypocrisy going around, and we all get ensnared in it. It is difficult to discuss virtue without making someone or some choice an example of the lack of virtue. We need comparative analysis to frame our understanding, but hot disputes indicate a lack of understanding.

### Silence is Not Harmony

A lack of conflict does not mean there is balance. A different priority could be the reason. There is no flash point to fight over. Similarly, silence is not an affirmation. Powermongers and their toadies attempt to silence criticism. Their success does not make them right, anymore than a complaint is always true. A boss can compel silence by non-verbal cues. If he threatens anyone who questions his choices, like vendors, then the workers internalize his behavior as a threat if they disagree. Fear compels silence. Workers may agree with a complaining employee, and will view him as a hero, or crazy, because of his courage to speak out.

Some people have the courage to speak out. Others do not. The same words that make him a villain for management make him a hero to others. To have empathy for a villain makes one the equivalent of a villain, so most people opt for silence. This is tragic. The only way to teach the next generation right from wrong is to stand up for what is right and speak out against what is wrong. The lack of a vigorous debate gives all errors the most opportunity to flourish. Yet, we need to disagree respectfully, or we are teaching that it is okay to be disrespectful.

Children are often indoctrinated to be afraid. They are taught to obey and not to think. Being wrong is not very different than being silent. Both error and a lack of courage have undesirable consequences for the formation of virtue in young minds. We learn the most when we disagree. While the goal is to agree, the means are to disagree. It is an odd tension. That is why free speech is so important. To have a right and to not exercise it is the same as not having it. The challenge is to be as intellectually honest with ourselves as we are critical of others. We have to be open to learning and being corrected, as much as to teaching and correcting others.

## Enlightenment

We have empathy for others, but we also make harsh judgments. That is the source of heroes and villains. We are usually more forgiving of our group and ourselves than we are of outliers. One person can be a mixture of many different extremes. Two people can be an ally on one issue and antagonists on another. Somewhere there must be cognitive dissonance present, because the truth will lead everyone to the same conclusions. Unfortunately, consensus is not proof of a truth. Many ill-advised choices have been carried forward through unanimous consent.

Enlightenment is a stage of redemptive and proactive forgiveness. We must forgive ourselves for our mistakes before we can forgive others for theirs, but first we need to recognize our mistakes. It is only in conquering our own unique cognitive dissonance can we see the same struggle in others. We heal others in the same manner that we heal ourselves. Hypocrisy and doublethink works the same way. We are apt to punish where the sins of another most closely align with our own. The merciless punish the merciless unmercifully, blurring the distinction between who is the victim and who is the crime. Might is not right, but neither is being a victim. In viewing the events of history, we need to be honest about the antecedents that created conflict. All is cause and effect. Blaming the victim is as absurd as claiming the victim is always innocent. We all have a shared responsibility for what occurs in society. We are victim and crime, a mixture of virtue and prejudices.

There are battles within organizations and within empires for dominance. For example, two factions within a church, political party or a business may develop. Each struggles to control the reins of the organization. This same organization struggles for dominance outside of the organization. For example, a church wants to control public opinion, or a political party wants to control the government. Certain businesses want to control their industry. There are also battles between the empires. The business community may want to control government, and government may want to control the business community. During war, people look to the government to protect them. During civil war, the government is regarded as the enemy or protector, depending upon which side you chose. When business and government unite for a common purpose they can be a formidable opponent. Non-profit organizations (religion) suffer, and they become the wedge force to divide government and business dominance. Control of government is desirable because of its ability to force others to obey your prejudice. Turf battles are fought with ferocious intensity. Dissonance exists whenever there is an inability to forgive. If there are heroes and villains, if there are conflicts, then dissonance is present.

**Directions of Conflict**

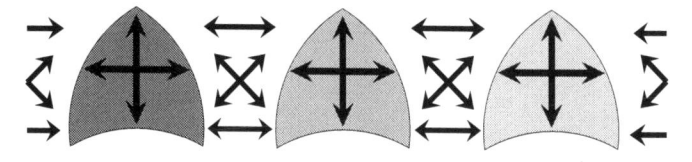

Every arrow represents an idea, organization, money and statistics. Conflict can exist (prejudice), even when there is no contact.

Does the previous graphic look familiar? It is a simplified version of the infamous PowerPoint slide regarding the Afghanistan War. (See next illustration) Upon seeing the original, General McChrystal remarked, *"When we understand that slide, we'll have won the war."* Everyone is the room laughed, but life and death is no laughing matter. Mankind has brought our troubles upon ourselves. We need to understand the nature of conflict if we are to defeat it. Eastern philosophy (Buddhism, Hinduism, etc.), with its many complex mandala representations, is trying communicate the same message regarding the importance of balance.

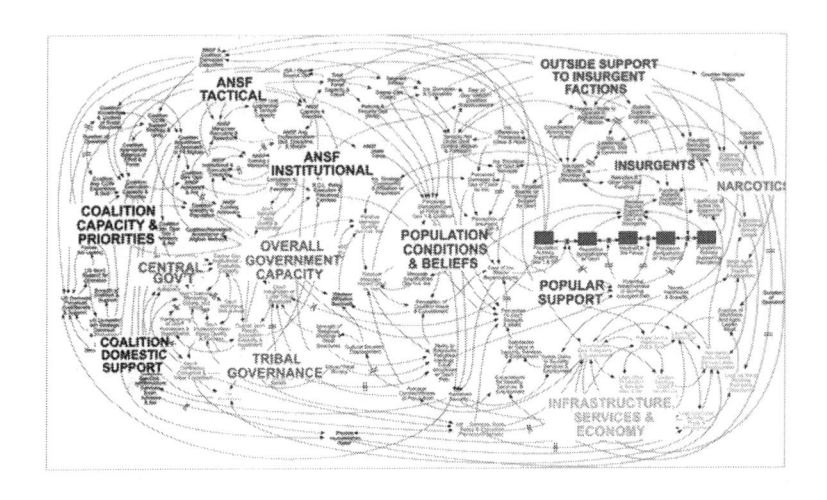

Another indicator of cognitive dissonance is the sense surrounding the relative importance of certain issues. The descriptions that people *'make a mountain out of a molehill'* is true. The lack of comparative analysis is also lack of perspective. A power-monger uses force disproportionately to the situation. For example, firing an employee for disagreeing, or violently silencing criticism by smashing a printing press. Electoral politics constantly seize upon minor issues as a means of attacking an opponent. Businesses take small design differences between themselves and their competition and cast them as huge advantages of their product. Olympic athletes are stellar performers, yet we are to believe a half-second of speed is a mark of significant superiority.

Before power corrupts, the lust for power distorts. Enlightenment is a world undivided into heroes and villains, or winners and losers. Socrates, after being found guilty, was required to propose a just punishment. His accuser recommended death. Socrates felt he should be housed and feted like the athletes. The molehill was worshipped, and the mountain of wisdom was destroyed. There are millions of petty squabbles over insignificant things. Money is a big one, but not the only one. True equality is the world's most radical idea: to see ones enemy as oneself.

### Know Thyself

People are ignorant about their dissonance, which is why Plato advised *"Know Thyself."* (Yes, Plato was ignorant of his own dissonance). We need to explore our own prejudices to find one another and ourselves. Everybody is exactly the same. We all share the capacity to mix up cause and effect, good and bad, true and false. We have all been indoctrinated into a unique set of half-truths that form our prejudices. Our heroes and villains reflect our unique challenges with dissonance. To be truly free, then we need to recognize the equality of mankind, regardless of skill, learning, position, pedigree or possession. Just as the planet is rich in resources and climates, we all have diverse gifts and temperaments, too. The challenge before us is, '*How do we exchange these gifts, that we fashion from the Earth and our community, with other communities?'* That, ultimately, is what the study of economics encompasses. Politics is supposed to make that process easier, not harder.

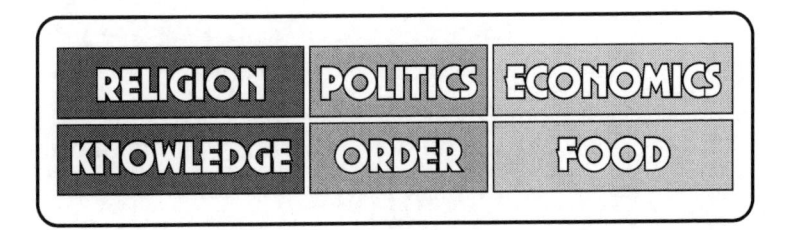

| RELIGION | POLITICS | ECONOMICS |
|---|---|---|
| KNOWLEDGE | ORDER | FOOD |

While a certain degree of simplification is necessary to understand the world, including these models, it is important to remember that everyone was, is, and will be tethered to the same 24-hour day. Our heroes and villains were both using comparative analysis in the best way they knew. They both sought to fix a problem, even if that put them in opposition to one another. They met with varying degrees of success over their lifetime, the same as us. We can do better. We have their experience to draw from.

Evolution is incremental. Just as we change everyday, so too do the ideas and institutions represented in the model. Time can appear to be like a pendulum in a repeating motion, swinging back and forth, but the pendulum is always moving forward as a single line. The line may intersect, but it does not repeat. However, the virtues that we ascribe to are timeless and accessible. A clock measures time, but it has no effect on time. Everyone is fully capable of living a virtuous life, but we need to ask, *'What is virtue?'* Virtue does not change. We need to hold ourselves, our heroes, our villains, and victims to the same standard.

We can start anywhere. Every point on the model is a definition of virtue. From there we can test it in every direction. Every idea is the center of the universe because ideas are a web. No idea is an island.

### The virtue model

The qualitative difference between opinions is how well they have been tested. Virtue is something that is true logically, emotionally and physically. Virtue works because it is in balance.

The Big History model is not in balance. It is a state of extreme imbalance, with the individual in the center of the confusion. A model in balance would have all three circles perfectly stacked one upon the other. There would be no difference between the ideas, the organizations and the individual. Perfect harmony.

**ALL IN BALANCE**

THE COMMONWEALTH
THE INDIVIDUAL
ECONOMICS
POLITICS
RELIGION
EARTH

**REQUIRES BALANCE**

In the current model, all of the organizations within the empires exist while ignoring the virtues of a particular philosophy. For example, politics excludes religious virtues, it is non-religious. Religion says do not kill, but governments decide life and death, and kill any challenge to its authority or threat to its citizens. Businesses are non-political. Even though it overlaps with religion, it makes no judgements.

Businesses sell anything to everyone. Governments try to restrict businesses from trading with its enemies, and religions try to prevent immoral commerce, but both have little success. Churches are non-profit. They do not try to produce or sell anything, but the non-profits enjoy some of the oldest and largest hoards of wealth. Every empire tries to impact the other empires, while enjoying the virtues that the other empires supply.

In practice, no organization is as cleanly separated as the model, but that is the point. The model attempts to expose the priority behind certain choices, the resulting struggle for success, and the dissonance trap that exists within all endeavor. Reality is similar to chaos theory. Humanity, like the Sun, acts like a flame, ever constant, yet never-repeating. Our fire is the interaction of solid matter, abstract ideas and emotions. New lives form the new embers. Time burns perpetually generating light and warmth, but it can just as easily flame out of control and burn, or reduce almost to the point of being extinguished, bringing cold and darkness. Ash and dust are generated during the burn, representing the discard of error, and the end of our lives, but the memory of light and temperature lingers onward. Just as the first chicken is an ancestor of every egg, so too is all light part of the same first fire, regardless of how or when humans became sentient. All is one, and one is all. We should not put man into boxes or stereotypical categories. **The purpose of using this model is to explain and illuminate, not to categorize and condemn.**

None of the empires are pure or logical, by any set of standards. If the goal of politics is to create order, the governments are constantly at war. If the goal of economics is to efficiently create plenty, businesses have created waste and poverty, too. If the goal of religion is to offer moral clarity, hope and salvation and brotherhood, it has created division and self-righteousness, too. Within themselves and between themselves the empires are full of contradictions. That is true generically and specifically for any organization. Everyone is in a constant state of difficulty. The virtues that they espouse (the real ones) are diluted by contradictions and the multitude of other forces that do not recognize their virtues.

As individuals, we all have our own sense of what is correct, which is usually slightly different than the organizations that we join or that employ us. This is not surprising, since none of the empires can address the complete needs of a whole person. The more the ideas are exclusionary in the model, the more it resembles a prison, rather than an organic machine. Separate but equal, like the division of church and state, is an intellectual farce. The empires have evolved to be contradicting what people need most: balance.

### The model in flux

There are ideas and organizations that attempt to move things towards a better balance. This occurs culturally as well as individually. Making comparisons between other nations and other times shows how the model can fluctuate. For example, by moving the religion disk more towards the center, religion has a greater influence on political and economic organizations. This can be good or bad, depending

**CHURCH & STATE DOMINANCE**
DURING AGRARIAN TIMES

CHURCH  BUSINESSES (Very Small)

GOVERNMENT

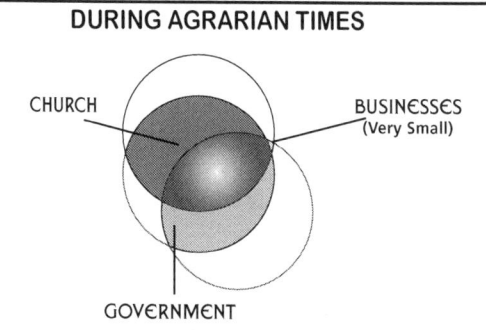

upon the nature of the political philosophy it is paired with. Is it a tolerant loving political philosophy or an intolerant punishing political philosophy?

When imbued with more political power, we could get an inquisition that persecutes heresy, or an enlightenment that encourages freedom of religion. Ideas from the religious realm can and should inform both our politics and our economics, but everything needs to be in balance.

Similarly, political ideas inform our economics and religious viewpoints. The term liberty can mean many things. The liberty discussed in the Bible is not the same liberty that is discussed politically. Political liberty is making ones own laws. Religious liberty is embracing God's laws. What one-person regards as liberty another may regard as slavery. That is a sure sign of dissonance, but if on one or both sides is unclear.

One of the big stories of the Bible is the political liberation of the Hebrews from slavery to the Pharaoh. Their faith in God gave them their political liberty. No sooner were the Hebrews politically free, and given the laws of Moses, did they start to make their own laws. They fashioned a golden calf and worshiped that instead of God. They deserted their religious liberty. Freedom gives one the ability to live up to, as well as to abandon, a standard of virtue.

Ancient slavery in Egypt was as much an economic condition as it was a political or religious condition. The Pharaoh's believed themselves to be gods. People like Karl Marx see religion as enslaving its followers to a blind obedience. The slaves of Egypt would disagree. Their faith in God led to their freedom. What they did with that liberation is a separate story. Because the Hebrews thought themselves superior, they lost their humility. That was the same failing as the Pharaoh. Egypt was not always ruled ruthlessly. It was Joseph who instituted the 1/7 tax to prepare for a drought seven years in the future. When the crop failure came, there was plenty of food on hand for all. Egypt provides an example of both wise and unwise public administration.

### Hierarchy: Slavery versus Liberty

The slave and slave-master relationship is found in religion, politics and economics. This suggests that the problem with liberty is not the realm, but the quality of hierarchical relationships within any empire. An organizational hierarchy of skill or experience is natural, but a hierarchy of inequality is not. A child is not inferior to its parents, or an object to be exploited. Obedience is blind when it is not a conscious or logical choice. Winston Smith, in 1984, was a slave of the status quo, as were his oppressors. It is the tenor of authority that is the problem, not the existence of authority.

There is always a tendency for us to become that which we oppose. That is the nature of dissonance. We are what we hate. Marx opposed religious virtues, but his brotherhood of comrades required the same brotherhood of community that religions hope to achieve. There is no 'right' side in history. This Big History model exposes the failings of every movement. We are all human, and fall victim to inconsistencies or double standards. Ideals are the only thing capable of being pure. Our challenge is first to understand virtue, and then to live up to that standard.

What we say is a measure of our understanding. Our virtue is as obvious as our dissonance, to everyone except ourselves. As followers, we follow those who share a similar dissonance.

Slaves, of course, have limited choice, but on any of a thousand nights they could have risen up and killed their captors. They chose not to kill. Marx, in advocating class warfare, did not recognize that the slaves were declining war, not justice. The slaves similarly rejected Moses when he killed one of the Pharaoh's soldiers. The ends cannot justify the means.

At the heart of all organizations are the concepts of property and justice. Both the haves and have-nots resort to violence to protect and enhance their livelihood, they only start at a different level. Violence can be a consequence of an imbalanced mathematical model. Reducing poverty and extremes in wealth will reduce the likelihood of war, but economics is only one possible cause of violence. There are two other causes: pride (the social realm) and fear (the religious realm). Equality needs to be political, economic, religious and, most importantly, generational. The freedom to live requires the responsibility to prepare for those who come after us.

All three empires are attempting to provide for the needs of the individual as well as the collective. To some degree, each empire exists to blunt the failures of the other empires. Religions exist to provide knowledge. Religions build schools to educate the social spirit, but not roads. Governments exist to provide order. They purchase roads for everyone and encourage productivity. It builds schools, but primarily to indoctrinate the population to trust the government and follow its rules, which is why the religions build their own schools. Businesses exist to solve the physical demands of production and consumption. It is contracted to build the roads and the schools.

Increasingly, business leaders make payments to schools and within politics to educate and indoctrinate their point of view. Businesses have the most money because they are free to create the most inflation. These owners believe themselves to be superior in society. People amass a personal fortune and then get involved in politics. The craving for wealth becomes a craving for power.

During and after times of war citizens turn to military generals as their political leaders. Usually, the rich are trusted to run things because they already have control. During wartime, the political leaders turn to private industry for their armaments. Either way, the businesses come out on top. In a financial crisis, the government turns to the banks to solve the problems, too. The people have no institutional power, even under a democracy. The Supreme Court recently ruled that corporations have the same rights as citizens. The Bill of Rights attempts to blunt the rough treatment of individuals, but with limited success. The empires themselves interpret their own rules of self-restraint, and they invariably fail to restrain themselves.

## Prejudice and Virtue

Individuals govern organizations, and their prejudices become the policy of the organization. The top individuals of one empire attempt to impact the top levels of another empire. For example, a popular entertainer may make comments about public policy. He could be pro or anti-war, support who should be President, or even run for office. Similarly, those in government might attempt to control or censor the entertainment industry. The Red Scare and Hollywood blacklisting of the 1950's was censorship. Religious leaders and organizations have often expressed their moral objections about politics and business. It is impossible to separate individual prejudices from the cultural currents. Generically, every empire, organization and individual (myself included) claims to have some special insight on what people need to be happy. There is some truth in these positions. We need the best ideas in all three empires to be in balance.

Language presents a problem because the same labels are sometimes used interchangeably, though they mean different things. The word liberty is a good example, but there are many others that can be viewed pejoratively. Some define freedom as unbridled capitalism, where others see unbridled capitalism as fascism, and the strong abusing the weak. Freedom is believed to be the ability of the good to limit the hand of the evil. People have different expectations of government, church and business. They all see their hand as the good hand, and all who impede them as the evil hand. When a church leader, political leader or business leader complain about the actions or choices of one another, that is the model in action.

There are multiple hands at work. In religion, there is the hand of God. In economics, there is the *invisible hand* of capitalism, as suggested by Adam Smith. And in politics, there is the *hand of government* and the *voice of the people*. There is too little appreciation for the *hand of man* in all these theories.

Everybody favors the good hand of their organization, as they have defined it. Using comparative analysis, and a set of principles, we can determine what are the best virtues for all empires, organizations and individuals.

In general, everyone has the same goal: peace and prosperity. While there is a divide between the tenor of optimists and pessimists, that should have no impact on virtue. Virtue should illuminate the best possible strategy. What is *The Good* must be good for all equally. The freedom to enslave others is not a freedom. Like math, virtue should balance, and be the same equation frontward and backward. It should be easy to accomplish.

**What are Virtues?**

Every virtue is a hybrid of thoughts, feelings and actions. For the sake of simplicity, and because of my desire to illuminate similarities and differences, it is necessary to discuss this topic using broad generalizations. The Big History model provides a good framework. In this section, intellectual realms and empires are treated as equivalent.

## Virtue in Religion, and its Opposite

The virtue of religion is faith; more specifically, love, forgiveness, trust and preparation for the future (stewardship). The abstract realm confronts the mystery of life, delves into the big questions of right and wrong, and encourages us to think. The non-profit organizations (universities and churches) provide educations to help children enter the workforce, adulthood and the afterlife. Faith is the virtue because we must have an open mind and a trusting spirit in order to be able to learn, and, later, question. Faith and reason are not opposites, rather, they are complimentary. We have faith in others and our conclusions, which we reach through reasoning. Faith is not only about a belief in God, but faith in our fellow man. Atheists go through the same exact reasoning process as believers to reach the opposite faith conclusion. It is as difficult to prove the existence of God as his non-existence. (For the record, I believe in God. God does not fix man's problems; he fixes the man who makes the problems. This book is a part of that process).

The primary element of faith is to trust our reasoning and one another, with or without God. This overlaps with politics and economics because a community is obliged to trust, otherwise it cannot function to govern or trade. The non-profits help us to determine who, what, when, where and why we trust. The vice of religion is fear. Fear spreads mistrust, anger, revenge and condemnation. Fear is the death of faith. When power is used to punish religious infidelity, political differences, or economic challenges, that is fear being expressed. Fear can exist high or low, with or without the power to act. Fear is a mental and emotional prison that clouds our judgment. Fear is pessimistic. We fear our conclusion. When we use a lock, we are both indicating what we value and our fears. The symbol of a lock represents our fears.

**NO FEAR!**

**RELIGION**

| VIRTUE | VICE |
|---|---|
| TRUST | FEAR |

### Virtue in Politics, and its Opposite

Government is the social realm. The virtue of politics is liberty. To say what we want to say and do what we want to do, and have what we need is liberty. The freedoms of self-determination, opportunity, movement, expression, and possession are all part of liberty. The vice in politics is authoritarianism, inequality or fascism. When one person or group controls another, they are unequal. Laws that divide, like the Jim Crow laws, are destructive of liberty. Legality often has a low moral standard. Laws allow stealing, predation, prejudice and many forms of injustice.

There is no universal victim. A black person may be mistreated in a white country or a white person mistreated in a black country. Similarly, Muslims, Christians, Jews, Buddhists and atheists can mistreat one another in their respective spheres. Citizens can mistreat non-citizens. The rich class can mistreat the poor class, and vice-versa. The employer can abuse employees. The unions can abuse consumers. The public servants can abuse the taxpayers. Every form of prejudice can be a government policy or a cultural norm. True liberty encompasses systemic equality and requires personal responsibility, not individualistic opportunism.

Authoritarianism is systemic inequality, which grants a privilege to one group or individual to exercise power at the expense of others. When Thomas Paine described society as a blessing, and government as a necessary evil, the dividing line was how power was used, not who was using it. Slavery and Jim Crow were as unfair as monarchy or feudalism. Plutocrats practicing democracy amongst themselves is not liberty. The peace symbol represents social harmony and equality whereas the fist represents violence and inequality.

**NO FORCE!**

**POLITICS**

| VIRTUE | VICE |
|---|---|
| LIBERTY | AUTHORITARIANISM |

### Virtue in Economics, and its opposite

The virtue of economics is production. Economics deals with the physical. Money, or finance, deals with the numerical values that we assign to the physical. We can live without money, but we cannot survive without work. We must produce so we can consume. The more we produce, the higher our standard of living, and the more people society can support. Goods and services are created through cooperation. No man is an island. As we step through the sequence of our lives, we need one another to fashion the physical world for our mutual benefit.

Distribution is an important element of production. Moving the wealth of land and labor between businesses, between the city and the countryside, and between nations, is at the heart of economics. Everyone lives a hand-to-mouth existence, and shares an immediate need for food, healthcare and shelter.

The vice in economics is destruction (war) or hoarding (selfishness). Both reduce the quality of life. When the goal of work is to make things difficult for others, to mutually destroy what others manufacture, or when we demand more than our share, we destroy economic balance. Selfishness (inequality) is a lethal act, but it works more slowly than a bomb. Greedy behavior mimics the slave-master who robs the productive labor of the slave. It is like an assembly-line worker who disrupts the line by not using the parts they were given. They have extra pieces, which serve no purpose, and everyone else suffers the consequences of inferior products and avoidable repairs. Economics is an assembly line on which we are all a participant. The happy face symbol represents hunger satiated. Through equality everyone's needs are met. In contrast, the percentage symbol with the embedded up and down arrows represent inequality and volatility, which eventually makes everyone miserable.

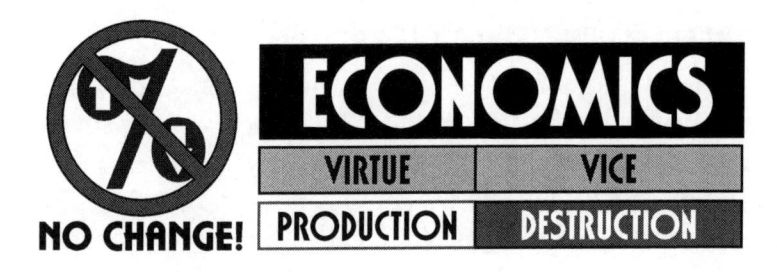

| ECONOMICS | |
|---|---|
| VIRTUE | VICE |
| PRODUCTION | DESTRUCTION |

NO CHANGE!

### Consistency

Commonwealth requires the understanding of a system, the recognition of our role, and standards of proper behavior for everyone. Commonwealth is more than just physical wealth; it is social harmony and intellectual enlightenment, too. Commonwealth combines faith, liberty and production.

In looking at the virtues and vices of religion, politics and economics, we can see that they are almost inseparable issues. Every criteria can be triangulated, which forms the pattern reflected in the Big History model. The virtues form a complete whole: faith, trust, equality, working hard, productivity, cooperation, sharing and optimism, whereas only a single vice is necessary to disrupt harmony.

| Realm / Empire | Wise | Unwise |
|---|---|---|
| RELIGION | MORAL | IMMORAL |
| POLITICS | LIBERTARIAN | AUTHORITARIAN |
| ECONOMICS | PROGRESSIVE | REGRESSIVE |
| Result: | Peace, Love, Wealth | War, Hate, Poverty |

There are very clear differences between vice and virtue, so why is there so much confusion? Comparative analysis can help us to understand the nature of dissonance and the failures of society. The problems are internally paired opposites before they are triangulated. In the religion empire we have immoral moralists or immoral morality. In the political empire we have authoritarian liberty or authoritarian libertarians. In the economic empire we have destructive production or destructive producers. Using these terms, we should be able to evaluate any topic that arises, and test every idea for both internal and connective consistency. The same as math, virtue and vice both balance. Virtue: Morality = Liberty = Production. Vice: Immorality = Authoritarianism = Destruction. In a mathematical equation, there are infinite numbers of incorrect answers. If we want a correct answer, then we need to work for it logically and consistently. Any one of the three virtues can be substituted with a non-virtue.

Ideas, emotions and action need to be in harmony for virtue to come to life. All opinions are not equal. Some are informed and some are misinformed. An opinion that is true is a fact, an opinion that is false is a claim. We need to separate the facts from the claims. Theories of cause and effect need to be tested. For example, *"Inflation is not caused by supply and demand; it is caused by the application of percentages."* I consider this statement regarding inflation to be a fact, but many others likely view it as either a new opinion or a false claim.

## Finding Balance

Any fact can be rejected by anyone. This book calls into question well-known economic 'facts.' New facts are no more absolute than the discarded facts. We are all our own judge of the evidence. Consensus is an invalid criterion for establishing truth. The laws of mathematics are not subject to consensus and neither are the truths about virtue. The challenge is not to get everyone to agree, or to follow; the challenge is to get everyone to understand yet continue to question and analyze. We must leave enough doubt that we can continuously improve our virtue, but not so much that we exit the path. We need to check the math, and not blindly follow procedures to confirm our bias. The procedures, the expectations and the math can all be wrong, but we can easily convince ourselves that we are in *'the best of all possible worlds'* while things are collapsing all around us. We need to be content without being complacent, confident without being condescending, curious without being incongruous.

We are all born ignorant. Getting a child to obey and believe is easy, but society moves forward based on the ability of the adults to improve. Deep thinking does not require a college degree, it only requires effort and doubt. We are all students and teachers of one another. Our collective problems are caused by our collective lack of understanding of virtue. A person who is forced to obey can not teach anything except to obey or rebel. It is impossible for a coward to teach courage, except as a negative example. A person who is forced to starve is forced to learn greed. Many of the richest people today were once among the poorest people. A person who understands virtue can spread virtue. It is virtue that sustains our humanity. With virtue, the ends and the means are in harmony. That is the balance that we all need. Doubt is required for questioning to exist. Indifference and complacency are as destructive to virtue as error. The child must grow into a fully functioning mature adult, not just be a cog in the wheels of an empire. Virtue is something that must be right and widespread for a society to advance.

The person at the center of the model is trying to grow, survive, understand and thrive. They are surrounded by many voices and organizations and culturally accepted bodies of knowledge with contradictory messages. Since we are all individuals, and involved with all three organization types, there are two types of dissonance we experience: personal and organizational.

The organizational hypocrisy has a clear distributive paradox. For a religion to promise salvation, it must also establish the damned. Morality needs immorality to define itself. Similarly, for a government to guarantee liberty it must impose restrictions using force. For a business to provide wealth it must consume resources of land and labor. Organizational dissonance can be an internal opposite, or formed by its indifference to whichever realm it fails to overlap. Similarly, personal hypocrisy occurs when we make a wrong or false judgment about other individuals or groups. All comparative analysis is a double-edged sword, which is why self-doubt must play as large a role as doubting others. A world divided into villains and heroes is like an acid. As it pours out of the container, it burns everything it touches.

## Money and the zero-sum game

Organizational hypocrisy is at the heart of the transactional nature of the monetary system. Everyone's gain can be someone else's expense, whether it is salvation, freedom or prosperity. It is not a zero-sum game in the traditional sense, but one of inner group and outer non-group. The same as numbers, the only limit of either virtue or prejudice is the imagination of the optimist and pessimist. We can build more schools or more prisons, have more hunger or more equality, and create more waste or more wealth.

All organizations use money for their own benefit, even if the organization nominally exists for the benefit of all. No organization can exist without revenue. In this way, revenue has become everyone's top priority, rather than virtue upon which they were founded. That is the deeper meaning of you cannot serve two masters. Money is the object that we think we understand. In fact, money is make-believe, whereas virtues are real. The ends and the means are in conflict.

Being miserly about money is to be like Ebenezer Scrooge. His *Quality of Life* was lost for an inanimate object. He was materially rich, but spiritually bankrupt, having destroyed all his social connections. Many organizations and individuals suffer the same self-inflicted wounds. They follow an endless quest for more revenue, as the richness in life fades away.

The trap that Scrooge fell into was partly a result of the structure of society. The future becomes something to be feared. In the absence of commonwealth, it is every man and organization for himself or itself. Once conditioned to take to survive, there is no conditioning to ever stop taking. Employees, vendors, citizens and customers are all something to be relentlessly squeezed and exploited. Whether it is political power or material wealth, there is no state of contentment. With inflation constantly nipping at our heels, one seeks to be rich as a means of maintaining order. Hoarding wealth and perpetual growth becomes the goal to avoid future financial stress.

Individuals slow down because of age and eventually pass away. Organizations, in contrast, do not age. Nor do they grow wise. Oftentimes, an individual with a conscience within an organization is forced out in favor of the more ruthless. Revenue rules. Organizations have the ability to improve or destroy the quality of life, both for themselves and those around them. The more consistently virtuous we are in all our roles, the happier everyone will be.

**Hypocrisy and Internal Division**

Dissonance can be understood as an intellectual-emotional condition. The root causes of dissonance are reflected in the exclusionary nature of the model and the internal conflicts within each separate realm. The same as the model, dissonance can be abstract, social or physical. In religion, dissonance is fueled by fear. In politics, dissonance is fueled by pride. In economics, dissonance is fueled by greed. Fear, pride and greed are all emotional states! Therefore, we can conclude that dissonance is caused by an emotional state that clouds our reasoning.

This is consistent with many studies that claim our sense of knowing something is a feeling. Dissonance can be understood as a bigotry that 'feels right' emotionally but is rationally incorrect. In other words, it is not just two incompatible ideas (accepting 2+2=4 and 2+2=5), but when ideas and emotions are in conflict, too. Virtue is when the head, heart and hands are equally informed. A virtuous society is when everyone recognizes and shares that balance. Peer pressure can encourage both healthy and unhealthy behaviors. Obviously, it would be best if individuals and organizations promoted consistently healthy virtues.

**Feeding the wolves inside of us**

There is a story of a Native American grandfather talking to his grandson. After purchasing a new knife and walking out of the trading post, some others boys surround the grandson, and trip him backwards. When he opens his hand to break his fall, he drops the knife. They tell him he does not deserve such a good knife; they steal it and run away. The grandson is full of rage and sorrow when he recounts the story to his grandfather.

His grandfather tells them that inside of all men live two wolves, one black and one white. The black wolf is full of hate, jealousy, revenge, greed and anger. The black wolf makes many bad choices. The white wolf is the opposite. It takes a longer view of things. He does not want to bring harm to those who harmed him, because in doing so, he will become small and petty just like them. The child is startled to think that he could become just like his enemy. He cautiously asks his grandfather, *"Which wolf wins?"* To which the grandfather replies, *"The one that you feed."*

Dissonant thoughts are triggered by our emotions and are easily recognizable. The black wolf is our dark emotions. The white wolf is our clear reasoning. We know which wolf we are feeding. Whenever we are angry, hypocrisy, or some element of misunderstanding, is nearby. The question is only whether the trigger is fear, pride or greed. When the knife was stolen, all of those issues were present. He was afraid because they ganged up on him. His pride was wounded because they tricked him, and he was also proud of his possession. His greed wanted the knife back.

He had worked for and saved for the knife, but he did not get his reward. However, the knife was not the issue. He had spent his whole life not owning a knife, and more days in the same state of non-possession have no impact. Rather, his expectations frame the issue. His disappointment, hurt, and desire for revenge were inversely proportional to his desire and expectations. As a baseline, everyone expects the reward of his or her labor and mutual respect. We do not expect hate or anger to be directed at ourselves, unless we have been conditioned by its frequent occurrence. We define our own ambition, which is our expectation. Our potential for disappointment is a reflection of our pride.

The discovery for the child was two-fold. First, not all people are perfect. Second, neither was he. We do not expect the rage that pours out of ourselves. We discover that we are like children, and do not have complete control of our emotions.

In a classroom, we discover a quantity of objective knowledge that is exciting to learn, but it is not a great epiphany. It is the discovery of ourselves that mark our epiphanies. They usually occur after a wrenching emotional moment. The rage spurred by fear, pride and greed is eventually exhausted, and a spiritual and rational calm fills the void. For example, former neo-Nazi skinheads have transformed into Buddhist monks. These transformations occur within everyone. No one starts out as a neo-Nazi or a Buddhist monk. We reach our current state through a process of emotional evolution. At some point we overreach, and then we begin the process of retraction.

The grandson could not change the boys who stole his knife, but he had to decide what he expected from himself. He could have easily planned a counter-attack by getting his own group of friends or adults. The decision centered on which wolf he would feed, and therefore who he would be in the world. We all bring some share of hurt into the world.

Everyone believes that their opinions are well reasoned, that their anger is justified, and their fears are common sense. That is why self-analysis is a critical element of enlightenment.

There are cabals that encourage the opposite. The gang of boys that stole the knife allowed themselves to be swayed by cruelty and greed. This is not the normal state of man. Every nation trains young men to glorify their baser instincts. Soldiers return from war zones with Post Traumatic Stress Disorder because they are unable to cope with the wide discrepancy between their emotions, actions and the intended goal. Love of comrades and hatred of enemies cannot coexist. The struggle to change their values causes the trauma. When the wolves do battle, the mind and emotions are tortured.

A house divided is when the means and the ends are opposites. Epiphanies are difficult. The capitalist and the socialist both have trouble accepting that they could be wrong about the economy, and that their enemy is more like themselves than different. The same is true of those would make moral judgements on others. The stone-thrower is not more righteous than the adulteress. He has simply adopted a different sin.

For everyone, it is our own unique dissonance that is our greatest struggle. When we form or join a group, we need to be careful about the assumptions of the group. The single purpose upon which it is founded may be doing as much harm as good. Recognizing contradictions, and the role of fiscal stress, is the first step in eliminating both.

# 13. The Anatomy of Hierarchy

Organizations share common characteristics with one another and with ourselves. Though nominally formed for different purposes, organizations share our struggle between selfishness and egalitarianism. The immediate needs of every group compete against the long-term good for the whole. How can both the individual and the collective be satisfied simultaneously? This question is the study of life in the form of religion, politics and economics. The challenge is the search for balance between the one and the many. The indoctrination we receive may make finding a solution more difficult, because we are learning false differences.

As soon as we are no longer one, we are a group or organization of some sort. Some groups are more formal than others, but as groups grow, they become more sophisticated in how they govern themselves. It is impossible for any organization to operate without a hierarchy. We divide by age and experience in the most basic of cooperative efforts, the family. The old guard must teach the newcomers. All too often, lies are taught with the truth. The next generation has no way of knowing how to separate the truth from half-truths.

Our personal imperfections infect every group endeavor. Leaders of organizations make choices for their personal benefit, rather than for the good of the whole. Even with the best of intentions, mistakes are easy to make, too. Organizations allow corruption, error and incompetence the opportunity to expand. Unfortunately, there is no alternative. We need to organize ourselves to survive. Any organization formed for a good purpose with good people can be corrupted, therefore organizational structure and things like checks and balances are not a complete solution. Both corruption and naive incompetence permeate government, non-profits and the business sector with a tragic regularity.

Virtue and enlightenment are a hard fought battle. It takes a virtuous and wise group to make virtuous and wise decisions. Unfortunately, the mathematical volatility of money breeds a moral volatility. Since only a virtuous people can infuse organizations with virtue, we must promote and uphold a standard of virtue, if we are to witness it in our greater society. Distinctions of age, skill and interest require a division of labor, but there cannot be a division of virtue. Our personal participation is fundamental. Patience is a virtue, but change relies upon redemptive self-analysis. The changes we are waiting upon in others, and in institutions, are also latent within ourselves. Do not wait for others to change before you do.

Organizations form the bulwark of our shared value system. Man cannot exist outside of organizations. We are co-dependent on the food, energy, and healthcare, educational and financial apparatuses. Our standard of living is considerably more complex than an isolated agriculturalist from a few centuries ago. If we are living at a higher level of sophistication, then logically we should be thinking and acting at a higher level of cooperation, too.

## Indoctrination as Prejudice

Virtue and prejudice coexist in dissonance. Progress requires rejecting the bad habits of the past, but the danger of authoring new bad habits is always present.

Reason and morality are not informing enough choices today. Rather than a logical system of division of labor, many want to trust 'free markets' and a perpetual battling for dominance amongst the participants. Competition is the baseline of our political and economic systems, which means that the one must always take precedence over the many: one winner, many losers.

The competitive approach has made the entire world subservient to the warrior driven by greed, rather than organized by the beauty of the poet, or the logic of an engineer. Of course, the warrior, the poet, and the engineer exist within all men. That is the nature of dissonance. We have to choose which voices we will follow and how we will follow them. We are the intersection of what is good for the self and what is good for all.

The free market competitive approach drives a reckless ambition that constantly destroys other organizations that are not infused with the same reckless greed. It is not the wisest and smartest that thrives, but the most ruthless and selfish. Those who reach the top in a competitive system may come to regret some of their choices, but at that point the damage has already been done, and new imitators are rising. Wisdom usually arrives later than when we need it. The challenge is to have a plurality of the population be wiser at a younger age.

It is difficult for the wise to disarm the reckless without being equally reckless. Democracy is a great idea in theory, but in practice is flawed. Checks and balances institutionalize competition and ambition. Wisdom gets suffocated. A time of crisis is often an opportunity for the wise to speak, but there is no guarantee of what will follow. Some crises bring enlightenment, but it is common for a crisis to bring a compounding of mistakes, too. Crisis repetition is indicative of which trend is prevailing.

## Chasing Revenue is desperate, not democratic

A large measure of what drives ambition is a response to inflation and inequality. Organizations sometimes start because the entrepreneur wants to solve a problem, but more commonly it is to solve the personal problem of unemployment. The economy makes people desperate. Forming an organization is a survival response, and the first priority of every group is its own future.

Inflation works against the long-term interests of humanity, but the short-term revenue gain is a necessity for groups and individuals. Waste and volatility are byproducts of organizations battling other organizations, making the economic situation incrementally more difficult. The cooperative endeavor becomes internal, within the group, and more ruthless. The real enemy is inflation, which conquers everyone.

Free market proponents claim that organizations failing is good an natural. They are abandoning reason and morality to chance and ruthlessness, which makes no sense. We want virtue, and organizations that are informed by virtue, to endure. The marketplace cannot and should not be trusted.

The true test of democracy is for choices to be made for the public good from various personal perspectives. The same virtues should inform all our decisions, regardless of where they are made. We can eliminate the stress between what is good for ourselves and what is good for everyone by analyzing the problems properly. All volatility, whether intellectual, social, or economic, should be regarded as failure. It marks the triumph of folly over wisdom.

Progress is change in a single direction, not the cyclical madness of boom and bust. Progress requires both personal virtue and organizational participation. *'The Good'* must be defined correctly and refined going forward. *'Changing with the times'* can be good or ill. An institution that was liberating yesterday could be enslaving today, and even worse tomorrow. Change is good when we are expanding our recognition of virtue. Only virtue can bring the one and the many into balance.

Every individual is a part of a family, business, religion and government. We are all laborers within a division of labor system. The more we battle, the less we produce. The more we cooperate, the more we succeed.

Certain principles should inform all our choices. We need intellectual, social and physical order to survive. Yet, many organizations exist to blunt the ill effects of other organizations. The righting of wrongs drives as much activity as the creation of wrongs drives inefficiency. Hypocrisy is the result of contradictory principles and false perspectives. For society to advance, it is necessary for individuals and all types of organizations to find the right balance. We are creating problems for one another, rather than cooperating. All organizations, because of the monetized and competitive hierarchal structure that exists, can fall prey to hypocrisy and corruption.

**Common Patterns**

Hierarchy has an anatomy, regardless of its purpose. Virtue and prejudice are the result of indoctrination. To contain dissonance, we need to analyze the tools of conformity. Substance is more important than process.

Leaders share a common expectation of followers, and followers have a common expectation of leaders. Everyone is expected to abide by the groups' definitions (abstract), values (social), and behavior (physical). Each organization has its own Big History model of ethics that it follows, just as we do as individuals. Both virtue and prejudice are taught the same way.

We can do a great job of teaching the wrong things. The same food nourishes the sane and the insane within us. A new government is formed after the overthrow of an old government. A new religion is born that overthrows an old religion. There is an attempt to replace dissonance with something new. The new thing may be, or become, a new dissonance. There is no systemic way to ensure that only the white wolf is fed. Courage, reason and compassion must be in balance. We all must set a better example for one another today and not live on yesterday's accomplishments. Tradition can inform us, but not guide us.

### False Language Distinctions

Organizations are structurally similar. There is a leader, administrators, workers, followers/clients, and outsiders. What is needed and expected are the same, but they get described differently. For example, the revenue streams in the non-profit realm are described as donations. The government's revenues are called taxes. A business' revenues are called sales. A bank's revenues are interest and fees. For an individual, revenues are wages. For an investor, revenues might be described as capital gains; for a gambler, winnings.

The process of collecting revenue is described differently, too. The church collects tithes, whereas a civic organization has dues. A magazine or newspaper charges a subscription. An insurance company has a policy premium. Once collected, the retained wealth after expenses can have a new name, too. In a non-profit, wealth is called an endowment; in a government, it is a stabilization fund; in a business, it is cash reserves; for an individual, it is their retirement savings. All these different names imply something different is occurring, but the behavior for all is the same.

## The Language of Organization

| MONEY | NON-PROFIT | GOVERNMENT | BUSINESS | INDIVIDUAL |
|---|---|---|---|---|
| REVENUE | Donations | Taxes | Sales | Wages |
| BILLING | Dues, Tithes, Tuition | Fees, Permits, Licenses, Tolls | Charges, Subscriptions, Premiums | Salary, Benefits |
| WEALTH | Endowment | Stabilization Fund | Cash Reserves | Nest Egg, Retirement, Savings |

The Cost of Living within a monetized economy requires a revenue stream. No entity is exempt. It is a peculiar thing to use so many words to describe the same thing. The Eskimos have many words to describe the texture of snow, but in this case, it is all just money. Money is money is money, and therein lies the problem. Money is being handled the same way (buy-low sell-high) by everyone. The labels imply a special circumstance, and imply a certain gravitas of the group, but these titles falsely mask the nature of common behaviors. Every organization must have a revenue stream, a collection receipt, cash holdings and expenses. Similar naming patterns occur with other organization-centric terminology regarding ideas, feelings and actions.

The leader's title changes based on the organization. In America, the terms president and chief are common. There is the President of the United States, the President of the Senate (the Vice-President), the Commander-in-Chief, the Chief Justice of the Supreme Court. The same terms occur in lower levels of government. The state supreme court has a Chief Justice. States have Governors who are the Chief Executive of their state. Cities and towns have a police chief and a fire chief. Businesses and non-profits have Presidents and Chief Executive Officers. Within religion, the terms Pope, Rabbi, Spiritual Leader, Mullah and Reverend are used. In all cases,

197

the terms are used to describe the top of some hierarchy, and that person is expected to act in a certain way in regard to the established ethos of the organization. The title reflects the broadness of authority. A district manager, or middle manager, oversees other managers and supervisors, and so on down the line. A big brother is in charge of a little brother.

Much like the chicken or the egg question, it is difficult to separate which came first: the person, the title or the organization? They spontaneously appear together. Once an organization is established, an individual can only rise to the top by accepting the indoctrination of the organization. This helps to explain why each empire and all organizations remain locked in a perpetual struggle. The individual can change roles, but the roles and expectations within the organizations are difficult to change.

Every organization has a desire for maximum revenue, maximum loyalty, maximum participation and maximum identification. Eric Hoffer, in his book *"True Believers: Thoughts On The Nature Of Mass Movements,"* wrote that the purpose of propaganda was not to convince others, but to convince oneself. Language and titles are a form of propaganda. Propaganda is considered to be a modern phenomenon, but it actually follows the ancient format of religious identification. Brand loyalty, nationalism, ethnicity and party identification are all held as dearly as any religious belief. We may change what we worship, but the nature of worship is unchanged.

## The Language of Organization

| IDENTITY | NON-PROFIT | GOVERNMENT | BUSINESS |
|---|---|---|---|
| LEADERS | Clergy, Educated | Elected, Kings | Owners, Investors |
| FOLLOWERS | Flock, Alumni, Supporters, Members | Citizens, Subjects, Activists | Employees, Vendors, Customers, Fans, Followers |
| SYMBOLS | Crucifix, Star, Crescent, | Flags, Shield, Seal | Logo, Trademark |

We are all what we love. We are also that which we oppose, or hate. Nazis were an extreme example of common habits of dissonance (love of Aryans, hatred of Jews). Individuals and organizations display some form of propaganda. No matter what we love or hate, it gets expressed. A grandmother carries photos of her grandchildren to show to strangers on a city bus; a nation builds museums and memorials celebrating itself. Fear, pride and greed cannot be eliminated from the human condition. In many ways, it is only our emotions that make us human and interesting. Unfortunately, the same emotions that can make us better can also make us toxic. This is why balance and virtue (trust, humility, sharing) are so critical. The belief that a conspiracy exists is why conspiracies form.

### The light and dark, young and old

A Nazi swastika is a symbol, just like any other symbol. Within their group dynamics, it models virtue, and they loved the strength and truth that it represented. It was their brand logo, the same as an American flag or the flag of any nation. We all believe in ourselves wholeheartedly, and do not question our pride. Leaders convince others to follow by encouraging their sense of pride and superiority. The group is *'the chosen ones'* to do what has never been done, and what no one else can do. Leaders make a judgment of how to survive, what is important, and how to prepare for the future. Within a group, the same virtues are always called upon:

sacrifice for the good of the group. The struggle between what is good for the self, and what is good for the whole, has two different dimensions, inner group and outer group.

There are two conditions here. First is the personal difficulty of sacrificing for others. Some people are selfish or afraid, and do not want to give up any advantage. They will only give a small amount or nothing. Second is the validity of the goal. People will make self-sacrifices for evil believing it to be an act for the good. The organization may be a religion, a nation or a business. *'My organization, right or wrong'* is always the first step on a slippery slope that separates virtue from virtuous action. Dissonance always has a subtle beginning. People can believe their sacrifice to be virtuous when their actions are not. When the blind follow the blind, it is not with ill intent, but dissonance is being expressed.

The first leaders in everyone's life are their parents. Our parents were exposed to the indoctrination of their time, just as we were exposed to ours. The generational sweep is both personal and organizational. Most core beliefs are a circumstance of birth. They are then adjusted based upon random experiences. Organizations, however, have the fortitude to endure across generations. This is why enlightened individuals are so important to society. Organizations are amoral, and become infused with the virtue or prejudices of those who join and control them. They are more powerful than individuals, are institutionally susceptible to dissonance, and are slower to reform themselves. Organizations are often spreading light with one hand, and darkness with the other.

The role of the head of every organization, whether the original founder or a successor, is to promote the reach of the organization. The hand of that ruler can be either gentle or harsh, depending upon both the amount of control and their personal temperament. Both internal and external forces limit the reach of their hand. Forces are interpreted as bad when they limit growth and good when they enhance growth. For all organizations, numbers are an important factor of success usually in the context of a fiscal budget, but not always. We are a number-mad society. Growth is measured because it is the criteria for success and survival. It affirms the budget myopia, provides the target and opportunity to define a vision, and affirms the organization's need for existence.

Leaders can be shortsighted because of their desire for immediate gratification and personal success, which translates into an organization that is impatient and greedy. Vendors, employees and even clients will be treated accordingly. The desire for competition to act as a force of 'checks and balances' is based on the assumption that organizational self-restraint is impossible.

The constitutional system accommodates, and thus guarantees, the perpetual existence of dissonance. That is why Islamists prefer sharia law. There is no Muslim Pope or hierarchy, but the moral code of a hypocrite (bin Laden) has the same footing as peaceful leaders. Substance and process are always separate tracks.

In the aftermath of the American Revolution, greed was redefined as a virtue. This was a conscious choice, made with hesitation, but was believed to be the best path to growth. Given the state of the continent, it was an unsurprising choice. Growth had long been the goal of every new society in the wilderness. Rigorous oversight was a practical impossibility, and the last thing anyone wanted was a unilateral power like the old monarchy. Checks and balances required little government overhead. Operational limitations were cast as virtuous choices, and selfishness became a patriotic duty.

Tyranny was someone else making a bad decision for you. This new system of trust based on mistrust left people free to compete, and ignored why the old system struggled. Somehow the King lacked personal virtue, but the personal virtue of greedy patriots mistrusting one another would self-regulate into an engineering marvel. It is hard to over-criticize this decision. It is akin to giving many monkeys a typewriter and expecting them to write War and Peace collaboratively. The modern pendulum-like swing between regulation and deregulation indicates that there was a deep flaw in Constitutional thinking. America was built on dissonance.

Self-reliance always requires self-restraint, but the bulk of virtue is in self-awareness and self-sacrifice. Greed does not fit anywhere in this paradigm. The creators of the new government failed to realize that self-restraint means failure under a competitive system. Nice guys who embraced self-sacrifice would always finish last. Rising leaders could win solely by intimidation. While genuflecting to a King may have been crazy, the new scripture was to encourage the crazy in everyone. The system favored the most ruthless, shrewd and greedy. Strong and stupid would blindly destroy the kind and wise. Not surprisingly, the genocide of the Native Americans followed, and America has been perpetually at war. The first promises of democracy, peace and prosperity, have never been realized.

It is the nature of violent rebellion and competition to never have mercy for the slow. The American Founder's failure of political analysis, of blaming the King for things he was not responsible for, migrated to economics. The goal was to create a society where what was good for the individual was good for the whole. Greed distorted commonwealth into a position where, *'What is good for me is good for you.'* Doublethink on steroids. Acts of charity attempt to blunt the effects of greed, but it is always too little too late. Philanthropy fails as a systemic solution. The concentration of wealth is a byproduct of imbalanced trade. Encouraging greed would accelerate the pace of the divide. The trade problem needs to be fixed.

Today, we have a unique problem. The status quo does not work, and there is no King to scapegoat. A high standard of living encourages domestic tranquility and prevents civil war. As a result, the inflationary numbers continue unabated. The Left and the Right attempt to blame the other, but both have had the reins of power and failed repeatedly. Their plans cannot work. We can only fix the economy with an extensive and conscious act of virtue.

## Organized Failure

Growing the economy is not a solution, since it will grow the problems, too. Growth squeezes more from others as well as from the land, and creates more debt to match inflation. The efficiency of production has been paired with the ruthlessness of social advancement. The landfills are bursting, along with obesity, pollution and excess. The American experiment, which started out as a family self-reliant on the land, has reduced everyone to a cog as a producer and consumer of industrial economic output. People have become the fodder of the organizations that they constructed.

Under Hitler, Germans were reduced to a cog in a system of Aryan self-infatuation. Centuries earlier, a serf labored under the Church and nobles. Millennia earlier, men were slaves to the Pharaoh. All unequal societies have a group that benefits from inequality through dominant organizations. Every organization promotes their narrow point of view, which is why there are attempts to prevent new organizations (unions, gangs, alliances) from forming. Nobody wants more competition in a competitive system. Eventually, the systems of inequality must collapse. False beliefs are not sustainable by pen or sword forever. The amount of violence the world has seen because of inner and outer group perceptions is shocking. Because of the lack of commonwealth, every organization needs to generate revenue, which guarantees that dissonance will be present in society. At some point, we will be unable to print money fast enough to cover the inflation being created by greed.

To think that one is superior because of the group they belong to is absurd. All groups are structurally the same and experiencing a similar rhythm of life. We are all a part of all of them, and they are all a part of us. The only thing we can be superior to is our past self. We need to recognize the distinction between better, worse and the same. Organizations make promises and threats to compel our obedience. The charts below show how that is accomplished.

## The Language of Organization

| POSITIVES | NON-PROFIT | GOVERNMENT | BUSINESS |
|---|---|---|---|
| PROMISE | Redemption, Knowledge | Security, Freedom | Comfort, Happiness |
| TRUTH | Moral | Consensus | Fact |
| OUTLOOK | Cooperate | Control | Compete |
| IDEAL | Mercy/Forgive | Justice/Punish | Conquer, Win |
| EPIPHANY | New Thinking | New Laws | New Product, New Marketing |

## The Language of Organization

| NEGATIVES | NON-PROFIT | GOVERNMENT | BUSINESS |
|---|---|---|---|
| FEAR | Punishment, God | Chaos, Men | Bankruptcy, Numbers |
| OUTSIDER | Unholy, Damned, Uneducated | Unpatriotic, Traitors | Competitors, Disloyal |
| CRISIS | Complaints, Low Attendence | Protests, Apathy | Anger, Low Sales |
| WORST BEHAVIOR | Break Commandments | Break Laws | Stop Consuming, Questioning |
| Threat | Guilt, Expulsion | Force, Incarceration | Inferiority, Fired |

We need the group as much as the group needs us, which is why there is the tension between what is good for one versus what is good for all. We cannot exist without each other. Human and civil rights arose because of one group being dismissive of the importance or equality of another group. Equality is a delicate balance, which embraces diversity without superiority or inferiority.

### Organized Success

Everywhere we go, it seems as if a line is forming to make a group, which assembles and then disperses. It is not difficult for the individual to serve the group, or for the group to serve the individual. At lunchtime, people are attracted to a restaurant, form a line, sit and wait, consume and leave. There is a constant need for the different types of nourishment that organizations provide. An organization needs some form of group habit to survive. Every group also needs a group to serve. Hospitals serve the ill. Schools serve the young. There is a symbiotic relationship between everyone and the groups that we need, which we can manage well or terribly.

Organizations need a location to operate and carry out their activities. They observe formalities regarding expected dress, spoken words, and group movement. The Internet has created a new location of global proportions.

Grouping patterns are common, regardless of the type of organization. We are the same as every perpetually migrating and foraging species, but, for us, the entertainment of one person is the work of another. In our head, they are dramatically different activities, but the similarities are present. Some people are paid to pick apples when elsewhere people are paying for the pleasure of picking them. The dress for a rock concert differs from dress for church, but in the same manner, the faithful gather to listen to words that satisfy. The fan and the flock choose their preacher.

The leader believes his propaganda. We need to unify the disparate propagandas into something consistent, peaceful and true. Unlike the natural world, we rely on one another to build and maintain a broad infrastructure. An infrastructure of competition is illogical.

Ambition is self-defined. It is usually a simple duality: Grow or die, win or lose, succeed or fail. Leaders want and need maximum participation and fidelity, which returns to them as an advantageous revenue stream, which can then be used to further the organization's purpose. The mission of every group is more growth.

There is a lust for wealth, power and fame within all of us. Everyone wants to conquer obstacles and feel good about themselves. We can attain self-esteem by being productive and creative within a virtuous group as easily as within competitive groups. Producing goods, satisfying others, and personal consumption all give us pleasure. It is trade that makes life pleasant spiritually and materially. Our labor should be guided by regulations that make success easier for everyone. Engineering and moral clarity require cooperation. Society should not abandon itself to chance and the reckless freedom of competition. It is well within our grasp to discern how our organizational and group behaviors fit into the whole, and act accordingly.

### Groupthink

Clothing and events serve to indoctrinate, promote and mark the mission of the organization. Gatherings take on significance for the participants. There is worship, recognition of the faithful, and the common joy of mutual identity.

Events are formed based on the nature of the organization. A Ku Klux Klan rally uses robes to establish self-identity the same as robes at a college commencement or a religious ceremony. The conferring of titles and awards marks the success of purpose, acceptance and legitimacy. All these activities serve to reinforce the authority of leadership. Leaders are careful to not betray the expectations of the followers. The organization defines what is important, not the participants. Our membership reflects an acceptance of tradition. A Klansman who favored racial integration would immediately be castigated. Any action (thought, word or deed) against the group's defined virtue would meet a similar fate. The propaganda must be supported. Once one rejects the propaganda, by association the group feels rejected, and the group rejects the individual. Brother can be divided against brother in an instant.

Saints are formed within every organization. A scripture is recognized. History is then glorified as a reflection of its own virtue. The flock follows and evangelizes a world-view. Invariably there is a sense of superiority and a greatness that is shared through association. The PC versus Macintosh favoritism was just as fervent as Catholics versus Protestants, Jews versus Christians, believers versus non-believers, nation against nation, or political party against political party. Group identity is a common part of self-esteem. The printed t-shirt, which is a recent phenomenon (1970's), proudly declares our many affiliations.

## The Language of Organization

| PRACTICE | NON-PROFIT | GOVERNMENT | BUSINESS |
|---|---|---|---|
| LOCATIONS | Chuches, Museums, Universities, Shrines | Assemblies, Offices, Courts, Schools, Military Bases | Stores, Factories, Farms, Malls, Skyscrapers. |
| EVENTS | Worship Services, Convocation, Graduation | Elctions, Meetings, Rallys, Parades | Shopping, Trade Shows, Farmers Market, Performances |
| ETHIC | Holy, Intelligent | Patriotic | Industrious |
| PRIDE | Chosen People, Best School | Greatest Nation, Greatest Party | Best Product, Best Company |
| MARKS | Degrees, Sacraments | Titles, Decrees, Proclamations | Awards, Recognition |

It is impossible to escape groupthink. We have to love and accept something. We cannot exist untethered. We will always be defined by what we accept or reject. However, the unwillingness to interact cooperatively with others indicates dissonance. It is as common to see multiple churches built on the same intersection of a city street as it is to see competing gas stations. The freedom to compete, and the freedom to organize, is also the freedom to engage in denial. Denial is tragic in the hands of omnipotent power, but it is the same denial when held by a powerless individual. The oak was once an acorn. Adolf Hitler is proof of how one individual believing a lie can grow powerful and infect an entire society. How we understand our group has consequences.

Groups inevitably form a narrow definition where survival is more important than purpose. Mergers often result when a crisis threatens survival. A bankrupt or struggling business will either merge with a competitor or expand through acquisition. Political coalitions similarly form after a mutual defeat. The enemy of my enemy can be my friend.

A group needs a group to serve, and too often, a group to oppose to form its self-definition. Groups separate themselves by generating propaganda to establish its identity. There is, of course, nothing wrong with having an identity. We are all individuals. The first thing we are given is a name, and our name is the only thing that we can take from this world. Our name is our only true possession.

Every organization has a name and a purpose. They use similar techniques to define and promote their group. Each one has a religious belief, a political culture, and a business-like practicality. The handling of money is just one of many common behaviors. Calling something by a different name does not make it different. The Big History model permeates all perspectives into an inner and outer group prejudice.

## The Language of Organization

| HISTORY | NON-PROFIT | GOVERNMENT | BUSINESS |
|---|---|---|---|
| ORIGIN | Saints, Prophets, Founders | Revolutionary, Fathers | Entrepreneur, Inventor |
| SCRIPTURE | Books, Bibles | Founding Documents | Invention, Recipes, Engineering System, Composition. |
| GESTURES | Blessings | Salutes | Hand Shakes, High 5 |
| CLOTHES | Robes | Uniforms | Suits, T-Shirts |
| OATH & SONG | Prayers/Hymns | Pledges/Anthems | Slogan/Jingles Mission Statement |
| EVENTS | Holy Days | Holidays | Sales Days |

People project their accepted virtues onto others that they like, and against those they dislike. For example, when a politician runs for office, he is trusted or feared because of his religious or business affiliations. Is he a common man or an elitist? The common man wants to be represented by the common man, and the elitist wants to be represented by an elitist.

We are all part of the three groupings of religion, politics and economics. Like the riddle of the Sphinx, we can start our day with a prayer, salute at mid-day, and shake hands in a business deal at night. We move from activity to activity easily. Compartmentalism and the division of labor plays a significant part in modern life. We experience a high level of confusing multi-dimensionalism.

Communication, industrialism and mobility have each created many possible affiliations. The caste system was destroyed by the productive capacity of tools. Only a few hundred years ago, steel kettles, horses and muskets amazed Native Americans. Today, we have cooking stores with thousands of gadgets, modes of transportation that reach deep into the universe, and terrifying new ways of violence.

Was the change primarily due to paper money or technology? It makes no difference. The modern world has collided with the old problem of inflation and debt. The only thing that can save any generation from themselves is themselves. We need to get control of the money, the organizations and the machines that we build. Tradition cannot be our guide when it is also our problem.

The problems in society are old. In our wise tolerance, we have allowed organizations that are fundamentally at opposition to one another to exist, but they cannot coexist as separate but equal. As they grow, solutions stagnate. We have had generations of split elections, income disparity, and institutionalized prejudices. The previous charts show how easy it is to make a virtue out of anything. Organizations, like people, need clear and consistent virtues.

### Build or destroy?

The Primary Dissonance has to do with killing. Ending life is the most extreme betrayal of the one over the many, and the many against the one. Tradition buttresses the revenge cycle. Killing results from ideas against ideas, and groups against groups. Killing should be wrong regardless if the target is an individual, a group or a government. We should be trying to grow together, but organizations are slow at admitting their sins. They are proud of what they should find shameful.

**The Primary Dissonance**

|  | NON-PROFIT | GOVERNMENT | BUSINESS |
|---|---|---|---|
| KILLING | *Bad: Sin* | *Good: Bravery* | *Necessary: Natural* |

Virtues and prejudices combine to attract like-minded believers to serve an organization. For all of them, money is the means to the ends and underlies the conflict. Violence elevates trade to a life or death situation. One lives or dies. Therefore, no agreeable trade is possible. A wall of false differentiation exists. Dissonance meets dissonance. The trade of money and goods is the same as the trade of emotions and ideas. Who lives and who dies? Who gains and who loses? Trade should be equally good for both parties, and all secondary parties. Every transaction needs to balance.

Balance is achieved when both the means and ends match. Individual actions should benefit the group and group actions should benefit the individual, both inside and outside of the organization. We need more virtue. Dissonance battling dissonance is the tragedy of mankind.

Balance was the driving force behind the Bill of Rights, but all rights also require responsibilities. Freedom is a diligent process that requires reason, humility and compassion. Just as roads are a public resource that is used by private citizens, we are all building roads for others with words and deeds. When virtue, cooperation and clever thinking combine, great things can be accomplished. Commonwealth is peace and prosperity for all.

In the modern world, it is easy for a man to produce far more than he can consume. There is no need for there to be a shortage of anything, but there are many difficulties because of a lack of virtue in our organizations. Commonwealth is a system that can endure for centuries once it is correctly designed and understood. Our religious, political and economic virtues must match, just as $2+2=4$ must always be true. We must question authority to improve it, but not destroy it. Substance must take precedence over process, and we need to stop indoctrinating delusions of pride.

# 14. What is Modern Finance?

### The social setting of Modern Finance

Old Europe was a hierarchal caste-like society. As in the Big History model, power was divided between the Church, State, and landowners, with the Church on top. Hereditary tradition and the threat of violence ensconced them all. Peasants paid their taxes with a share of the harvests. The landowners were rich, but the least powerful. They were required to support the status quo through loans and gifts. Gold was held in high regard, and wealth derived from owning land, but privileges were the root of power. The Church and State had more privileges than the landowning nobles.

In agrarian societies, war was conducted on a limited scale. The more a nation fought, the less food was grown. An army needed to plunder to survive. The goal of war was to infuse the treasury, but more often than not, war led to depletion. The reach of government was limited by practical considerations. In the long-term, a generation of young and strong producers could be lost. The nobles, therefore, were fair-weather friends to the state. They only wanted to support winning wars. It is the nature of war, however, that debt and inflation will conquer both sides off the battlefield. Lives and plunder were only one measure. War creates many secondary social pressures.

A study of the exchequer, written in 1180, reveals a limited financial system. It required little effort to manage the accounting needs of an agrarian nation. Like today, a problem could be shifted temporarily and claim to be solved. A reading of the *Magna Carta* (1215) however, reveals many issues concerning debt, taxes and inheritance. Money was a problem of growing legal, fiscal and social complexity.

The landowning families had two paths of advancement: the military (the black) and the church (the red). A lack of war, or distaste for it, meant fewer opportunities for advancement. People adorned the cloth for less than holy reasons. The church, state and military can resemble a conspiracy of the craven.

As agrarianism waned, middle-class artisans in the form of guilds grew. They were the pillars of the fledgling military-industrial complex. The government needed swords and shields, as well as the other accoutrements of pomp and circumstance. Consumption by the government and the ruling class, for war or peace, drove much of the economy.

Technological skills enhanced the importance of the artisans, and their own appetite became an economic force. The Bible was printed in the common language in 1456, and literacy increased. A burgeoning middle class began to question ecclesiastical and political authority.

The monopoly status of a guild, or a royal warrant to supply the crown, arouses resentment. A discussion of rights, fairness and economics, which was practically moot under feudalism, began to be explored. Modern finance caps all these discussions. A society based on class of birth was eventually obliterated. It was not replaced with commonwealth; it was replaced with the friendly competition of a gaming table.

## The Rise of Commerce

Mercantilism encouraged trade, self-reliance, invention and personal ambition. The luxury of nobility was having food and servants. Entrepreneurs began to own factories, gardens and hire their own servants. After many centuries of battle, man felt that he had the upper hand over nature. He could engineer perfection through the power of reason and labor. The caste system fell away and ambition was freed from tradition.

Modern finance was an outgrowth of the first joint-stock corporations, the tea-trading companies. A joint-stock company embraced the idea of common ownership and pooled resources, like commonwealth (or communism), but it is non-cooperative amongst the owners. The stockholders are only interested in their share, not one another. The gamblers bond of betting on the same horse holds them together. Gamblers want predictable rules and 'controlled risk.' Commercial settlements, or colonies, were granted by favor of the State. They expanded the claim of the nation, and required military protection. The state expected a share of the gains, and the investors expected protection. Investing in colonies was expected to supply a high return without the cost of war, resources or lives. The Lords of Trade would manage a system.

Like an army, a corporation has a predatory outlook and needs to plunder to survive. Trade becomes more aggressive and efficient, and less cooperative with outsiders. The farther it reaches, the larger its size and overhead, which increases financial pressures. Governments have always had fiscal problems, but it was corporations that gave birth to the modern budget mentality. Managers can only measure quantitative results. The Quality of Life for laborers was not a factor. Unlike government, a corporation has no duty to the many. A hierarchal society generally has a low regard for those on the bottom. Corporations reduce all members of society to a source of revenue, including its own people.

For a growing economy to function, more money needs to be in supply. Finance is the money-side of the chit-for-product exchange. A lot more money was needed to support mercantilism, which is why the initial expeditions were primarily interested in gold and silver. Only later did the resources of the new continents become apparent and desired.

The exchequer system was inadequate. A new modern approach was needed, in part, *'to keep the poor and idle employed.'* With the discovery of the Americas, more capital, financial, physical and human, was needed to explore and exploit the new lands. A radically new vision of ambition was formed. There was literally a new world to conquer. The serfs were freed from their crops. A changed vision of the future took root in all classes. The future would not be the same as the past.

The intent of modern finance was to create more money. It was believed that an increase in cash would be enough to solve the fiscal problems once and for all. Money would be manufactured. The same as with other items, plenty was better than scarcity. Paper money would finance expeditions, promote the expansion of material wealth, allow society to develop, and provide income for both the government and investors. It was the perfect winning formula. Because of boom and bust, it did accomplish these goals temporarily, and then it made all the original fiscal problems worse.

Modern finance expanded the taste for individualistic economic freedom, provided the means for growth, and attempted to set uniform rules and expectations for all members of society. Unfortunately, it also made everyone subject to a mathematical absurdity. Like an addiction, no matter how much you have, it is never enough. After the pleasure of self-determination, the second most common experience has been panic and addiction withdrawal. Inflation ensures that people will get less, when they want more.

Modern finance broke the social bonds between the individual and the group. It was every man for himself, whether he owned shares of stock or not. The pace of inflation, which was always present, increased significantly. Fear and illogical choices define the history of modern finance. Society migrated from a caste system to one of greater social mobility combined with fiscal instability, forming a twisted meritocracy based on the thrill of gambling with your life. Win or lose, the process demands more gambling. The addiction won.

### The Origin of Modern Finance

The architect of modern finance was John Law (1671-1729) of Scotland. He was born to a family of goldsmiths and bankers. He was an avid and successful gambler because of an ability to count cards and quickly calculate the odds. Law drew on his artisan and financial background and argued in favor of a new financial system: a national bank and a paper money supply. His outlook was infused with the habits of a gambler.

Coining money with the face of government had been common since Caesar. Credit and debt had been around as long, too. The new system would replace colored dirt (gold), which was in limited supply, with printed paper, of which there was a more flexible supply. The government would issue banknotes backed by precious metals. Using paper would allegedly solve many problems. Britain rejected his proposals. His having killed a rival, allegedly in self-defense, did not help his cause.

He moved to France, and the government there was receptive to his ideas. He was appointed Controller General of Finances in 1716. This was a time of crisis in France. Louis XIV had recently died, as well as many others in the line of succession. King Louis XV was only four-years old. The country was governed by what might be considered to be the platonic ideal: a board of regents. The regents essentially abdicated control of the economy to John Law. He came to be in charge of the bank, the currency, the stock market and the largest corporation simultaneously! There may have never been a more powerful individual. He was an extraordinary exchequer.

JOHN LAW

This period presents a fascinating historical timeline. Louis XIV had built The Paris Opera (1675), and recently expanded Versailles (1688-1697). Peter the Great was building St. Petersburg (1703). In 1729, a 23 year old Benjamin Franklin would write an essay advocating the need for a paper currency in Philadelphia, which was adopted. The history of each nation is both common and dramatically different. On three continents the seeds of revolution were planted. They all revolve around money. We will explore the beginning of modern finance in France, and the twists and turns of American history.

## France

Before his death, Louis XIV was deeply involved in a lifestyle of art. One's social standing was based on how well one could perform the ballet. The nobles were busy dancing, gossiping, and gambling. King Louis XIV was an accomplished dancer, and the sets for performances became increasingly complex. He was a King of self-indulgent luxury, not the Chief Executive Officer of a country.

The Mississippi Company was a French joint-stock company. This settlement would come to be known as The Louisiana Purchase (1803) by Thomas Jefferson. France eventually abandoned the property it could no longer support, the same as a business closing. The Mississippi Company got its start before John Law came on the scene, but he transformed that outpost into the world's first stock bubble and bust. It is a pattern that continues to this day. He was the world's first millionaire, and the world's first bankrupt millionaire. Many others rose and fell with him.

On paper, the Mississippi Company made many people rich. Being new, the system was significantly less regulated than today. A noble would give his coachman shares to sell at 20 Livre, on what was essentially a street corner that served as their Wall Street. When he arrived, the coachman might actually sell the shares at 24 Livre, and he would pocket the difference and buy shares for himself. There was a tremendous amount of upward mobility generated by unearned income. Former coachmen were hiring their own coachman. Profits were used to buy more stocks to generate more profits. Like a ponzi scheme, it works easily at the beginning. The stock keeps rising and new money keeps pouring in. People were willing to pay more and more for the same sheet of paper. New investors were drawn in by the success of others, and the avarice of the original players kept them involved.

An editorial drawing from the time shows people pouring gold, silver and jewels into the open mouth of a crouching John Law, while from his exposed rear-end he excretes paper notes. The future losers were warned, but they choose to believe the impossible, rather than common-sense. If someone had a piece a silver, or a dollar bill, and was told it weighed more than what it was stamped, or was worth ten times its face amount as printed, then nobody would believe it. With stocks, having no value printed on its face, people accept that it can have any value. Money is an intellectual agreement, but stocks seem to be based solely on the gullibility of a child.

There were a lot of problems. The first, obviously, was that the bubble was not real. The Mississippi Company was consuming resources, not producing them. People and supplies went west; nothing valuable came back. The number of ships involved in French export went from sixteen to three hundred. Secondarily, nobody wants to let go of the boom that they artificially created. The game, once begun, is difficult to end. Initial success removes the last traces of self-restraint. People want to believe that the good times will last forever, and that was what John Law promised. Unearned wealth is the world's oldest seduction, whether through gambling or war. With wealth comes a sense of superiority and invincibility. They were enjoying a self-fulfilling prophesy. The same as on a battlefield, an early victory does not mean that the war is won. The costs will rise as time passes.

The French financial experiment collapsed in 1720, just a few years after it began. The economy experienced a tremendous boom before the tremendous bust. The entire world took notice of the boom.

### The Problem with Gold

The system wobbled the moment it started, and steps were taken to prevent a collapse. To sustain growth, more money was needed. Just as today, the solution was to create more debt to cover the old debt, aka *'prime the pump.'* The stocks were frequently recalled and reissued. The investor's faith in the value of a piece of paper was constantly assured. Every change was characterized as an adjustment yielding a new profit opportunity. The few people asking probing questions were ignored. John Law was regarded as a genius and a hero. He made France, society, and individuals significantly richer. There was no way to argue against the buzz of activity and the productive wealth being created. Waste, pollution, illness and inequality were not a pressing problem.

The paper money that purchased the stocks was supposed to be backed by hard currency (gold, silver, jewels). Buyers were guaranteed that at anytime they could be redeem their notes for gold. As the price of the stocks went up, that was materially impossible, unless the value of the gold went up just as fast. The first solution was to change the rules. Notes could only be cashed for gold in a limited amount, but eventually that was not enough. The increase in the stocks value created a problem with the amount of money in circulation. The shortage of money issue had returned.

By definition, borrowed money is immediately spent; otherwise there is no need to borrow. It is impossible to repay the lender, without re-borrowing or extracting money from someone else. Time is required for the inflationary spiral of buy-low sell-high to shift the burden onto someone else. Therefore, it was impossible to guarantee to return what was borrowed within a narrow time frame. The 'backing' of a bank or business was the ability to borrow more money at will, which led to the need for a central bank. A problem occurs whenever people expect their money returned or sell their stocks. The 'run on the bank' can be from a lack of trust or another economic condition, but the results are equally volatile, and cascade. The hedge fund collapse of 2008 was a re-enactment of the simple math of 1720. Once one person cannot borrow to pay a bill, the entire system collapses. The only reason a nation can stay afloat is because of its capacity to increase its debt. Doing so does not increase the amount of gold it has, however. The value of the gold must rise.

The gold the Mississippi Company received was spent purchasing supplies for the expeditions. That was the real boom. Gold formally held in vaults was spent and recirculated. If one ignores inflation, and the future bust, the prime the pump model of Keynesian economics does work temporarily. Money greases the wheels of progress. However, there can never be as much money in the system as the values imply. Debt must correspond to the size of the boom. The gold in the vaults of the rich was lent, not spent, within a casino-like structure. The consequences of this subtlety between spending and lending eventually appear. The structure of modern finance and a ponzi scheme are exactly the same. The system can only continue with a perpetual supply of new money masking the mathematical truth. Any interruption of revenue, for any reason (like a natural disaster, illness, mistakes), and the whole thing collapses. Inflation makes sustaining overhead difficult, and losses can quickly become fatal.

To deal with the gold-to-paper exchange problem, France made the ownership of gold illegal. The original gold backing paper agreement had collapsed under the weight of its own contradiction. It was claimed that centralizing ownership of gold would solve the problem and prevent the old money from competing with the new money. Everything would be paid in paper, which the government could regulate and create at will.

The prohibition of gold ownership obliterated any sense of decency in what was already a heady society. A ransom was to be paid to anyone who reported illegal hoarding. The expanding society of the rich people turned from joy to fear. Their pride combined with anger and paranoia. Corruption by the police took every form: accepting a bribe, demanding a bribe or planting evidence. A friend would turn in a friend, a spouse would turn in a spouse, and competitors or enemies could use the prohibition to seek an advantage or revenge. It turned their society into a fascist hell, resembling the totalitarian societies of the twentieth century. Paris became a police state. Everybody was afraid. Just like the prohibition on alcohol in America, the cure was worse than the disease.

The government's zeal was salt in an open wound. Old money was lost, new money was lost, and those cautious souls who sat out the boom were now targeted for having precious metals. Why would anyone want to turn gold into paper, based on what they just witnessed? Fascism is the climax of many small steps of folly. The birth of modern finance destroyed the social fabric. It is easy to understand the brutality of the French Revolution sixty-nine years later in the context of these events. The caste system was increasingly anachronistic, and the problems with money were only going to get worse.

Just as with the *Monopoly* game, the boom was imprinted on everybody's psyche. The French treasury got rich, allowing the settling of war debts and expansion of government. Other nations witnessed their early success and copied this public financing solution.

The new export industry of colonization increased the material wealth for everyone. It seemed like the perfect solution. Goods went out, and profits were generated. The collapse was not blamed on contradictions within the system; it was blamed on the decisions of specific people. John Law received a lot of the blame. He zigged when he should have zagged. Collapse was viewed as a management problem, not a systemic failure.

Two dramatic intellectual shifts had occurred. First, paper money was real. Second, profit was the new panacea for the financing of society. The government would be sustained by taxes, and the private sector would be sustained by profits. The chit had eclipsed the product. Increasingly, taxes would be paid with money, not harvests.

Nobody was questioning whether the experiment with paper money and stocks had failed. Despite the results, the experiment was regarded as a success. *"Everything that fails brings you closer to what works."* Like the game *Monopoly*, one person winning, and three people losing, was regarded as acceptable. Under monarchy, only the royals won. It was a marked improvement to be able to compete as equals, regardless of the terrible odds.

France's financial disaster became the blueprint for the modern world. The failure reinforced the idea that those with merit and skill should hold power, not people by tradition of birth. The collapse was not just John Law's fault, but also the failure of the unelected Regents. The young king's son, Louis XVI, would eventually pay with his head for his father's handlers mistakes. Today, in both business and government, people are routinely replaced because of economic pressures. Heads still roll when profit expectations are not met.

### Cognitive Dissonance in America

Ben Franklin, like John Law, was interested in solving problems, and correctly saw money as an obstacle for society. His essay, *A Modest Enquiry into the Nature and Necessity of a Paper Currency* (1729) frames his views.

The beginning of the essay argues that credit and risk-taking are necessary for a society to advance materially. We still hear the same arguments in defense of Wall Street. Like John Law, he was arguing Keynesian economics 200 years before Keynes: a shortage of money stifles trade.

Franklin was astutely critical about the role of interest. He argued that a guaranteed return from lending creates a disincentive for taking a risk in commerce. Loaning money for a mortgage had a guaranteed profit, but did not materially advance society. In his view, artisans and tradesmen were more useful to society than bankers. They needed the credit which was difficult to acquire. Local banks could alleviate the money shortage by providing its own paper currency to merchants.

He draws the conclusion that if there were more money in circulation, then there would be more mercantile-type trade, which would be advantageous for everyone. Paper would be an ideal substitute for metal. He blames the Crown, which was true, of restricting the amount of hard currency available in the colonies. He does not recognize that they are also struggling with a short supply.

Franklin's gets attacked on the idea of a paper currency because he will be the one to supply the printing, but there were no better ideas being offered. In retrospect, Franklin was very wrong. A money shortage was not the problem. If merchants issue credit to one another, which undoubtedly was already the case, the amount of currency in circulation was moot. His goal, like every merchant, was to get paid. Having money on the books was not as useful as real cash flow. It was certainly a win-win for him. Not only would he get the job printing the money, but there would also be enough money circulating so he could collect debts and pay his creditors. However, this self-interest is not dissonance.

His dissonance was that at the beginning of the essay he complained about how money was handled. At the end of the essay he suggests only changing what money was made from. He fails to recognize that more money in circulation would not change the behavior, but make the same behavior more prevalent. He sensed the problem, but did not manage to solve it.

### Robert Morris: America's version of John Law and Solon

Besides Franklin, the other key figure in American history was Robert Morris Jr. He was one of two people that signed all three founding documents. He was a true merchant, a gatekeeper of goods moving in and out of the country. He was the richest man in America. Logically, he should have been a loyalist, but he was repulsed by the violence of the government against the citizens, and instead sided with the rebels.

At the start of the American Revolution, the first act of the Continental Congress was to issue a new currency. Morris was the financier of the revolution. He used his personal fortune and credit to fund the fledgling government. He contracted the building of the US Navy while living in British-occupied Philadelphia. At one point he issued his own currency, Morris Notes, which were more readily accepted than the Continentals. His home served as the first White House. He launched the first trade ship to China. On one of the ships, the commodity was ginseng. Ginseng at one point grew abundantly wild in the colonies. Its price became so astronomically high that it was harvested to the brink of extinction.

The export of the natural resources to elsewhere was the promise of settling the colonies. Free-market pressures, even in colonial times, prevented the proper management of natural resources. The *Magna Carta,* written 300 years earlier, struggles with the same issues of natural resources depletion. In the same way that more currency did not change how money was handled, more land (colonies) did not change how the land was treated. All the same problems with money and the stewardship of society existed prior to and after modern finance.

## Power and personal opportunity

Shifting political power did not change how people treated one another, or what they considered important. The habits of Kings, nobles and the Founding Fathers were similar. They ran the country as if it were their personal property. Just as Tsar Peter would poach ideas for his gardens from King Louis XIV, George Washington poached ideas for an ice cellar from Robert Morris. An underground patronage system of cronyism continues in modern government. Partisan politics may fuel the prejudices of class, race, income and nationality, but alliances formed based on the nature of hierarchy (as discussed in the previous chapter) are stronger.

One day, Robert Morris learned of an impending flour shortage. He immediately set about purchasing as much flour as he could. When the shortage arrived, he increased the prices, and made a handsome profit. There was an outcry that he manipulated the market and was gouging the citizenry. As today, personal choices impact the public mood and eventually policy. An investigation was ordered. Thomas Paine was appointed to audit Morris' books, and he concluded that no manipulation or gouging had occurred.

Paine was a relentlessly honest critic of society, but he probably would have been merciful to a man that did so much for the new nation. It is doubtful that Paine had a merchant's eye, and knew where to look. The American Revolution never questioned the appropriateness of buy-low sell-high. Like the militarization of society that occurred because of how the white settlers treated the natives, profit margins were a ubiquitous and invisible part of trade. Who is to say what is a reasonable mark-up percentage, when we cannot determine a fair exchange of chickens for eggs? Whatever Morris paid for the flour, the following mark-up percentages could be considered reasonable and not gouging. Profit is the way of the market, and conventional wisdom cannot be sued.

Morris was unanimously appointed the first Superintendent of Finance under the Articles of Confederation. Alexander Hamilton, who later became Secretary of Treasury under George Washington, was following the roadmap that Morris created. Morris' business partner eventually became the head of the First National Bank, what we today call The Federal Reserve.

Like the French bank that financed the Mississippi Company sixty years earlier, the managers would engage in smoke and mirrors to create the illusion of stability. If you visited the new bank in Philadelphia, then you would see piles of gold coins in continuous motion passing by a barred window. It gave the impression that there was plenty of gold backing the new currency, when in fact it was a small amount rotating on a turntable. The facade of a con man, advertising, and the gambler's bluff all intersect with banking. Modern financial advertising continues to sell an illusion on the Sunday morning talk shows and during sporting events. The illusion of financial stability has endured for centuries. The Treasury cannot logically be called a treasury, with a debt of trillions of dollars. .

**Developing a Currency**

Part of the history of modern finance is the history of currency. Philadelphia's experiment with paper money set a precedent. Banks throughout the colonies issued their own banknotes, and a huge counterfeiting problem quickly developed. The counterfeiters became more sophisticated as time passed. They would intentionally insert a mistake on a note so there was an easy 'tell' that it was a fake. Then they would print more notes with the 'tell' removed, ensuring its acceptance.

The counterfeiters thrived. Fraud is the easiest way to secure unearned income. Their final assault was to create notes for fictitious banks. They looked real, and there were no warnings regarding that note, and it was only when someone tried to redeem the note was it found to be for a non-existent bank. A similar fraud now occurs with stocks issued by a business, which is the fiscal equivalent of a bank issuing its own currency.

The Constitution eliminated the different currencies. The problem that Franklin envisioned originally had shifted. Instead of there not being enough currency, there were now too many forms of currency. The underlying problem of how the money was handled was ignored again in framing a new government. Franklin's first solution made fraud easier. The Constitution only attempted to solve the problem that he had created earlier.

### The Temptation of Speculation

After the Constitution was ratified, plans were made for the development of Washington D.C. There was a heady confidence about the new city. America would have its version of St. Petersburg. Robert Morris, after a lifetime of trade and political activism, resorted to the same 'safe' speculation that Ben Franklin had originally recognized as the problem. Morris tried to use his alleged knowledge of future developments to his advantage. Instead of trading in flour and ginseng, he would trade in land. He borrowed heavily, purchasing land in the District of Columbia. Unfortunately for Morris, the new nation had a slow start. He lost his fortune, and unable to pay his creditors, landed in debtors' prison (1798-1801). His fall, like John

Law almost one hundred years earlier, is perhaps the best example of the failure of democratic political institutions, and of the American Founders, to solve what was essentially a mathematical problem in economics.

Debtor prisons goes back thousands of years, and debt was a common story that neither the revolution, nor modern finance, solved. The father of Confederate General Robert E. Lee also landed in debtors prison (1808-1809). Harry Lee was a revolutionary war hero and later a federalist. Like Morris, he speculated on land values, but this time in the South and West.

The problems of public debt and business difficulties were the impetus for attempting modern finance. It failed, but the newly created marketplace led to democratic reform. The problems of society can no longer be blamed on tradition or the top of the hierarchy. We all share responsibility. The freedom of opinions, and the power to decide, do not matter as much as the truth of mathematical facts.

As Franklin observed, interest has a guaranteed return, as long as the borrower does not default. Most borrowing originates from the need to purchase land. Flipping real estate is a high-risk path to great wealth, and is one of the defining characteristics of modern finance. When the King and nobles owned all the land, prior to modern finance, land transfers were few and not speculative. Robert Morris and Harry Lee engaged in the same behavior that caused the Savings and Loan collapse in the 1980's: borrowing money to flip real estate. It is not much different than borrowing money to buy stocks. It is a bet that the market will rise, not fall. Unfortunately, the rise will force the fall.

All borrowing is based on a predicted future gain. All lending is based on the expectation that the borrower will pay the lender back. Corporate takeovers are a financial version of war. Private equity firms, venture capitalists and angel investors are flipping businesses instead of land, or stocks, or merchandise. The scale of what is being bought and sold changes, not the behavior.

Public credit allows the government to wage endless war on whatever citizens or nations it fears. Private credit allows endless war between businesses. These events are not the marketplace adjusting itself by an invisible hand, but the hand of credit dividing winners and losers. The entity with the most credit wins because they can borrow more after every failure. Only when the flow of credit stops does collapse follow. The recent automobile manufacturers' bailout revealed that they were in debt to bankers for billions of dollars. They had burned through all the free money available through stocks and needed to borrow more to stay afloat. They got their bailout, as did the bankers. Homeowners were no so lucky. Not being an organization, they have no representation in the Big History system.

### The Civil War and Banking

Wall Street got its start in the early 1800's. With the establishment of a single currency in 1798, trading could be more earnest. The nation expanded toward the westward shore. Businesses needed a way to trade with one another. Unfortunately, while there was less counterfeiting, there was still fraud. People could buy on credit with no intention of paying for the goods. The issue of trust has shifted from 'Is this currency real?' to 'Will this person pay for their goods?' Wall Street began as a credit-reporting agency. An unpaid invoice was no better than a counterfeit bill.

Financial intelligence resembles a gossip mill. Person X pays his bills, Person Y does not. Business managers have always decided whom to pay fast or slow. Some suppliers are coddled while others are bullied. Negative information (paying slow, late or not at all), true or not, changes relationships with vendors and makes business more difficult.

There was a growing need to keep information confidential and private.

Everyone acts as both a buyer and a seller. They want the truth when they issue credit, and a positive rating for themselves when they are purchasing. Businesses needed a source or reliable information. Wall Street began with a few businesses acting as credit reporting agencies.

As businesses expand, the issue of credit and cash-flow become greater. Even with a guarantee that your customer will pay you, you may need additional capital to ramp up capacity to service new orders. Growing businesses lack enough credit with vendors to offer credit to their clients, too. The era when someone like Robert Morris could use his expansive network of credit to build a fleet and a nation had come to a close. The 18th century was the merchant's world. Men like Rockefeller and Carnegie found themselves in credit pinches as they grew, as did all the merchants of the growing empire. Everyone wanted to sell, and everyone needed to get paid. Profit, not liberty, was the predominate discussion of the day. The Big History model had shifted from politics to economics.

Manufacturing has a ceaseless urgency, which differs from the seasonal fluctuations of an agrarian economy. Industrialism introduces new cultural divides, like blue-collar and white-collar workers. War follows trading routes, and the Civil War follows the same pattern. Trust was waning between the modern factory-driven North and the traditional agrarian South. Abolitionists never dropped the issue of liberty for all. They found an ally in the industrialists, who, like the sophists of two millennia earlier, opposed unpaid labor. They saw slavery as unfair competition. The 19th century economy ran through a number of seizures, and people were then looking for something or someone to blame. The number of self-employed dropped about 50% between

1776 and 1865. The myth of the rugged, self-sufficient individual was dead. There was a growing co-dependency on the federal financial system. In the North, slavery opposition combined both moral and economic issues, but the call for Southern secession added a new political issue to the mix. All the major organizations of Northern society could see a public good in war.

Wall Street transformed from a credit-reporting agency to a credit-providing agency. The ability to make money on money was well known. Rather than tying money up in mortgages, a new form of property was being created: intellectual property. As Franklin wished, money would be lent to merchants and industrialists, which seemed to offer the same surety. His views resonate today, where lending is regarded as a public service. Too few are asking 'Why is there so much debt?' Lending is characterized as helping businesses and individuals through difficult times, but the original goal was to finance the future. This later reason being the one most commonly promoted, from John Law to the current Chamber of Commerce and Small Business Administration. Investing is always promoted as win-win, even though it is obviously a gambling table where someone must lose. A new business (winner) will displace an older business (loser). The seduction of unearned income gets wrapped in a dissonance where preying on one group is seen as helpful and healthy.

The selling of joint stocks was the equivalent of a business taking a loan from a group of different individuals, rather than directly from a bank. Just as a bank would use credit information to assess if a loan was a good risk, the ability to be listed in the stock exchange was a mark of creditworthiness. Using the framework of a joint-stock company, risk was theoretically mitigated and depersonalized for the lender and the banks. In theory, like democracy, the many hands involved make the process safer for everyone. Risk was diluted, and 'owners' can enter and exit their position without disruption to the business. In practice, neither the promise of democracy or of stocks has been realized. While centralization can yield tyranny, decentralization can yield multiple risks.

For a business, there are major differences between a bank loan and selling stocks. A bank loan is for a fixed amount, interest must be paid, and a payment schedule to reimburse the bank is initiated with the loan. None of these things occur with stocks. Selling stocks is an influx of free money for the business to spend. Going public is a cash windfall, and a huge temptation. There is no day of reckoning when the note becomes due, but everyday becomes a day of reckoning to keep the share price high, which is in the best interest of everyone who owns shares. Any criticism of the business must be tempered to protect the stock value, and nobody else really cares.

For the business founders, stocks are better than the difficult business of buying-low and selling-high. Issuing stocks are far more profitable than selling a product. If the stock rises, the stocks they withheld are worth more, and easily redeemable for more cash. If the share value falls, they incur no loss. The business can perpetually capitalize on the manipulation of stock value. The cash infusion gets used to bully vendors and competitors, which appears to make the business more profitable. Not surprisingly, those who sell stocks and are inside the company during the early stage can get very rich. If the business is profitable, it is a double win-win. The corporation can also adjust what it pays in dividends, if it pays dividends at all, for its own convenience. It is easy to see why there is a push to take a business public.

The investment banks benefit from a huge influx of money as deposits. Whether the stock value rises or falls has only a secondary effect for them. Bankers are going to hold all the free cash as it moves between buyers and sellers of stocks. Either way, they win. The greater the activity, the more fees they collect. Banking was lucrative before stocks. Now it was more so. The newly created value is used to make new loans.

The buyers of the stock assume that there will be other buyers of the stock, which will inflate their share value. As we saw in the Mississippi Company, it makes no difference if the actual business is profitable or not, the stock itself is a separate commodity issued by, but not directly controlled by, the business. Its value is based on the psychology of the stockholders, who use real money to engage in a make-believe trading world of stock certificates. This virtual world has accelerated with the advent of computers, but, it only needs imagination and the habit of culture to fuel it. Stocks are an extension of the belief that money is real, and not just a chit.

The stock market has winners and losers. Those who create stocks are the winners. Those who buy stocks are the losers. Any rise in share value is mimicked in the inflationary spiral. Those who buy stocks see their money devalued, whereas those who create stocks have their invented paper revalued as money.

Generally, people are advised to purchase stock as a hedge against inflation and to plan for retirement. In reality, the stock market drives inflation. Selling stocks for profit, just as in a ponzi scheme, requires a new participant to play the game that will fund the gains of another participant. The issue of timing becomes critically important. The game is about anticipating changes to group psychology, not about marketplaces, society needs or businesses. It is just as easy to lose money, as it is to make money. The late investors are at a perpetual disadvantage, unless they are purchasing after a collapse of share value, which belies the advice to invest.

Of course, it is also critically important that the original business remain solvent, otherwise the entire scheme will collapse.

In the aftermath of the Civil War, many new banks were founded. They were primarily mutual, savers or cooperative banks, not commercial banks. In other words, they were formed with the noble purpose of helping the community. The goal was to provide a bridge between generations, and harness the wealth of the community for the social good. At the same time, many social and civic organizations were formed. There was clearly a desire on the part of many people to reduce the social and financial antecedents that led to the Civil War.

A new breed of bankers went into the countryside to convince farmers to take their money out from under the mattress, and instead deposit it in their banks. They were often shocked to discover the amount of hard currency that was being held on what appeared to be a ramshackle farm. In return, the bankers offered an interest payment on their deposit. Money would 'grow' just like the crops on the farm.

The result was an economic boom, as all this new money flowed into the economy. Unfortunately for the farmers, they seeded their own destruction. The Roaring 20's arrived, and in its aftermath, the Great Depression, where many families lost the farm. More money and more interest create more inflation. This is why the discovery of gold and silver on the new continents, rather than making the old empires rich, worked silently to destroy them. The same thing had occurred in America with the Gold Rush of 1849. More money does not solve the ancient economic problems, regardless of whether its form is gold, cash or stocks. The traditional practice of buy low-sell high does not work. More money creates bigger problems. With the rise of the banks and the stock market, more and more people were paying and receiving unearned income, putting themselves and the future at risk.

Earned and unearned incomes are two rails of the same track. Ben Franklin claimed that earned income is productive, whereas unearned income was destructive. Interest, and the dividends paid from a joint-stock company, are predatory mechanisms. For someone to earn money without labor, then someone must be laboring without pay. The stock market was an evolution of the original slave and serf systems. What goes around must come around.

## The Income Tax

Inflation is a benefit when selling, and a squeeze when buying. Eventually, there is never enough revenue for individuals, business or government. Inflation always wins. The income tax got its start during the Civil War, was eliminated in 1872, then reinstated fourteen years later in 1894, only to be declared unconstitutional the following year in 1895. In 1913, the Constitution was amended (#16) to allow a permanent income tax. The revolution and its democratic ideals would seem to be officially dead. Government had made war on its own citizenry, and now taxation was permanently fixed from above. Local representation, taxation and spending was surrendered to a centralized authority, much like to the Lords of Trade a century earlier. Washington D.C. was closer than London, but the same bad habits ensued. Rather than tariffs (as on tea), the entire economy was subject to taxation. The forms of taxation were multiplying (sales, property, income), which each level of government adding more taxes in a mindless search for more revenue.

The new income tax paid for World War I. The dissonance of production for destructive purposes had reached a global scale. Unions and workers rights issues were coming to the fore. Corporations were having great success by abusing the non-slave labor force. Child labor supported the craving and gluttony of unearned income on Wall Street. During the 20's, self-sustainability on the farm became less and less common. People were forced into the industrial workforce in search of wages. Excessive wealth and poverty cannot coexist. Businesses cannot sell only to the rich; workers are also customers. With the crash of Wall Street, the factories were idle. Only the need for daily consumption kept people and the economy working. The Great Depression represents a colossal accounting failure.

**Dissonance of Ownership**

Conditions have improved for the American worker since the New Deal was instituted, but things are still very bizarre. Some of the largest holdings on Wall Street are the pension funds of union members. American workers have become slaves of themselves by proxy, often owning stock in the company that employs them, and watching their jobs be outsourced overseas for greater profit. Because of their high income, insurance companies constantly target union workers. Investing brokerages seek to abscond with their savings, too. Better-paid workers do not understand economics any better than under-paid workers or the owners themselves. The brutality of the 1920's child worker system was exported to faraway countries. Foxconn, a subcontractor for Apple, has a million employees. The harsh garment factory conditions, which led the Pilgrims to flee Europe before modern finance began, has spread around the world.

Many young adults are working for start-up companies for the promise of future stocks options when the company goes public. Like the blue-collar union worker, they have combined a craving for effortless wealth with our own labor. Marx's distain for the bourgeois middle-class was because they are so blinded by their love of money. Being in the majority, they have the political power to fix things, but lack the moral and economic insight to act. Marx, for his part, failed to realize that the lower classes would copy the middle-class, the same way that the middle-class copied the upper class.

## Wall Street and the Role of Gold

As we know today, there is no shortage of currency, but there is still not enough money. The problem was always how money was handled, not what it was made from. Modern finance is the same buy-low sell-high system that has been with us for thousands of years. Paper money was gold once removed. Stocks are gold twice removed. Modern finance has been a failure, and any alleged gains of industrial and political advancement pale in comparison. Every generation has had an opportunity for peace and plenty, but lost it in pursuit of unearned income. The Biblical story told in *The Book of Nehemiah* details the same story. Unearned income is a merciless process. Older citizens take advantage of young laborers. Today we do it across national boundaries. Because of stocks, we live in a perplexing multi-colonial world, where the slave and the master can be the same person, paying interest with one hand while trying to collect it with the other.

The French (1720) desired to gather all the gold because of failures in the stock market. America (1933) tried to do the same thing, but FDR's attempt fell flat. The law was generally ignored. They both operated on the false assumption that centralizing a problem was the same as solving it.

Richard Nixon eventually abandoned the gold standard (1971). He never understood the complaints of the communists, but attempted to use their solutions by introducing wage and price controls. His attempts at regulating the oil supply through geo-politics and regulation failed miserably, leading to the rise of Islamic terrorism. Financial volatility continues with or without gold in the mix.

Oil stocks have dominated the market for almost a century, and stocks have eclipsed money in importance, leading to attacks on Wall Street and oil facilities.

The stock market is a not very well disguised international slave system, where the desire for unearned income rules men's imagination. The slave-master is not the 1%, but a familiar evil that resides in all of us. The attempt to use evil for good was illogical. The promise of modern finance was that it would solve the money problems, reduce conflict, and allow art and the common good to flourish. It failed primarily because of a mathematical flaw, and grew into the FIRE economy.

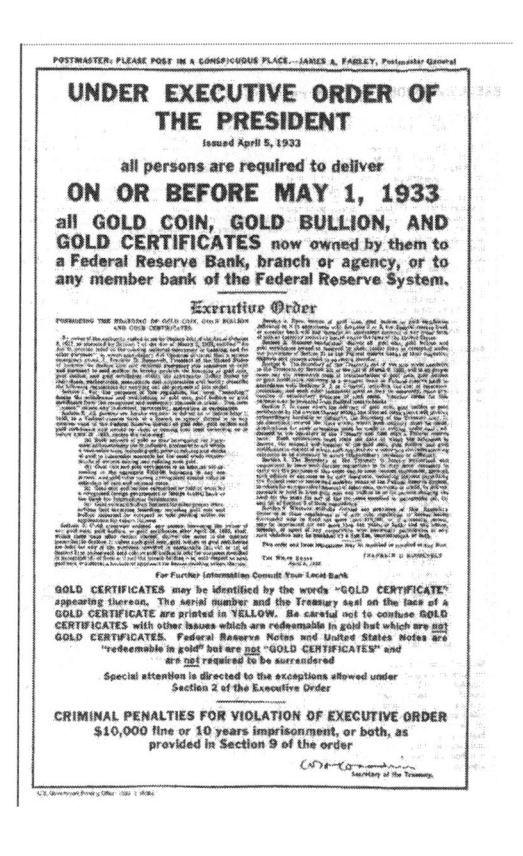

# 15. The FIRE Economy and C=M+L

The FIRE economy is an acronym, which means Finance, Insurance and Real Estate. It is a parallel to the Big History paradigm, as outlined in Chapter 11. Finance is the abstract, insurance is the social, and real estate is the physical. The FIRE economy appears to be modern finance, but its roots are in feudalism. In the past, serfs were bound to the land. They worked and gave a lion's share of the harvest to the landowners. Today, the worker is bound by their mortgage (or lease) and they pay cash. It is common for fifty percent of income to go toward housing alone, but that is just one of many housing expenses. The high nobles are banking corporations. Secondary nobles are the utilities, communications, insurance and government.

In other words, the modern world is a masquerade of a feudalistic system with the same large inequalities of wealth and structural imbalances across generations. Rigid social castes have been relaxed and a large middle-class has developed in industrialized nations, but on a both a national and global scale, feudalism continues to quietly reign. Even the habit of toll roads has endured, along with fees on strangers passing through, which are found in meal and hotel taxes. What we call capitalism and democracy has the same mathematical framework and cruelties as feudalism and parochial monarchy.

The feudalistic housing market is dominated by the thirty or forty year mortgage. People pay banking corporations for most of their working life. When they pass on, the property will transfer to someone new, who will pay again for years. Excluding brief breaks, the banks own most property in perpetuity.

Landlords are a smaller version of the banks, pressing the advantages of ownership directly. Landlords rent space, whereas banks rent money used to purchase space. The New World unconsciously followed the habits of the Old World. Modern history is a tale of global colonization and the clash of a European hybrid merchant-feudal system with indigenous sharing economies.

Banks exist to finance housing, support other banks, and to finance development through both the public and private sector. The only competition to bankers and landlords are government-provided elderly housing and subsidized rental housing. In some locales, there is an attempt at rent control, too. Housing covers a wide spectrum of prices. People are passively forced to migrate to housing that they can afford. In general, the more one earns, the more they pay for housing.

The role of government is to promote the public good. The existence of foreclosures, bankruptcy, slums and homelessness indicates a widespread systemic failure. Our land management system satisfies no one, even the wealthy, who is forced to live a guarded life full of fear, and often become victims of the volatility that allowed them to rise into riches.

Underlying the promise of democracy is the expectation of a stable sharing economy where all contribute and gain. The monarch was believed to be greedy and incompetent.

Perhaps true, but we can now see that economic imbalances also stemmed from a mathematical source: the nature of how we buy and sell. The growth of homelessness is directly related to the nature of how we sell real estate, just as hunger is the result of how we sell food. The free market is grotesquely inefficient and unfair. Land and housing management is the central problem of modern society. Hunger was the result of crop failures under feudalism, whereas today it is a systemic failure of equality.

### Interest: the control of land and money

Under feudalism, land was bought and sold infrequently. Under capitalism, land gets bought and sold constantly, or so it appears. In fact, what moves is the bondage of mortgages. Modern serfs are free to roam to find housing they can afford, but must pay the banks or landlords wherever they go. Landlords are often indebted to the banks, too, so renting is generally paying a bank through proxy.

Native Americans, in contrast, never had such a problem. Land was occupied but not owned. Ownership was unnecessary, and men were naturally equal with the land and one another. The American Revolution contradictorily attempted to establish political equality with private ownership, when the central privilege of monarchy was a claim to ownership. They removed the king and kept the inequality of privileges (like slavery), which makes the financial continuation of feudalism somewhat unsurprising. They democratized the problem.

To their credit, many of the Founding Fathers wanted everyone to own land. They recognized that those without land were unequal. The landless had no voting rights in the new society, but that was seen as a temporary condition. Europeans never grasped the native inhabitants understanding of land. The colonists saw the land as a resource to be exploited, rather than as a garden which provided.

The rise of industrialism destroyed the dream of a nation of yeoman farmers. With the decision to issue copyright law and patent protections, the meaning of property and privilege had changed fundamentally. Today, we have two unworkable property systems, once based on land, and another based on ideas.

### The Land Bondage System

Key to understanding our modern land bondage is the combination of interest rates and real estate appreciation. The higher the land and housing valuations, and the higher the interest rates, then the greater the mathematical duress on society. Everyone has become enslaved to this system. Exploitation is not necessarily willful, but a survival response driven by fiscal pressure.

Modern bankers have control of both the land and the money, in much the same way that the feudal lords had control over the land and the food. The interest paid on a $100,000.00 loan, at 5% for 30 years, is $93,255.78. Let's assume the $100,000.00 home then sold for $200,000.00, a 100% gain. After paying the interest, the original owner comes out almost even, and someone else is bonded for the full amount in his place. The bank took all the proceeds of his thirty years of labor. The owner got a place to sleep; the bank got everything else.

The $200,000 in proceeds from the sale then becomes his retirement fund, which he must spend. He can downsize, but he still needs housing that must be purchased at the currently inflated rate. After purchasing new housing, anything remaining from the windfall will be deposited in a bank, where it is lent to bind another buyer, including the buyer of his old property. Anything left over at death will be an inheritance, but the bank always has control of the money. Housing appreciation benefits the banks and harms the people.

Other professions and institutions skim off the rising cost of real estate. For example, local government, realtors and insurance companies. A realtor commission generally runs six percent of the purchase price. The more the property costs, the larger their pay. The more transfers that occur, the more opportunity for all the lawyers and sellers involved. Realtors occupy the role of the previous slave-trader, moving the bondage between the banks. Others offer ancillary services like title search, home inspection, databases, advertising, signage, repair, etc. A very large industry of self-help gurus exist, too, that proclaim a mantra of flipping real estate for profit.

Local government benefits from housing appreciation, and often suffer when it drops. Towns generally tax the value of property. With housing appreciation, they stealthily get additional revenue without resorting to a tax increase.

Insurance companies also benefit from housing appreciation. The more everything costs, the more they can charge to protect it. None of these groups contribute materially to the well being of society, but by acting as financial gatekeepers they can earn a good living. They are all in favor of high prices and a brisk market.

The more housing costs, the more interest must be paid. Terms of the note determine how much the bank earns, and how hard and long the borrower must labor. Loan rates have mimicked Jim Crow laws. Credit scores are a shield for prejudice. Subprime mortgages fell mainly on minorities, who were expected to pay more to rent the same amount of money. The difference is huge. A mortgagee at 8% pays three times more in interest than a mortgagee with a 3% rate.

## The Power of Interest

| BORROWED | INTEREST PROFIT 3% | INTEREST PROFIT 5% | INTEREST PROFIT 8% |
|---|---|---|---|
| 100,000 | $51,777.45 | $93,255.78 | $164,155.25 |
| 200,000 | $103,554.90 | $186,511.57 | $328,310.49 |
| 400,000 | $207,109.81 | $373,023.14 | $656,620.99 |

**Bank Profit on a 30 Year Mortgage**

The more one must pay to cover living expenses, then the more one must charge for their labor. Young people have large income demands because they are entering into an inflated real estate market. The financial pressure of the young increases pressure on the elderly, who experience a fiscal gap from the opposite direction: rising expenses and no income. The generation gap and the fiscal gap intersect at labor and real estate costs.

All the profit generated by labor and land appreciation eventually migrates to the banks' balance sheet, giving the banks almost absolute control of the global economy. Such power does not make the banks invincible, however. Inflation puts them at risk, too, and defaults cause individual banks to collapse. A chain is only as strong as the weakest link.

### The Social Consequence

The American Revolution is generally regarded as a world-changing event, but it actually marks a moment of tremendous error. We can witness the generation and fiscal gap in the father and son relationship of Harry and Robert E. Lee. The father and son both waged war against their respective governments, but for astonishingly opposite reasons. The cure for one was the poison of the other. Going bankrupt did not make Harry Lee blameless. Private real estate speculators like him destroyed the economy in the years after The Revolution. Winners and losers in the competitive marketplace gamble with both their lives and the lives of others, including their own progeny. The father's revolution ended monarchy but not inequality or economic volatility. Had the son's revolution succeeded, it would have fared no better.

Both misunderstood the problem, and blamed government for their personal failures. Forcing others to accept our contradictions cannot be a substitute for analysis and enlightenment. The merchants that led the American Revolution created the conditions that they were complaining about. The King was not perfect, but he was blamed for crimes for which he could not possibly be responsible.

Conflicts with the Native Americans stemmed from the colonists desire for profit. Had the colonists traded fairly, maybe history would have been different. Of course, the colonists could not do so. They were under the yoke of the European model, and the Discovery Doctrine, which gave all newly discovered lands directly to European governments. Treaties with Native Americans acquired some lands, but the land's distribution internally followed the old pattern requiring bondage. Speculation covered the continent, finally reaching the Pacific shore with the Gold Rush of 1849.

Speculation and land appreciation have often led to the genocide and civil war. The same economic pressures continue unabated for the victors and survivors. Everyone has experienced some manner of financial insecurity. Every generation finds itself desperate for money and land. The monetized marketplace is merciless. The only safety net has been deficit financing directed toward social programs and tax credits. The National Debt is both the pressure relief valve and a source of pressure. The King is gone. There is no one left to blame but us. We have reaped what we sowed.

Few are willing to think of themselves as a slave-master or feudal lord, therefore a dissonance must be maintained. The marketplace is regarded as an objective challenge, and a natural phenomenon, rather than something man-made by us. In this way, amoral and immoral behavior gets externalized. Dissonance has created a civilized cocoon where economic problems fester unimpeded. In contrast, the Native Americans enjoyed a stable lifestyle for thousands of years. We need to combine modern technology with their 'primitive' land-sharing economy. It was much more advanced than generally recognized.

### Government's equal: the Bank

During many historical periods, the taking of interest was considered immoral. Today it is a widely accepted cultural norm. As a result, the modern banking industry has grown huge, and cannot lose, even if individual banks falter. A geometric progression constantly compounds the banker's advantage, slowly separating the wealth from the worker, and dividing banking corporations from the citizens. Families get divided, too. Modern finance is the tragedy of perpetual inequality: the wealth of the parents is the debt of the children, or the wealth of the children is the debt of the parents.

People can attempt to downsize or live frugally to stretch their dollars, but the banks, in contrast, will ride the wave of inflation. Their omnipotence is stunning. Because they also offer second mortgages, they can enjoy an equity rise before the owner sells or dies. No matter what strategy one pursues, saving or spending, investing or working, it is to the advantage of the banks.

Interest payments reveal the same power of doubling as the mark-ups involved in selling an apple, as discussed in *Chapter 4, What is Inflation?* The selling of money creates inflation just like the selling of a product. We are doing the same thing with land values. We cannot live without land, food and labor to trade. Everyone alive and every organization is caught in the same trap.

Banks exert control of the economy by lending or not lending, and they create another set of winners and losers by the rates they use. Also, there is always a new generation entering adulthood and independence. The banks have a captive population. Slavery and child labor have given way to a perpetual debt trap in America, and youngsters in third world countries have lost their agrarian livelihood to become the new equivalent of America's early 20th century child labor. Living standards may have improved in America, but the underlying systemic injustice of feudalism and slavery endures and spreads.

Banks thrive from the constant flipping and inflating of real estate. If the homeowner sells before the terms of the note, then the bank gets to restart the loan at the newly inflated property price. If the buyers pays off the note early and stays in the home, most of the interest has already been collected. The contract structures repayment by the Rule of 78's. Half of the interest will have been paid in the first ten years of a thirty-year note. Refinancing and new mortgages are always to the bank's advantage. Even when the interest rate drops for the borrower, the bank can come out father ahead by adding more years.

Banks are willing to fund risky speculators in real estate and business because lending is how they survive. Businesses need customers, bankers need debtors, and their needs intersect. Banks will loan to a landlord to build a mall, and then fund the businesses that rent the space, and finally fund the buyers of the goods at the stores. It would seem that nobody could live without banks, which is why we need to make major changes.

## Bubbles and Real Estate

Economic bubbles begin within a particular sector of the economy and eventually affect the local real estate. For example, the first technology bubble fed the real estate boom of Route 128 outside of Boston, Massachusetts and the latest one drives real estate prices in Silicon Valley, California. The real estate of Hollywood and Los Angeles, and much of California, are supported by the multiple bubbles of the entertainment industry (movie, TV, cable, music), whereas New York City is the center for theatre and banking. The more expensive the land, then the more expensive the product created there, and vice-versa. The rise and fall of Detroit followed the fortunes of American automobile manufacturing. Boom and bust are never absolute. There are always multiple small and large bubbles building and bursting.

Despite all the advantages that banks have, they are still subject to conventional budgetary pressures. Ponzi mathematics is the bias of modern finance, and even banks need perpetual growth to survive. They too get drawn into the volatility of foreclosures, bankruptcies, and changing demands of the marketplace. We all must reap what we sow. Banks, however, have an extra lifeline. As the bailout of 2008 demonstrated, banks benefit from their direct relationship with the Federal Reserve System. Under capitalism, the winner is determined by who has the most credit. Nobody has more access to ready credit than the banking industry. At the height of the crisis, they got an infusion of almost one trillion dollars overnight. The same amount could have forgiven every mortgage in the nation. The government and the banking industry are ensconced within a gilded cage.

## Understanding Wall Street

Wall Street manufactures its own chit, called stocks, that are sold in exchange for the government's chit, money. Most businesses buy and sell a product, or buy and sell labor as a service. A business privileged to be listed on the exchange has a new secondary product: stock certificates. These are sold alongside its main products. Secondary buyers purchase these new chits in an attempt to sell them to other secondary buyers for a profit. Wall Street is involved with the constant selling of stocks whose cost changes by the minute! There is no other product like it in the world. There is no mathematical reason why the values change, they just do.

Value changes are determined wholly by the opinions (delusions?) of the participants. While nominally tied to the health of the business, it is very common for a stock to rise while the business is struggling or losing money. In this artificial world, bad news can be when expectations are not met, even if the actual profits of the business have increased. Conversely, there is no bad news, if expectations are met. Even losing money can drive up the share price. Long-term, everyone wants the stock price to rise.

Only relatively recently has a new breed of investor arrived, where they bet that the stock price will fall. They gain by finding and convincing someone else to believe that the price will rise, and getting a commitment to purchase future shares at the current price. That way, when/if the price falls, they buy them at the new lower price and sell them at the previously agreed to price, which is now higher. The buyer is betting that the opposite will happen. They think the price will rise, and will be able to purchase a block of shares at a low price, and immediately sell it at the high price. They are not betting within the marketplace, per se. It is more like a boxing match; each side is trying to harm each other. It is an odd double jeopardy, because their buying and selling is altering the market they are trying to predict and manipulate.

Wall Street has many tertiary levels of players' playing-the-player-playing-the-player. Even without intentional fraud, it is a marketplace of the make-believe. Only because a real business is associated with the stock does it seem plausible. Dividends from the business reinforce the illusion of joint ownership. Bitcoins represent a new territory. They are stocks being represented as currency, and devoid of any association with an actual business.

The kindest explanation of the stock market is as a system of perpetual interest for a loan that cannot be repaid. Investors do not own the business; rather, the original owner(s) have signed a mortgage for the cash they received. Stocks are then traded in the same way debts are sold to a collection agency. There is no demand date: the shares are just sold. Dividends on the shares represent an interest payment, and the principle is never paid off.

Proxy binds the workers at the public companies to these mortgages. They must generate the profit to pay the interest dividend. The original founder and Board of Directors control a lot of the shares, giving themselves multiple sources of revenue: wages, dividends and stock value. The same is not true for the workers. They are wage-slaves. A 'shareholder' of a business is actually a 'slaveholder.' For them to profit without labor, then someone must labor unpaid. Public corporations are a modern version of slavery. The chains are fiscal rather than physical.

When employees own shares of their employer, which is quite common, they are in the odd position of being slaves of themselves by proxy. The only exception being the original employees who were promised shares before the company went public. In general, that group was overworked and underpaid as a condition of the promise of a future windfall. Those who follow are overworked and underpaid, and never get a windfall.

Business is difficult under capitalism, and the seduction of free money through selling stocks is strong. The second major survival response is to turn to the government for protection or revenue. Unfortunately, it was government that started the cycle of distress. Once debt became institutionalized through the issuing of a fiat currency, everyone needs perpetually more revenue. Fiat stocks are a defense mechanism to a national currency. A sharing, barter or trade economy is stable. Profit and debt, in contrast, put us out of sync with nature and with one another.

Social problems follow the mathematical challenges of capitalism. Having money to spend engenders a sense of entitlement of what can be reasonably demanded from others. Capitalism lacks grace. A transaction mentality has eclipsed the personal nature of our relationships.

## Wall Street as Community

Wall Street did not arrive in a vacuum. It was built upon old banking habits that predate modern finance by thousands of years. Ancient and current generations both have the same challenges: As inequality compounds, society becomes divided between lenders and debtors, the rich and the poor. Oftentimes wealth is an illusion, since it is based on borrowing. The middle-class only exists because of our debt apparatus.

Money proceeds can be productive, like building a factory, or consumptive, like building a palatial estate. Debt flowing through the economy allows people to buy and sell. Modern money was an accounting gimmick intended to promote productivity, but the aristocratic habit of excess privilege and consumption continued, keeping workers, like serfs, at a systemic disadvantage.

There is a structural difference between paying taxes with money and paying taxes with a share of the harvest. Any money that a nation first issues is debt, and that debt must grow. Political equality cannot be achieved when there is a structural economic contradiction, which is why democracies have failed to create societies of peace and prosperity despite widespread consensus and tolerance.

The growth of Wall Street reflects the increase in populations, the pace of industrialism, and the presence of an infinite supply of electronic money. It represents the debt as wealth model as much as government does. Wall Street has been responsible for global depressions and world wars. It was attacked twice by Islamists (February 26, 1993 and September 11, 2001), and the target of protests by the Occupy 99% movement. Scandals, volatility and excess color its history. While powerful and influential, it has no authority. It exists because it allegedly serves a critical role to help businesses do business. Wall Street is a masquerade for a desperate gamblers paradise. People voluntarily infuse Wall Street with cash, the same as at a gaming table. Investing is loaded with betting language: winnings, loses, hedging and splitting. Only cheating is illegal, the games themselves are regulated like a professional sport.

Government does not mandate investing in Wall Street, but government does a lot to protect and encourage its existence. Since Wall Street has caused economic depressions and recessions, one would think that government should see it as in competition with the public good, but most statesmen are fully vested in Wall Street personally and politically. Their ties to public corporations and financial services are why most members of Congress are millionaires. They are not questioning the system that gave them success, which makes it difficult for them to analyze problems or find solutions.

The same people who are bonded to Wall Street also try to benefit from it. The middle-class behaves strangely; it is bound by mortgage debts, yet also invests through IRA's, 401K's and mutual funds. Financially, they are slaves of themselves, paying interest with one hand while trying to collect it with the other. Even the large unions, which nominally are on the side of the worker, are supporting corporate management by having pension funds invested in Wall Street. The problems with dissonance run deep.

Crime and gambling involve a calculated risk, the same as investing. The better you calculate, the lower your risk. Not surprisingly, Wall Street is the intersection of crime and gambling. It is the financial version of sport and casinos. Anyone can rob a boxcar, but it takes special skill to accomplish theft with a pen. "Managing wealth" through financial instruments is an oxymoron. Even if the people are honest, the system itself is not.

Amazingly, many claim that everyone can win together on Wall Street, which is impossible. Gambling, like sports, is predicated on winners and losers. Somebody must buy high for somebody to sell high. Some believe that they can beat the odds, but that is impossible, too. Nobody can keep pace. Banks cannot win every gamble, and neither can casinos, even with all their advantages. Both systems create a maximum number of losers. In the long term, the only winner is inflation. Overhead cannot be sustained within an inflationary spiral. The left hand is working against the right hand.

## Housing Reform

Just as the birds in the sky must have a nest, we all need a place to lay our head every night. We cannot live without some form of real estate to call our own. The Earth is certainly big enough to accommodate everyone, but we have imposed a false scarcity upon a world of plenty. Native Americans never had the problems we have.

Capitalism and socialism have both failed, and we need to move forward into a new system. Wall Street, seemingly, acts as impartial marketplace between government and citizens, but in reality it objectifies the flow of money, and demands a nonsensical efficiency, which results in a subsurface feudalism. Indifference to our unhealthy housing market is destructive to the population in a myriad of ways.

Population growth and the demand for land cannot explain current financial pressures. The problem is not supply or demand, but our method of accounting. The FIRE economy exists because of one simple behavior: speculation. The FIRE economy was imported from Europe and was part of colonial times. As the natives tragically discovered, the act of speculating draws everyone alive into the game. Separate but equal is not an option. The system has an inherent hunger that cannot be checked by past agreements.

Criticism of Wall Street is nothing new, but the real enemy has always been inflation. The big winners on Wall Street were industrialists, men like John D. Rockefeller or Henry Ford. It is simplistic to call the rich evil, like many are prone to do. Ford was more than a tinkering engineer. He was also an idealist, and searched hard for a better plan for a better society, just as Washington and Jefferson sought a better plan for yeoman farmers a century earlier. There is plenty of compassion in the upper ranks of society, what has been missing is better analysis.

### Stewardship

Wall Street has its own unique dissonance. It speculates on the future, but never prepares for it. It is now devoid of any concept of stewardship, while managing the funds whose purpose is stewardship. The poor cannot afford to gamble in this marketplace, but are forced to pay the winners through the profits of successful businesses. Wall Street deserves criticism, but it must be based on how the system works, and not be based on individuals or corruption within the system.

Both Main Street and Wall Street can be accused of indifference and bullying. The owner of a small business gets to decide how much employees can earn and how much customers must pay. The primary difference between Main

Street and Wall Street is the former buys and sells products, whereas the later buys and sells businesses. The scale of property ownership changes, but not the behavior. "Buy low-sell high" is everywhere.

Wall Street defenders claim it is a solution for young or expanding businesses, but it acts primarily as a tool for profiting from inflation for those not involved with the business at all. The IPO's (initial public offering) and new stock issuances for fresh funding are a masquerade. The real game being played is the creation of a third inflated 'property' to compete with inflated real estate and intellectual property. If money is real, then it follows that ideas can be property. Stocks follow the intellectual acceptance that money has value and are regarded as equals to cash and gold. Democracy voided hereditary claims, but capitalism has preserved the acts of claims through contracts, and enshrined copyright and patent laws as a new hereditary claim. Could anything be more contradictory to a freethinking society than treating ideas as perpetually owned property?

**What is Value?**

Our inability to define 'fair' is at the root of our fiscal, social and political distress. The question of "How many eggs is one chicken worth?" cannot go away. We need to trade eggs for chickens, and we need to trade between generations. The choices of Harry and Robert E. Lee demonstrate the problem. Speculation pre-dates Wall Street. Wall Street was never a workable solution for funding the next generation of entrepreneurs or inventors. Regulation was an attempt to make speculation safe and for the pubic good. It was a typical oxymoron.

Ironically, the FIRE economy is the antithesis of self-reliance. It is based on unearned income, and it underlies the buy low-sell high nature of the merchant economy. To some degree, earned versus unearned income is the fundamental difference between Wall Street and Main Street. Earned income cannot coexist mathematically with unearned income. Separate but equal never works. Unearned income now takes various forms: capital gains on real estate, interest on loans, stock value changes or insurance products. The essence of slavery was unearned income. Lincoln may have freed the remaining slaves, but the bondage endured. Wall Street gets going in the same era as the Civil War. Volatility eventually leads to war. The damage from land speculation was too great to be contained by a secondary level of speculation like Wall Street.

The promise of consensus politics was that multiple groups of producers could make good decisions, but the ancient divide between farmers, fishermen, ranchers and merchants was never resolved in Athens. Government can make a bad situation better or worse, but it was always the greedy choices of private individuals that drove conflict and destroyed the economy. If the conventional wisdom of business was flawed, then the conventional wisdom of government would fare no better. The planet does not belong to the indigenous tribes any more than it belongs to the banks, the church or the government. The land is for all people. The claims of hereditary ownership are false regardless of the source. The FIRE economy is both proof and cause of economic failure, and like the root cause of inflation, it is based on percentages.

### The Power and Place of Percentages

Percentages make our lives unnecessarily difficult. The greed of a single man can spawn millions of imitators who are seduced into competing with him. Many hands should make light work, but the overhead of competition, profit, government and the avarice of individuals eventually make everything difficult. Even if you think you are winning, eventually your labor will get lost to the fiscal gap. Inflation reigns as the only victor. We are caught in a trap by our collective behavior. It will take a collective effort to free us.

Equality requires a willingness to be equal. Nobody gambles with the goal of breaking even, yet that is how we need to think. To break even is to win. Otherwise, your gain is someone else's pain.

A system of winners must create losers. Instead of planning to gamble, we need to engineer money and recognize that the Earth is for the benefit of everyone. Structural deficiencies will ensure that there will be rich and poor, but your place is mobile. If democracy does not change the rules, some form of violence will change the operating conditions.

Within this context, it is ironic and tragic that savings can serve as the failure of stewardship. Everybody only needs to have their daily needs met. If we accomplish that, then there is no need to be overly worried about tomorrow. We are fully capable of taking care of one another; we just need the courage to do so, and to discover the logic of a wiser accounting.

### C=M+L: Capital equals Money Plus Labor

Trade can exist without our accounting habit of recording profit. Trading eggs for chickens is trading earned income without using money. The challenge is how to trade using money, and without lapsing into the unearned income (inflationary) phenomenon.

The first challenge with trade is that it requires the possession of something with which to trade. When people are born, they own nothing. Others control everything that exists. The only way to acquire anything within a monetized competitive system is to trade unequally. Usually, the first thing someone trades is his or her labor for money. By working more and consuming less, one can generate a monetary surplus, which can be invested. Investing is only possible when one has more than what they need to survive. An imbalance has begun, and the goal is to widen the imbalance.

Our development follows a predictable pattern. People work so they can separate from their parents. They want to rent and furnish a place to live independently. The next major expense is when these children have their own children. The last concern is having enough money to retire, and leaving an inheritance for the children.

Saving and investing, like budgeting and gambling, implements a plan to quietly shift a burden onto others. In general, people are taught and follow the economic strategy that their parents experienced. Economics, as much as cooking, politics and religion, are part of conventional familial wisdom. The rich teach their kids how to stay rich through calculated risk. The poor teach their kids how to keep their job. Rich or poor, the baseline plan is to have more money than our needs. Since all income is someone else's expense, the burden has to fall somewhere, and it will continually shift onto the next generation and into our alchemistic accounting ledgers.

The struggle we experience when starting out as a young adult remains constant. People want to maximize their positive budget ratio in the hopes that when/if it starts decreasing, that they will die from old age before they run out of money. The fixation on retirement within our culture is a symptom of the lack of stewardship and commonwealth. The competitive marketplace offers no comfort for anyone, even for those who seemingly have all the advantages of age. Transactional economics indicates that our needs will change as we age, and that our experience is dependent upon the role we get to choose. There is a generic formula that explains all activity within the economy: C=M+L. Capital equals Money plus Labor.

Capital is an all-encompassing word. It is both the means of production and the result of production. It can be the services we provide to one another, a durable or consumptive product, a short-term want or a long term necessity, physical or intellectual, a man-made or natural resource. Capital is the sum of all our activity to produce and consume, and at the micro level of a single transaction. Capital requires Labor to come into existence. Because we have made the commitment to use Money, M needs to be part of the formula, too. Hence, C=M+L.

If there were no money, then Capital would equal Natural Capital plus Labor. (C=NC+L). The Native Americans understood the value of Natural Capital. They could produce and consume in rhythm with nature. Money has an innate risk, which can lead to the depletion and extinction of resources and species, and create tremendous imbalances within society. The abuse of power and privilege is a social risk for society with or without money, but money introduces a mathematical risk, where the numbers end up running the people, rather than people running the numbers.

Survival always requires a division of labor. The next choice is to use money or not. If we are to use money, then we need to be clear on how it is to be used. The youth need to be trained and become active contributors within both types of society (C=M+L or C=NC+L). However, the unemployed, underemployed, and overworked are common symptoms of a money system. Distortions within M cause distortions within L. Being young or old was not a problem under the C=NC+L system. One contributed as one could, and whatever they produced was enough. It was not necessary to hoard indiscriminately for ones entire life, or to fear retirement. There was no distinction between life and labor. In a system without money, aging and labor are symbiotic.

Before modern finance and paper money, C=M+L did not work because the M value was based on any possible number (2+2=?). Modern finance attempted to fix the M problem, which was believed to be a shortage of money, rather than an issue with valuation. With more money, we still had the original problem.

We can clearly see the challenge was in how percentages were applied. Under a barter system, the problem would have been hidden under haggled negotiations, with one side wanting more or less eggs exchanged for a single chicken. A fair trade is difficult to define because of human emotions. Trading labor, time and skill are difficult to quantify, but the root problem is still mathematical in nature.

Karl Marx focused on the creation of value, but his formula of M-C-M+ ignored the labor component, ironically. He claimed that the fundamental economic conflict was between management and labor, but actually the contradiction is between buying and selling, a dual role that we all share.

The emotional component of an economic system is critical, too. A system must be accepted spiritually. Revolution is a common habit of mankind, and it is always in response to some inequality, real or imagined. A system can only endure if it balances the abstract, the emotional and the physical. Dissonance must be purged, and the laws of mathematics respected. Sensitivity to commonwealth makes all things better, which is why the prophets have perennially warned about profits. It is as easy to do the right thing for the wrong reason, as it is to do the wrong thing for the right reason. Enlightenment is doing the right thing for the right reason.

Modern finance has had some successes. It got everyone busy and changed the quality of life and the standard of living. It put an end to the belief in alchemy, as it was no longer necessary to turn lead into gold. The process of discovery shifted to a more useful purpose like science and manufacturing. We are significantly savvier about the world around us than previous generations, but the ends cannot be used to justify the means. Discovery has been a permanent part of mankind's journey, and it has not been dependent on democracy or capitalism.

Some wisdom cannot be improved upon, and adding to it becomes a loss. As Leo Tolstoy put it: *"Truth, like gold, is to be obtained not by its growth, but by washing away from it all that is not gold."* In the same way, adding percentages destroys value. There is a tension between what we should add or subtract, like separating the wheat from the chaff. Improvement requires rejection. We should be rejecting percentages.

Modern finance made the problems with inflation and debt considerably worse. Valuations become the new alchemy, particularly in regard to real estate. Every nation in the world now uses deficit financing, and it is mathematically impossible to prevent the debt from compounding. We have old problems, but with much larger numbers. Computers are programmed to wrestle with the administrative overhead of inflation and debt. A tool that could make life easier is commonly used to make it worse.

More money increased the levels of corruption, war and poverty, rather than eliminating them. Democracy removed the figurehead that was easy to blame. Instead of commonwealth, we have had more division. Salesmanship and propaganda replaced wisdom. We are now discarding materials almost as fast as we produce them. We have created cumbersome procedures that are regarded as efficient. On a colossal scale, there is a waste of human and natural capital. The FIRE economy does not work.

## The FIRE Economy

Money is an invented thing, and it needs a connection to something that is real. As the name implies, there is nothing more real than real estate. Man needs the Earth to survive. It is our womb and tomb. Surplus money gets pumped back into the FIRE economy, either directly or indirectly.

The FIRE economy keeps institutions strong and people weak, and forms a barrier between society and its hopes. Corporations are like zombies, neither living nor dead. Even worker-owned business, which Marx envisioned, need to follow the same behaviors of capitalism. People are now trapped between debt and inflation in the same way that society was previously trapped between violence and scarcity. Issues of violence and scarcity are still common in poor neighborhoods and in poor countries. The focus remains on individualism rather than commonwealth.

The transfer of real estate increases its value in the same way that the price of an apple inflates on its journey from tree to table. In this case, the land, transfers from the current generation to the next. Every generation confronts the rising cost of real estate. Deflating real estate values are commonly regarded as indicative of a failing economy or catastrophic. Speculators fail when land or building values depreciate.

To purchase a home, whether for living or for profit, money must usually be borrowed. A strange thing occurs as a result of lending. When an apple is sold and resold, it increases in value. When money is sold and resold, it decreases in value. It takes more money to purchase the same good. As land value inflates, and money value deflates, it drives a demand for ever greater percentages. Whether in the form of taxes, interest rates, profit margins or wages, the need for housing feeds the mathematical disease of inflation.

The *Monopoly* game is a simplified version of the real estate market. In the real world, only inflation and corporations can win. Inflation wins because of the math. Corporations win because they cannot consume, suffer or die like humans.

Some institutions are regarded as 'too big to fail,' but the real problem is that the concentration of wealth within corporations (including non-profit corporations) has no release. A particular corporation may fail, but their wealth will transfer to another corporation. When people die, the wealth gets redistributed amongst the living. When a corporation ceases, the concentration of wealth favoring the non-living continues unabated.

### The problem with insurance and government

Insurance, by definition, is a ponzi scheme. The premium pays for the overhead of those who manage the company. If you get back more than was paid in, then it was taken from someone else. Insurance has progressed with inflation. We have insurance purchasing insurance, insurance guaranteed by other insurance, insurance that avoids liability and insurance for small items that need no insurance. Insurance is more complicated than taxes, and has more fraud than stocks. Both taxes and insurance keeps millions of people pointlessly employed.

One of the original taxes of ancient Egypt was a seventh share of the harvest, to prepare for a drought that Joseph envisioned in a dream that was seven years off. When the drought arrived, a full years harvest was on hand. Nobody suffered. Government should be a system of planning, and can be a natural part of the division of labor. In contrast, government today is a failed system of insurance.

The accounting ledger is not a substitute for reality. What gets destroyed is gone, and desired harvests will continue to fail. The Supreme Court's ruled that national healthcare insurance is a tax, but it is only slight of hand. Administering invented numbers is not real work. Rather than protecting people, insurance and taxed money wastes both human and natural resources. Nothing in the economy should be difficult to replace, unless the Earth itself fails to provide. Mandatory insurance (of all types) is outsourcing by government, and marks the failure of commonwealth.

When the federal government bailed out Wall Street firms by buying their stocks, and then sold them for profit, it was only able to do so by increasing the National Debt by trillions of dollars. The gigantic sums of money involved in the 2008 bailout were not real. Money is an intellectual agreement. The numbers we record (2+2=5) constitute intellectual fraud, the same as alchemy or the divine superiority of the king's blood. Fake numbers are protecting fake numbers. It is a false security.

On the skyline of most cities, there are insurance companies and banks towering over the region. The FIRE Economy dominates the globe, not manufacturing. A religious-like faith in numerical alchemy has reduced all men to be servants of the corporate balance sheet.

### Moving Forward

2+2=5 (percentages applied) has an adverse effect on the C=M+L formula. Inflation changes M, which exerts pressure on C and L. This is why both the land and people are abused. As inflation advances, the abuse gets worse. The economy is full of struggle and failure, rather than of commonwealth and ease through cooperation.

In the apple example, we saw how the price of an apple increased as it moved from tree to table. The same thing is occurring with the land as it moves between generations. We want the price of the apple and the land to increase as slowly as possible, if at all.

# 16. What is to be Done?

### The Choice: Fascism or Commonwealth

Economic history reveals a constant battle between commonwealth and fascism. Under commonwealth, people are happy and productive. Under fascism, people are stressed and destructive. Much of human history lies in the grey area between these two extremes. Our challenge is to recognize in which direction we are heading and choosing where to lead others.

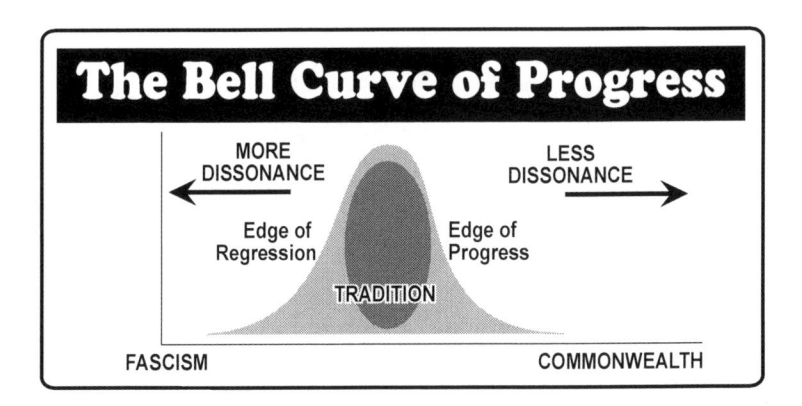

**The Bell Curve of Progress**

MORE DISSONANCE ←    LESS DISSONANCE →

Edge of Regression    Edge of Progress

TRADITION

FASCISM    COMMONWEALTH

The difference between fascism and commonwealth is sometimes claimed to be a choice between good and evil, but the choice is not about *'them.'* It is our own level of self-awareness that determines what we choose. The *'evil'* is sure of their choices, and believes them to be well reasoned, even at the extremes of fascism. There was an entire body of science that the Nazis created to *'prove'* to themselves the superiority of Aryans, and they had similar evidence that proved a worldwide Jewish conspiracy that needed to be stopped. People can convince themselves of anything, no matter how ridiculous. Similar bodies of work self-certify the superiority of monarchy, religion, democracy, capitalism, Islamism and socialism. If any of these systems worked as claimed, there would be no point to writing or reading this book.

Unfortunately, only by the testing of ones own beliefs can wisdom be discovered. Claiming others to be inferior is a bit too easy. We need to untangle our own contradictions. Under such circumstances, a little humility will go a long way.

A society shifts the status quo toward commonwealth by refining its values, removing prejudices and thinking consistently across the religious, political and economic realms. Man is his own worst enemy, and dissonance is *'the enemy within'* that leads to fascism. The pairing of contradictory ideas has no limits. Money plays a key role because it is the common tool through which we all interact. Ownership and rights stretch across generations, but there can be no rights without an equal share of responsibility to the collective that grants and protects those rights. Commonwealth is not a concept of shared ownership, but one of a shared existence.

Tragically, the math we commonly use when handling money exhibits its own dissonance. Previous chapters dealt with the nature of these mathematical contradictions, by removing them we can lay the foundations for commonwealth and build a peaceful and prosperous society.

### The Problem: Inflation and Debt and Inequality

Let's be clear on where the problem lies: inflation, debt and inequality are the problems that we must eliminate. Individuals, government, businesses and non-profits must all change how they handle money. This is an accounting methodology problem as much as anything else. We are all feeding a vicious cycle of "percentages added" that can only lead to more inflation. Taxes, Profit and Interest are all the same thing mathematically. It will take everyone to change the direction of society, but reform always begins at the bottom, with one person with a new idea. It takes time for ideas to spread, and individuals to take action to guide others.

What is missing is a Universal Code of Conduct for how money should be handled. This is both a moral and a mathematical imperative. A machine must be engineered using standards of predictability. Consistency is the basis of trust, and without trust and standards, a society cannot function. Freedom is a group effort, ironically. Obedience to law is only half of the equation of a free society. The other half is good law, and they have been in short supply for many generations.

Because we are divided by age, wealth, position, skill and realm, a reform strategy must begin in many places simultaneously. Change can be thought of as a giant migration. As ideas spread, individuals will slowly change direction forcing the stampede to alter course slightly. This process will continuously repeat until eventually the stampede has completely changed direction. As Thomas Paine wrote at the opening of *Commonsense*, *"Time makes more converts than reason."* We all constitute a pressure point that can enable change. By having the courage to begin, success is assured, but in which direction is the bell curve moving?

### Reforms for the Individual

A virtuous society requires virtuous people. There is no way around this fundamental, and our personal finances must illuminate virtue before our laws and institutions can reflect them. The most common dissonance of the large middle-class is paying interest with one hand while trying to collect it with the other. Long-term loans are taken for education, cars, and housing; short-term loans exist on credit cards. Meanwhile, long-term planning for retirement is based on saving and accruing compound interest and investing in stocks.

Our banality with this contradiction is the root cause of why we were attacked on 9/11. Thousands of lives have been lost, trillions of dollars spent, and a gigantic surveillance state has been erected because of this habit. A similarly sized apparatus exists attempting to audit the fraud possibilities inherent in this type of banking, too. We waste a lot of resources perpetuating a complicated system, when a simple system could serve everyone well.

The sufferings of society are caused by greedy money decisions recorded in private, which are akin to the quiet burdens individuals carry because of money. As Pogo observed, we are our own enemy. A huge legal and institutional structure must be maintained to allow debt and profit from debt to exist. This is not a predator versus prey situation on the open savannah, but a willful choice of the numbers we record. This is a centuries old problem, and we can see the results in the compounding of inflation and frequent wars, which represent the collapse of trade, freedom and liberty. We must personally be part of the change that we have been waiting upon. Our check books are more powerful than the ballot box, contracts or peace treaties. We create a social environment by how we handle money. Our use of a surplus reveals the continuum of innocence lost.

The only way to eliminate the problems caused with paying interest is for people to stop trying to collect it for themselves. For example, student debts are related to teacher pensions. To think otherwise is to be in denial. Everything and everyone is connected.

We often hear the term *'enlightened self-interest'* bandied about as the delicate balance required for a free society. The greater part of this wisdom is self-restraint. Unearned income is a huge and destructive temptation. What goes around must come around, and we have all been indoctrinated by tradition to accept what should be unacceptable. If it is possible to make money without labor, then someone must be laboring without getting paid. A large part of banking and financial services are nothing more than slavery by proxy. All interest is usury. Any amount more than zero slowly cascades and drags society into a slave system of growing misery. Fascism advances, commonwealth recedes.

Eliminating interest will not solve all the mathematical problems in society. It is only one of three sources of 'percentages added.' Further reforms are needed.

However, rejecting interest personally is the easiest place to start. Only a surplus can be lent or invested. There is nothing wrong with saving or planning for the future. The problem is in trying to manipulate money. It creates the very problem hoping to be avoided: inflation and volatility. We cannot escape the consequences of our own actions, for better and ill.

If the middle-class were to forgo trying to collect interest via CD's, 401K's, mutual funds, and annuities, then it would be a dramatic change in philosophy and behavior. It is not that hard to do. Pick up the phone and sell your (slave-) holdings. Transfer the funds to your local bank. Even if you pay a government penalty for early withdrawal, it is a wise choice. Pay taxes this year instead of later on. Never care again about what the stock market is doing. If you own the stocks of your employer, then you are actually a slave of yourself, which is a common example of extreme dissonance.

The middle-class, particularly the worker unions, have the power to free themselves and challenge the wage-slave system, although in many cases they have negotiated away the right to control their own pensions. More dissonance. Everyone should use their savings to pay their own debts or the debts of their children. To be debt-free, and innocent of predation, is the wisdom behind the Poor Richard's Almanac entry: *"Neither a borrower nor a lender be."*

While this idea may seem radical and unworkable, in fact, what we are doing now is already radical and unworkable. Social Security was created because of the collapse of Wall Street. Now, people are trying to supplant their Social Security by investing in Wall Street. This is partially why programs like Social Security grew to be inadequate, and why pension plans became unworkable. We have made the original disease into a cure!

It a ridiculous amount of fear for people to spend their working years worried about retiring. People growing old is not a new phenomenon. A more stable and logical system is possible, as will become apparent. Just as we can plan better for the youth, we can plan better for the elderly.

We have misused the genius of computers, and have programmed highly sophisticated habits of hoarding and investing. Every percentage that can be found or created is squeezed. Numbers are the new alchemy, and the wizards are full of self-delusion. Accounting is a simple thing, but it has become unnecessarily difficult. With paper money and electronic accounting debt is infinite. 2+2=5 will never be true.

A domestic divestment movement from Wall Street is the single best and easiest thing the middle-class can do for themselves. This is not a *'run on the banks.'* It simply shifts funds from Wall Street to Main Street. What people have today they will have tomorrow, but the stampede of the rat race will begin to turn.

Insanity is doing the same thing over and over and expecting different results. Either expectations need to change, or behaviors. We cannot act like misers personally and expect to enjoy the public liberty of a strong commonwealth. The only way that *'We The People'* can lead the government and business community is by setting an example. The middle-class can make the manipulated money markets dry up by refusing to participate. By lowering the cost of living, we will raise the standard of living and the quality of life, but people must have the courage and faith to build a better society, and let go of the status quo.

There are two faces to the scourge of inflation. One is the price of the goods going up, the other is the value of the money going down. Inflation will always outpace interest. Higher yields lead to even higher inflation. Compounding interest devalues the currency. While the numbers seem bigger, the purchasing power of what was accrued is diminished. Of course, what we should not be doing as individuals, larger institutions should not be doing either.

The poor and young, as they manage to rise up the economic ladder, quickly fall into the bad habits of the middle-class. The rich, of course, have luck on their side (not skill). But, even when they become philanthropists, they seldom question the process that brought them to the top. It is not how much money you have that is important, but how you handle it. Money should always be a tool and never a weapon. Taking interest is to exploit the poor and young. Prophets have long warned about profit (interest is profit on money) with good reason. Forgoing interest is the easiest step to take, and it can begin with every individual.

Abolishing profit, and eventually abolishing taxes, are a bit more complicated, but equally necessary to create a debt-free and inflation-free society. The trillions of dollars of deficit value already in existence is more than enough money to fund the economy perpetually, but only if we constrain inflation. Otherwise, not even a googolplex of zeroes will be enough. Computers will just be documenting the absurd.

### Reforms for Local Government

Taxes have always been a hot point of dispute and with good reason in modern times. They are a 'percentage added' for which someone must suffer a 'percentage subtracted.' All revenue is someone's expense.

We have three levels of government (local, state and national) and three forms of taxation (income, sales, and property). We are taxed for earning money, for spending money, and for owning what was purchased.

You are taxed for owning a home, renting a room, eating food at a restaurant, traveling on a road and for buying a car, owning a car and when fueling the car. You are also taxed for parking the car or crossing some bridges. You may be taxed for buying clothes, or fined and imprisoned for removing them. So, where do we start in fixing such a ridiculous mess? We start at the bottom, of course.

Of the three forms of taxes, property tax is by far the worst. You are taxed for what you own. You do not own your home; you live in it under license from the local authority. If you miss some tax payments, then they have the right to seize the home. The punishment is grotesquely disproportionate, and captures the most fundamental problem in our society, how we manage land and property.

To reform local government, we must reconsider not only issues of cash flow but the concepts of ownership and stewardship, too. This is an old challenge. Even the *Magna*

*Carta* dealt with issues regarding abuse of the environment. Clear-cutting, pollution and over-harvesting natural resources to the point of extinction are one of the glaring problems of a profit-motivated system. The interest and profit associated with real estate drives much of our economic madness. It can be eliminated with local control and a shift in tax policy.

The first reform every town should adopt is a shift to income tax and away from property tax. That way, taxation can be progressive. The rich pay more and the poor pay less. The elderly on a fixed income, and those who lose their jobs, are less pressured to move or downsize because of financial issues.

Second, a local public bank should be established. All mortgages need to be held locally. Funding for the bank can be from public pension funds, individual citizens and non-profit endowments. There will be a giant sucking sound as money moves from Wall Street to Main Street. These mortgages should be rewritten at zero percent. The public bank can be set up new, or existing local banks can handle the duties. The issue is to move the money and change the percentages. It is not necessary to have it be a publicly run bank, as long as it is acting in the public interest and not for shareholders.

Next up is the problem of housing appreciation, which is at the core of all our troubles. Willful speculation and background appreciation needs to end, and steps taken to reduce all land and housing values.

Housing is not an 'investment,' it is a necessity. Developers should not be allowed to manipulate the market by flipping real estate or converting everyone to renters. Housing should have a fixed price, but more importantly, everyone should have a place to sleep and call their own. Housing should be inexpensive, plentiful, and easily exchanged. The Earth is more than big enough to fit everyone. The cost of building should not be prohibitive. Ensuring and coordinating the time and talent to build adequate housing is a basic function for government. Why join together collectively under a government if our most basic needs cannot be met?

Jefferson wrote: *"it is the Right of the People to alter or to abolish it, and to institute new Government, laying its foundation on such principles and organizing its powers in such form, as to them shall seem most likely to effect their Safety and Happiness."* A government that fails to house, feed, cure and educate its people has failed in its role of administrating the public good.

Native Americans never had the problem we are experiencing. Adam Smith called them savages. Who were the real savages? The legacy of hypocrisy is clear. Clever technology is not a moral standard. Might is not right. More importantly, we must recognize that our fear, and the fear of our enemy, are not very different. We are experiencing a shared dissonance. Two wrongs do not make a right, but double the amount of wrong.

While private ownership is maintained, the private real estate market as we know must be transformed. Every town government should act as a clearing house for real estate sales. If you want to sell and move, then property is sold to the town. When you want to move to the town, then housing is purchased from the town. Apartments essentially become condominiums. There is no gain or loss possible in the housing market. The price you buy for is the price you sell for. It was real estate prices that caused the collapse of 2008, the S&L of the 1980's, and so on back into the 1700's. Every boom is a bust.

To force prices down, governments can use deficit financing to 'buy high and sell low.' Some minor adjustments can be made for improved properties, or penalties for damaged properties, but as a whole, a housing purchase will become as complicated as buying a loaf of bread or renting a room. The town acts as the buyer and the seller of property. There should be some special conditions, too. For example, universities should be required to provide all housing for students. A stable economy requires real estate prices that are as rock solid as the land we stand on.

Commercial space should also fall under the control of local government. It would be best for all commercial space to be owned by the town and leased rent-free to all businesses. The need for this favorable reduction in overhead for business will become clear later, but if there are any conflicts, the people will have the upper hand. The need to give tax breaks to attract businesses will be moot. Ideally, people will live and work in the same town. Such a system will make moving easy for everyone, and relieve many financial pressures in society. Inflated real estate values and mortgage interest are the two largest sources of inflation.

### Reforms for State Government

State government should likewise abandon multiple taxes and defer to a single income tax. They should also make it illegal for towns to borrow. If a town needs more funds to operate, or for a special expenditure, than the state should supply all the funds. States generally support their towns by diverting some share of sales tax and income tax revenues. Taxation methods differ by state primarily based on whether there is a bold effort to fleece the tourist or not. This approach demonstrates another example of how public policy degrades the quality of life. By making entertainment expensive for tourists, it also makes it expensive for local citizens.

The race to the top is also a race to the bottom, which is the inherent nature of a vicious circle. More dissonance leads to more dissonance. That is the domino effect that we should fear.

States divert federal funds to the towns and towns likewise apply for federal and state funds. All this nonsensical reporting and begging and largesse is based on the presumption that money is in short supply, when the real problem is that there is too much inflation.

State governments expend a lot of time on the budget process, trying to predict and respond to revenue fluctuations. All services and problem solving take place under a budgeting umbrella. Expediency, short-term thinking, and personal avarice color management decisions in government just as they do in business. Organizations do not have to be structured like this.

As the towns rely on states, the states should rely on the Federal government to balance any shortfalls. Borrowing at the state level should be illegal, too. The demand for pork spending and special interest dollars and privileges stems from the nature of the cash flow. The man-made scarcity of funds drives the panic. It is nonsensical to have three levels of government all borrowing and taxing in a different manner.

Ultimately, all money flows from the National Debt. By controlling prices within the state, dollars will go farther. The need for more funding is because we blithely allow inflation to advance. Even worse, real estate inflation is generally regarded as desirable. As with the towns, pension funds can be used to fund a public bank that enable the transition to a better system. There is no money shortage, only a failure of accounting sanity.

### Reforms for Federal Government

The purpose of the federal government is to create a currency, act as the clearing house for debt (all money is inherently debt), to set principles, and ensure standards or fairness in the states. Any system can be corrupted because checks and balances have a tendency to make a wider and wider circle of collusion, which is what we have with three level of government each duplicating taxes and debt. A chain cannot be stronger than the weakest link. If housing, jobs, food, education and healthcare are not secure at the local level, then the chain is broken.

Too many 'separate but equal' systems have been established. For example, Social Security for citizens, various plans for union workers, and pensions for government workers. Everyone needs to be treated the same. The Universal Code of Conduct needs to constrain wages, prices and retirement benefits so there is a tighter parity. We see the same dissonance with the requirement that everyone purchase health insurance. Universal coverage should be based on a simple universal plan, not preserve 'separate but equal' confusion and duplicity.

Benefits should not be tied to careers. All positions are necessary and we all have the same basic needs. Our access to the output of the nation should be equal. How grotesquely unfair is it to overpay some people their entire career, and then overpay them in retirement, while others spend their entire lives underpaid, and are underpaid again in retirement, too? The support for the elderly should be as uniform and consistent as the support children receive in school, or the healthcare we receive in a hospital. We need to remove prejudices and privileges. With reforms at the personal and local level constraining debt, inflation and real estate values, establishing standards of conduct by law at the Federal level will be easy to implement and maintain.

It is possible for government(s) to eliminate taxes completely by relying on deficit spending. In many ways, that is already what we have done. Tax receipts are trillions of dollars behind the citizenries' ability to provide. We are engaged in a game of numerical alchemy. The experiment in paper money that started 300 years ago is an abject failure in terms of accounting and social equality. However, we can use deficit spending as a tool, if we would just admit that most of the economic assumptions that we are operating under are false. Money is primarily an intellectual agreement. If we agree on fascism, then we will get fascism. If we agree on commonwealth, then we will get commonwealth.

Money can be a useful tool of measure for both fairness and demand. An income tax can provide an auditing framework to an industrialized society to ensure that trade is easy, plentiful, equitable, sustainable and in balance with nature. Conceivably, money could be rendered obsolete. Maybe there will be a language shift, and money will be called credits, which is more appropriate to the needs of the coming generation. Bottom Line: there can be no consumption without production. We must work and create useful things. We are all part of a cycle that sustains everyone and us together. Inequality between generations, whether in the form of slavery, child labor, or youth debt, all mark the failure of that cycle.

Whether we call it money or credits, trade involves an exchange, and money can facilitate that exchange so we have freedom of choice. The problem is not the object of money itself, but our accounting contradictions, which pre-determine the flow, giving some people lots of choices and other people none. Trade is stewardship and healthy. Profit is disruptive, competitive and destructive. Laws requiring 'fiduciary duty' are the equivalent of mandating treason to the body politic. They institutionalize fascism in the same way that slavery, Jim Crow and child labor were institutionalized. The Federal government should be passing laws that mandate a sharing and cooperative economy of equals.

### Reforms for Businesses and Banking

The dominate philosophy of our culture is to 'buy low and sell high.' This behavior is fueled by fear and the conditions of economic volatility. Living requires a constant demand for new consumption. A monetized and inflationary economy therefore constantly demands more profit. Overhead and expenses quickly consume revenue. Businesses are inherently fragile because of the volume of buy and sell. Size does not make them stronger. Increases in prices from suppliers (or taxes), or decreases in demand from consumers, send their balance sheet into an immediate collision course with debt. In general, only the businesses with the most credit survive the boom and bust waves. Many large businesses are absorbed by other large businesses, whereas as small businesses simply cease to exist.

The volatility of business is directly related to the volatility of housing prices. As real estate increases, citizens need more revenue. Raising wages will eventually raise the price of goods, which will further increase real estate prices. It is an old but strong vicious circle, and entirely man-made. By stabilizing real estate pricing, we can begin to stabilize prices on other goods.

Modern manufacturing has made it possible for everyone to produce far more than they can consume. To see the economy as a problem of scarcity is nonsensical. The landfills are bursting. We are throwing stuff away as fast as we can make it. What is called a shortage is really just an imbalance that has plagued man for centuries. That imbalance has always been created by the act of 'buy low-sell high' compounding. The new operating philosophy has to be 'buy low-sell low.'

The government needs to set standards. It does not need to set prices, but it does need to control the profit percentages used and establish a framework of what is acceptable and unacceptable behavior. How much should an apple cost, 2 cents, 8 cents, 14 cents or 32 cents? The current retail price is often close to and over a dollar each. The pricing difference reflects pricing habits, not the apple. As more people touch the apple, each working on a similar mark-up percentage, the more the apple costs. There is a dramatic price difference between a small mark-up percentage and a large one! The cheaper the apple; the fewer hungry people and more equality and tranquility. When it comes to pricing, less is more.

Eliminating rent and property taxes for a business is a huge step in making it possible for a business to 'sell low.' Now all that are needed are the machines, raw materials and labor to produce the products. Machines are a one-time expense. Labor is at whatever rate we determine. The volatility of the market has ended. Cash flow is no longer a perpetual crisis. Banks still exist to lend money for start-ups and expansion. Wall Street becomes obsolete. It's closing has no negative effect on the next generation needing capital for a new idea.

By maintaining low profit margins, products can move to one side of the world to the other without a significant price change. There will be no financial risk associated with running a business, and best practices can be followed with fear of cost. We can have safe industry, clean industry and efficient industry. The waste caused by competition will cease as well as the incessant advertising. There are many differences between a trade-driven system and a profit-driven system. Cooperatives and employee-owned businesses will flourish in a non-competitive business environment, allowing democracy to spread to the workplace. The stress of jobs, and of losing jobs, will cease. All will have full and satisfying employment. With profit, imbalances grow. With a trade system, many hands make light work.

Ending the sales tax eliminates the false competition of places like Amazon with local stores, or cross-border state competition. But a lot of fault actually lies with manufactures that sell to distributors at different prices. For example, by giving Wal-Mart a better price, the manufacturer creates a self-fulfilling condition that Wal-Mart will be its largest customer. Two businesses selling the same product, and working on the same profit margin, will have a pricing disparity because of the manufacturer's favor. The solution to this is to make any business classified as a manufacturer to sell the same product to everyone at the same price, including delivery. Utilities can be distributed for free on a quota system. These changes captures the entire market except for food and labor.

The idiocy of copyright and patent protections needs to be abolished. Ideas and inventions needs to be shared freely, not artificially constrained. The creator has no need to fear for his financial future.

The reward for labor is a huge problem. The gap between the highest and lowest within a business is too large. That needs to be regulated to be no more than a fixed ratio, perhaps 3:1 in a small business and 10:1 for a large corporation.

Ideally, however, it should be 1:1. There is no need to generate profit; there is only a need to generate value. If everyone were given a $1000 at birth, they could conceivably have more money than they could spend in their lifetime.

Pricing as we know it could be drastically different. We have seen this just in our lifetime. The cost of tuition and room and board at my college was $6000; today it is over $60,000. Same buildings, same location, same food. What changed? Thirty years of compounding inflation, homelessness, joblessness, gangs, corruption and pollution. What did I learn? The universities are setting the worst examples of how to handle money. What they and others are doing is not stewardship, but a corruption of our hopes and dreams. The ends and the means are incongruent.

Universities not only teach 'buy low-sell high' but created hedge funds and many other forms of money manipulation. These institutions exist at the grace of the taxpayer. Their hoards of wealth invested in Wall Street are destroying our community both by example and by accounting. Many universities pre-date government and many were funded by the original wealth of tea-trading corporations that subdued and exploited the planet. We need to purge contradictions at their source. In ourselves first, but also in our institutions: government, business and non-profits.

## Liberty

By eliminating inflation, all of the good ideas that people have can be fully implemented. It will not be necessary to hold fund-raisers to cure cancer; just build the labs and train the scientists. Businesses do not need to compete, or struggle with rising prices from suppliers. It is the work that has the value, not the price assigned to it.

We can eliminate the constant worry about retirement and healthcare. Just build the hospitals and staff them. Pay a uniform pension to everyone when they reach a certain age. It is unnecessary to prey on the next generation by charging them interest. Time does not have to be money. Let time be time and money be money. Banking becomes a provided service that we pay for. No more free checking, and no more interest on loans, and merchants no longer pay a fee per transaction. Credit flow is a national utility, not a private kingdom. Every bank has always been a franchise of the Federal Reserve. We can use the deficit as a smarter tool by not trusting the marketplace more than common sense.

## Personal Responsibility

Personal responsibility is not getting a job and paying your own way, and viewing the struggles of others as a failure of self-reliance. Personal responsibility is working together as part of a group. That was what *'We the People'* was aiming for. Accepting personal responsibility is accepting that you are part of the problem when there is a problem, not assigning blame and declaring ones innocence or superiority. Money cannot be a measure or proof of success, and holding it in excess is certainly a failure of personal responsibility. Greed is not wise; it is a violation of the standards of liberty and community.

As a business owner, I recognize that 'buy low-sell high' is a structural problem that I cannot fix on my own. We are all responding to the math we are given. What I am suggesting is a fundamental reworking of the entire accounting system, using the idle cash within the system to smooth out the transitions. Our current accounting traditions are nonsensical. Inflation will continue to destroy everything and everyone in its path unless we move proactively to stop it.

Obviously, there will be some wrenching displacement in the financial sector, but every community will have the resources to deploy solutions. Employment will shift to activities that add true value to the quality of life, whereas now high profit products spend almost fifty percent of their revenue on advertising. We are in a "waste time for profit" cycle.

Under this model businesses will be able to staff without fear of overhead expenses. Goods will be affordable, and we could to return to a single-income family. The workweek can be shorter for everyone. Art and the accruements of a renaissance will be the new routine: No war, no debt, no misery.

America has long been a leader of the world. We must accept personal responsibility for its conditions, make peace with our enemies, and reform our personal banking habits. Every citizen has the power to reform his or her local government. By implementing these ideas, or some variation of them, commonwealth can spread.

## One Caveat

I suspect many balance sheets are false. If one were to actually liquidate many of the pension funds and endowments, then it would be discovered that the values claimed are untrue. There is also the other problem of to whom these securities would be sold to, if everyone were exiting the market simultaneously. Depending upon the speed of the transition, it may be necessary to begin fresh with a new currency.

In the interim, a date of 5 years prior could be used to establish a current value, and the government could use deficit financing to purchase unwanted securities. The need for a new currency step will probably present itself eventually. When it does, we can then establish universal wage standards. Employers should not be setting wages.

With a new currency, it will also be necessary to revisit established property valuations. There is little from the existing marketplace that we will want to carry forward.

The excessively rich will slowly become non-existent along with the excessively poor. People will only want to live in a house that they are willing to clean themselves. Servant-Master relationships will cease. We will be equal and, as George Washington envisioned when he wrote to the Jewish congregation at Newport: *"every one shall sit in safety under his own vine and fig tree, and there shall be none to make him afraid."*

Large estates will be managed by the local town, and can be used for functions, vacation rentals for families, weddings, conferences and other activities as appropriate. Everyone will be able to afford vacations and to travel, but rather than preying on tourists, which is the current policy, towns will be welcoming the opportunity to share.

We are by nature a social species. Trade should be a great source of pleasure for everyone. Only the accounting system we are using stands in the way of a better future. If we trust one another, and recognize the value of a common good, then we can live a full and rich life without fear or worry.

The ideas of wage and price controls have been around for a long. Even the rabid anti-communist President Nixon suggested them. Business-owners and free-market believers will probably complain the loudest about the reforms presented here, but business-owners already have complete wage and price control! The system does not work for them because they cannot control one other. Competition has no internal logic. Pricing habits drive fear and desperation. We live within a mathematical madness. The invisible hand is a self-delusion.

The numbers we write down creates economic volatility. The laws of mathematics have no mercy, and care nothing about intent or majority rule. If we write down different numbers, then we will have different results. Commonwealth is as simple as that.

Made in the USA
Charleston, SC
28 April 2016